P9-CDJ-838

# The Role-Play Technique:

## A Handbook for Management and Leadership Practice

(A revision of
*Supervisory and Executive Development:
A Manual for Role Playing*)

Norman R. F. Maier

Allen R. Solem

Ayesha A. Maier

University Associates, Inc.
7596 Eads Avenue, La Jolla, California 92037

Copyright © 1975 by University Associates, Inc.
ISBN: 0-88390-104-8
Library of Congress Catalog Card Number: 74-30943

The materials that appear in this book may be reproduced for use in educational training activities. Special permission is not required for such uses. However, the following statement must appear on all reproductions:

> Reproduced from
> *The Role-Play Technique:*
> *A Handbook for Management and Leadership Practice*
> by Norman R. F. Maier, Allen R. Solem, and Ayesha A. Maier
> La Jolla, Ca.: University Associates, Inc., 1975

This permission statement does *not* apply to: (1) use of these materials for systematic or large-scale reproduction or distribution; (2) inclusion of these materials in other publications for sale; or (3) *any reproduction whatsoever* of materials previously copyrighted by another source. Any such reproductions may be done only with prior written permission of University Associates or where applicable, the original copyright holder.

Printed in the United States of America

# *Preface*

Experience in human relations training and executive development programs is making it more and more clear that learning the principles of human behavior has little value unless it is supplemented with skill practice. As with any skill, book learning and demonstrations are needed, but they never will replace practice. The best kind of practice is performing under competent supervision. The greatest need in all training programs that involve the ability to relate to other people is the opportunity to practice without being hurt or without hurting anyone else.

The present volume is designed to give two kinds of practice. In the first place, it deals with role playing, a method that furnishes an opportunity to practice a human relations incident in a lifelike setting. The cases incorporate conflicts, differences in power and responsibility, and practical considerations. Participants soon discover how real these situations become. Because they are play situations, participants can experiment and try out new methods without running the risks that such experimenting entails in real life.

In the second place, the present volume is a casebook, and this approach to human relations invites practice in discussing and analyzing crucial issues. Discussion stimulates a group to explore a problem actively from many points of view; what might have been passed over quickly in reading can become an issue that participants find to be basic to their everyday jobs. Discussion also reveals various attitudes that can be clarified, evaluated, and modified through group interaction. Reading, with no discussion, may have little or no influence on attitudes. Finally, a discussion permits persons to compare their thinking with that of other members of a group. It is important for each person to know how his views compare with those of others, if he is to relate effectively with people in a community or organization.

Both role playing and discussion methods approach human relations issues as problems; the emphasis is on skills in solving and preventing problems. These methods differ from the lecture and textbook approach in which emphasis may be placed on principles and determining the "right" answer. The answer approach is so ingrained in our educational and training methods today that participants insist on the teacher's giving the answer. Nevertheless, the "right" answer will not necessarily be accepted and utilized. Quite the contrary: giving answers arouses arguments and stimulates people to think about what is wrong with the answer. Disagreements of this sort lead to ego problems, and new conflict issues are introduced.

This volume avoids giving answers. Some principles and facts may be introduced, but basically the aid supplied is in the form of suggested questions and issues. With these aids, a group of persons should come up with good answers; as training proceeds, the answers should become better. Improvement, not perfection, then becomes the goal.

The book can be used as a manual for supervisory and executive training; it requires no highly skilled leader. It can also serve as a handbook for a group of persons who wish to form a study group and have no designated trainer or leader. Since human relations problems arise in the home and in the community as well as in industry, these cases have universal interest and value.

Norman R. F. Maier
Allen R. Solem
December 1956                                       Ayesha A. Maier

# *Preface to the Revised Edition*

In attempting to write a new preface, we realized that we could not improve on the old one despite the fact that we now have much more experience behind us. We are now even more convinced that the skill-training value of role playing and the opportunities to observe differences in reactions are unique kinds of learning that cannot be gained in other ways. Narrowing the gap between training and life situations is a must if training is to be effective. The greatest failing in most supervisory programs is the shortage of opportunities for practice and discussion. Too often we expect to make good supervisors with a week's introduction to principles, but we may spend months training a machine operator.

A life situation happens only once, and one can never be sure it was handled in the best way. By means of simulation, one can be exposed to the same situation repeatedly and one can determine whether one is practicing or violating basic principles of behavior. Was the supervisor really listening to understand or was he busy persuading the subordinate? Did the leader really want to learn the subordinates' opinion about the problem or did he have a particular solution in mind? Role playing also becomes a research instrument for testing various behavior principles because the same situation can be repeated.

Generating ideas and evaluating ideas are as different as night and day, but only by observing role playing and being personally involved do we understand the degree to which the evaluation of ideas stifles the generation of ideas. The difference between posing a problem and posing a solution goes unrecognized in untrained groups, but the difference in the effect the two approaches have on problem-solving behavior is tremendous and apparent to all. Only practice makes us sensitive to interpersonal skills and expands our behavior repertoire. It is not uncommon for trainees to appraise role-playing exercises as the most valuable of their training experiences.

Norman R. F. Maier
Allen R. Solem

May 1975

Ayesha A. Maier

# Contents

# Introduction

## The Integration of Role Playing and Case Studies

The case-study approach to human relations was initiated at Harvard[1] and made a unique contribution to the educational process. Cases force one to think in terms of particulars. Whether a theory or broad generalization is sound can be determined only by applying it to a specific set of facts. When placed in an institutional setting, the facts must be considered in relation to power structure, personalities, and time pressures.

The case-study approach assumes group discussion, and the cases are sufficiently involved and detailed to produce a wide range of opinions concerning (1) who was to blame, (2) what caused a person to behave as he did, and (3) what the best corrective action is.

The fact that a group of persons with similar backgrounds and aspirations should disagree in matters of simple behavior often comes as a surprise to participants. However, since a case merely describes a series of sample events, each stating what someone said or did and how others reacted, it leaves a big gap between theoretical solutions and practical action.

The more important contributions of the case method to training include the following:

1. It discourages making snap judgments about people and behavior.
2. It discourages believing in, or looking for, the "correct" answer.
3. It graphically illustrates how the same set of events can be perceived differently.

---

[1]H. Cabot and J. A. Kahl, *Human Relations: Concepts and Cases in Concrete Social Science* (Vol. 2, *Cases*). Cambridge, Mass.: Harvard University Press, 1953; J. D. Glover and R. M. Hower, *The Administrator: Cases on Human Relations in Business* (2nd ed.). Homewood, Ill.: Richard D. Irwin, 1952.

4. It destroys any smug generalizations one might have about right vs. wrong answers, management prerogatives, the attitude of labor, the best methods of discipline, the younger generation, the place of women in management, and many other issues.
5. It trains one to discuss things with others and to experience the broadening value of interacting with one's equals.
6. It stresses practical thinking, so that such considerations as cost, convenience, deadlines, attitudes of top management, and the feelings of other persons prevent solutions from becoming idealistic.
7. It causes doubt as to whether there really are basic human relations principles.[2]

Although human relations principles may exist, it is wise not to come into a problem with foregone conclusions. If a program is well handled, some general principles should develop in the process of training.

The technique of role playing is an outgrowth of the work of Moreno,[3] who initially developed the method while working with the mentally disturbed. The purpose of the technique is to give the patient insight into some of his relationships with others by having him play the role of these other persons. A patient might be asked to act out his father's behavior while the clinical assistant plays the part of the patient. The technique is recognized and accepted as a training method in interpersonal relationships and can be modified and extended in a variety of ways to suit specific purposes.

The unique values of role playing include the following:
1. It requires the person to carry out a thought or decision. From a case study, for example, a conferee may conclude that Mr. A should apologize to Mr. B. In role playing, A would go to B and apologize. Role-playing experience soon demonstrates the difference between *thinking* and *doing*.
2. It permits practice in carrying out an action and makes clear the fact that good human relations require skill in the same sense that playing golf requires skill.
3. It accomplishes attitude changes effectively by placing persons in specified roles. This demonstrates that a person's behavior is

---

[2]F. J. Roethlisberger emphasized the need for more skill and less talk about verbal principles in his article "Human Relations: Rare, Medium or Well Done," *Harvard Business Review*, January 1948, p. 107.

[3]J. L. Moreno, *Who Shall Survive?* Beacon, N.Y.: Beacon House, 1953.

not only a function of his personality, but also of the situation in which he finds himself.

4. It trains a person to be aware of and sensitive to the feelings of others. This awareness functions as feedback on the effect of his behavior.

5. It develops a fuller appreciation of the important part played by feelings in determining behavior in social situations.

6. It enables each person to discover his personal faults. For example, the person who enjoys making wisecracks may discover that these often hurt others.

7. It permits training in the control of feelings and emotions. For example, by repeatedly playing the role of a supervisor, a person can practice not becoming irritated by complaints.

Role playing combined with the case method should yield the benefits of both methods. A situation is created that contains practical considerations beyond those involved in the interpersonal relationship. For instance, the question of whether or not a foreman can take time off to listen to an employee under a given set of conditions involves not only the matter of how to deal with an employee's request, but also other demands that the situation makes on the supervisor at the time. In this way, practical considerations and good human relations skills must be integrated. It is probable that new insights will be achieved because of the new relationships created. Certainly the discussion of how something was said or done in a role play can lead to insight into skill requirements as well as to better decision making on what should or should not be done. Discussions of case studies, at best, remain at the intellectual level—a great deficiency that role playing can correct.

Further training values are achieved by using different types of role playing, thus placing persons in new and strange situations. One learns not to act as another person would, but to act as oneself would in varied situations under many conditions. In this manner, the role playing of cases comes very close to practice in the solving of actual interpersonal as well as industrial problems.

## Selection of Cases

All the cases have been tested with various management groups and college classes, and a large number of them have been used extensively for training and demonstration purposes. The role-playing participants have included all levels of management in large and small companies representing many industries. Similarly, the college-student participants represent various levels of academic training in many areas of study.

The cases selected for this handbook have been effective in reproducing the conditions of a life situation with a minimum of detail. This fact encourages participants to act as themselves and experience motivations and feelings similar to those in real life, rather than to attempt to portray other persons. Under these favorable conditions, role-playing experiences frequently have considerable impact on a person's perception of a problem; the new attitudes and behaviors experienced in the scene tend to carry over into life situations.

Much of the training value of a case depends on the scope of the generalizations that can be drawn from the results. For this reason, two important factors in screening a case were the extent to which it typified a broad range of management problems and the extent to which it illustrated and highlighted the methods and principles for dealing with those problems.

A third factor in the selection of a case was its interest value and the kind of challenge it offered. Role playing may be boring if the case used lacks conflict and variety.

In addition to these considerations, each case was selected for its unique contribution to an overall training program in human relations. A relatively small number of cases therefore provide comprehensive coverage of human relations problems as they occur in industry.

It is sometimes felt that cases should be based on conditions within the company in which the training is given. It is the experience of the writers that this can be done successfully only after there has been a considerable amount of training with general cases. When cases are based on company experiences, the following unfavorable conditions may be created:

1. Irrelevant facts are introduced; these disrupt discussion as well as role playing.
2. Defensive behavior often is shown by persons involved in the company situation.
3. Persons who know the company situation may disagree on the basic issues in the conflict.
4. Participants become *solution minded* rather than *process minded* and speculate on whether the company made a mistake.
5. Company cases may be imbedded in a complex situation wherein the human relations issues are obscured by other factors.

Once the group becomes accustomed to role playing, has acquired a familiarity with the basic skill principles, and appreciates the constructive interaction that occurs in group discussion, it is good practice to try to role play company situations. It is best, however, to use problems that have not been resolved, both because face-saving difficulties and the betrayal of confidences are not involved, and also because the insights gained in the role playing can be utilized in solving the problem. When a group is ready to role play company problems, different members of the group should present their own case data for the group's consideration.

## Sequence of Cases

There has been some attempt to introduce variety by mixing group and individual cases but, in general, their order of presentation follows a developmental sequence of principles and skills. Each case involves the use of partially new and increasingly complex abilities. It should be understood, however, that any of the cases may be made more difficult merely by increasing the degree of competence expected. The multiple role-playing procedure[4] is emphasized initially because it is easier to handle and discuss. This fact made it necessary to feature cases that readily lend themselves to multiple role playing in the first half of the book. The transition to single-group role playing is made in cases 9 through 13.

There is no content or special knowledge in the cases that requires that the sequence in the handbook be followed. Rather, the order and number of the cases used may be determined by the requirements of a particular training program. In one program there may be a need for practice in a particular skill, such as interviewing in connection with performance appraisal; in another, the desire to demonstrate and practice the principles of group decision may be in order; and in still a different instance, there may be a wish to stimulate discussion on methods of handling a particular problem such as clarification of coffee privileges. Limitations are often imposed on the use of all the cases. Lack of sufficient time or suitable space, or an insufficient number of group members to play the roles may require selectivity. In such instances, the problem is to make the most appropriate and complete use of the material that is possible. These and other initial obstacles frequently can be overcome after a few of the cases have been tried.

If there are no special requirements, it is recommended that the

---

[4]N. R. F. Maier and L. F. Zerfoss, "MRP: A Technique for Training Large Groups of Supervisors and Its Potential Use in Social Research," *Human Relations*, 1952, 5, 177–186.

cases be used in the sequence in which they appear. This order illustrates a progression that has been found useful for general training both at various levels of management and in many organizations.

## Plan of Case Organization

All cases are presented in the same basic format. Each is divided into four general sections with the same major headings. Beyond this, minor variations in form are made in order to meet the unique demands of each case. It is hoped that this consistency of presentation will facilitate the use of the role-playing procedures in the different cases and will make it convenient to locate and identify the various parts of the cases.

The four general sections and the nature of the contents under each one are as follows:

1. *Focusing the Problem:* This introductory section contains a description of the general class of problem illustrated by the case. Some indication of the primary training functions as well as the nature or degree of skill required by the trainees is also given, in order to establish a favorable mental set.
2. *Role-Playing Procedure:* The recommended role-playing procedure is indicated in this section and a step-by-step description is presented for setting up the role-playing scene. Additional instructions are provided for conducting the role-playing process. Questions and discussion topics are included for facilitating the subsequent analysis of the developments in the role play and for highlighting the applications of the new learning to problems on the job.
3. *Materials:* Background information on the role-playing problem for all group members is furnished in this section, as are the individual roles for the participants. Special instructions are provided in some of the cases for group members who act as observers. When the role-playing procedure provides for the collection of data and comparison of results from several groups of participants, sample tables are provided to illustrate the method for recording results.
4. *Comments and Implications:* Under this heading is a discussion of the types of errors most likely to be made and the usual consequences of these errors. However, the main purpose of this section is to point up the principles involved in the case and the kinds of skills required for dealing with related problems. These aspects of the case are presented within the framework of an effective approach to the type of problem that the case illustrates. In this manner, applications of the new learning can be made to other job and life problems.

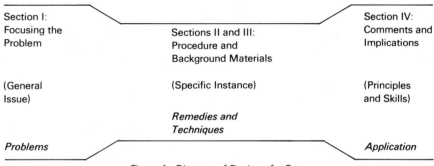

Figure 1. Diagram of Design of a Case.

Taken together, the four sections conform to the design shown in Figure 1. A general problem issue, such as "how to be fair to all employees," is raised in Section I. In order to test the adequacy of principles or points of view, one must go from conceptual thinking to a particular set of circumstances without getting sidetracked by exceptions. In any particular case under consideration, there are no exceptions. This process of funneling the thinking from a *broad* classification of problems to a *particular* one is shown in the left portion of the figure.

Since the role-playing experience and the discussion that follows are concerned with a particular situation and set of facts (background and role instructions), Sections II and III are shown as the narrow middle part of the diagram. This is the stage in which ideas, skills, and viewpoints are tested. It may also include discussion of the best way to handle the particular problem.

Once there is clarification of the problem, it is interesting to speculate on the ways in which the skills, the attitudes, and the thinking about a specific case may be transferred to other situations. This generalization is a different sort than the one discussed in Section I: remedies and techniques rather than problems are generalized. It is possible that the boundaries for transferring techniques might be quite different from those for classifying problems. Section IV bridges the gap between the lessons learned in the particular case and human relations principles. The communication established between participants in the discussion of particulars will facilitate communication of generalized principles. Although communication is most faulty in the conceptual area of thinking, careful discussion of a situation will aid the group members in communicating and understanding each other when they attempt to generalize the findings from the case.

## Types of Role-Playing Procedures

Two role-playing procedures are featured in this casebook. Approximately half the cases utilize the multiple role-playing procedure; for the remaining half, the single-group role-playing procedure is prescribed.

Using two procedures for role playing instead of one has an important advantage in that different kinds of training objectives are achieved by each.

When the multiple role-playing procedure is used, the entire audience is formed into role-playing groups, the size of the groups depending on the number of participants required for the particular case. All groups role play simultaneously. There are several advantages to this method.

1. The multiple role-playing procedure is a particularly effective method of training by doing because it maximizes opportunities for the members of the audience to try out new attitudes and behaviors.

2. It provides data from each of the several groups so that comparisons of the results can be made. Discussing the findings and relating them to various actions of the role players are especially convincing because the conclusions are based on the group's own experiences. Since the roles are the same for all groups, differences in outcome result from variations in group interactions.

3. The multiple role-playing procedure is a markedly effective way to involve all members of an audience in a problem. This, in turn, quickly dispels any shyness or self-consciousness among members who have not role played previously. When all persons are involved in a similar activity, no one feels that he is being observed. Rather, the spirit of interacting causes one group to stimulate rather than to inhibit the performances of others. Embarrassment and face-saving problems are eliminated.

When the main purpose of the training is to develop skill in sensitivity to the feelings of others, the single-group role-playing procedure is most effective. This procedure is preferable for intensive training or advanced work with small groups and for certain types of demonstrations. Because the procedure permits only one role-playing group to perform, other members of a class can participate as observers. (A variation of the method is to have the observers function as consultants to the role-play leader.) When no progress is being made, the role-play can be interrupted for a brief discussion and consultation. Afterward, the action is resumed.

When the scene has been completed, discussion methods are used for analysis and evaluation. There are several advantages to single-group role-playing.

1. Since all persons observe a single performance, it is possible to discuss the details that led to a particular effect. For example, the group can discuss the first appearance of defensive behavior of the part of one role player and then attempt to determine what behavior on someone else's part caused it.

2. Participants in the role play profit from the analytical discussion of their behaviors, since they often are unaware of the effect of their actions on others.

3. Observers can develop sensitivity to the feelings of participants. If one person in the role play indicates that he will improve his work, the observers may be asked to tell whether or not he means it. Since the role players can report on their true feelings, it is possible to check the keenness of the sensitivity of observers.

It should now be apparent that one of these two procedures is not preferable to the other, but that they perform different training functions. These functions effectively complement each other in the development of all-around proficiency in human relations. It follows, therefore, that the decision to use one procedure or the other on a particular occasion should be determined by the specific training objectives and by the size of the group.

Within the framework of both procedures, a number of variations are possible. In Case 10, the skit-completion method[5] is illustrated. This variation uses a skit to create the situation and carry developments to a specific conflict point. Role players must pick up the action from this point and complete the drama. This approach determines events up to a certain stage, thereby controlling the type of conflict to a great extent.

Another variation is the dramatized case method,[6] in which a previous incident is furnished by means of written dialog. From this point on, the subsequent contacts are role played. This approach is illustrated in Case 13.

Both the skit-completion method and the dramatized case method supply background data in a more interesting and dramatic way than can be achieved by role instructions. The description of a conflict situation may affect different role players in different ways, but when previ-

[5]N. R. F. Maier, *Principles of Human Relations: Applications to Management.* New York: John Wiley, 1952.

[6]N. R. F. Maier, "Dramatized Case Material as a Springboard for Role Playing," *Group Psychotherapy,* 1953, 6, 30–42.

ous lines are supplied, the kind of emotion established in a role player is more effectively controlled. It is possible therefore to increase as well as control the range of problems and emotions that can be incorporated into a role-playing episode.

## Types of Role-Playing Problems

It is possible to divide human relations problems into two general types, those having to do with individuals and those having to do with a group. Giving a job assignment, correcting an individual, interviewing a person, dealing with a complaint, and calming an emotionally upset employee are examples of face-to-face relationships with individuals. These require skills in interpersonal relations on the part of the supervisor.

When a supervisor has more than one person reporting to him, he not only has many face-to-face relationships, but he must deal with an additional problem: the relationships that each employee has with the others. Problems of favoritism, discriminatory practices, status, fairness of assignments, and regimentation fall into this category. Insofar as the supervisor is in charge of a group, he is a leader and certain leadership skills are demanded of him.

In some cases it is difficult for the supervisor to know whether he is dealing with a group problem or an individual problem. An individual's violation of a safety rule may actually reflect the attitude of the entire group.[7] One of the skills of a supervisor in his ability to make a correct diagnosis of the type of problem that confronts him. It is also important that he be ready to change his diagnosis if new and relevant factors are disclosed.

The descriptive chart on page 19 shows the type of problem illustrated in each case. It will be noted that both types of problems are represented almost equally and that both the single and the multiple role-playing procedures are used with each type of problem. In a few instances, it is difficult to diagnose the type of problem; both the individual and the group approach seem to be adequate, although they yield very different results.

The cases that contain group problems are primarily aimed toward training in various conference leadership skills. Considerable research

---

[7]In a large power plant, the safety department had great difficulty in getting electricians to wear hard hats for protection. Finally it was discovered that the electricians resisted because hard hats made them look like construction workers; the underlying difficulty was thus a class-status problem. The simple solution was to provide different types of hard hats for the various groups of workers.

evidence indicates the effectiveness of certain leadership attitudes and participation techniques. Important leadership functions can determine whether or not a group will work together, accept improvements, and try to develop better ways of doing a job.

The cases concerned with problems and dealings with individuals focus attention on the practice and outcomes of various interpersonal procedures and skills. These include creating an atmosphere in which an individual feels his supervisor is a willing helper rather than a judge; discovering an individual's needs, aspirations, and attitudes; avoiding defensive behavior; responding to feelings rather than facts; and improving the effectiveness of interviews.

It is not within the scope of this volume to present an adequate discussion of the principles of group leadership and interpersonal relationships with individuals. Those who desire to explore these areas further are referred to related publications.[8]

## Number of Role Players Required

The number of participants needed for role playing varies with the case and the role-playing procedure. Many of the cases require only two role players; the largest number requested is thirteen.

The number of participants needed for each of the cases is shown in the descriptive chart on page 19.

In addition to the role players, provision is made in the cases for other group members to participate as observers (when single-group role playing is used) or to form additional role-playing groups (when the multiple role-playing procedure is followed). Special instructions and details for involving all class members are provided separately in each of the cases, and in some instances, suggestions are supplied for role playing a case with fewer than the number of participants indicated.

Although cases may be used with only the minimum number of persons required, this should not be regarded as the optimum condition. Observers perform a valuable function as critics. Because they are not emotionally involved, they can be objective in their observations and evaluations. Everyone should have the opportunity to serve as both a role player and as an observer, since the learning is different in each instance. Observers readily increase their sensitivity to feelings because they can devote full attention to watching and need not be concerned with responding.

## How to Role Play

People are good actors when they make up their own lines—this is one of the most impressive facts one experiences in working with role playing. One need not train participants in voice intonation and gestures. The role player remains himself and merely behaves according to the situation described. If he is placed in the role of a union steward, he should consider himself to *be* the steward and not act the way he *thinks* a union steward would. The role player is expected to accept certain facts about his length of service, sex, family ties, friends, and previous experiences. He should adopt these as his own and let his feelings and attitude change as these imagined events or factors require.

All of us conduct ourselves differently depending on the situation in which we find ourselves. The conduct of a supervisor on the job is likely to be very different from his conduct at home with his family. This does not imply a personality change; behavior is altered in response to the situation in which the person finds himself.

The role-playing instructions describe the setting in which a particular attitude will be formulated. Because they set up a state of mind that serves as a point of departure, the roles should not be re-examined by the players once the interaction has begun. It is important to realize that the initial attitude adopted by a role player need not remain static. Subsequent events or experiences, as they occur in the process of role playing, may alter these attitudes and create pleasant or unpleasant feelings. As a result, the persons involved may have some of the same emotional experiences that occur in real-life situations. This emotional arousal is one of the most important values of role playing and serves as a rehearsal for practical problems. As persons become more experienced in role-playing situations, they learn to feel the part, and role-playing behavior becomes more and more authentic. The fact that role playing can simulate real-life situations makes it possible for one to try new ways of handling problems without suffering any serious consequences if the methods fail.

In the process of role playing, questions that are not covered by the instructions to the participants may be raised in the discussion. When this occurs, the person questioned should feel free to make up facts or experiences that are appropriate to the circumstances. For example, if the foreman in a case asks a worker a question about the health of his children, the worker may answer it in any one of several ways without altering the spirit of the case. However, the player should not make up *3ï* experiences or facts that are inconsistent with his role.

In conclusion, it is perhaps worthwhile to repeat certain points in order to warn against two common mistakes in role playing.

1. Do not consult your role while playing a part. Doing so tends to make an attitude a static condition and not subject to alteration. Real attitudes are dynamic forces and are subject to change in direction as well as intensity.
2. Do not behave the way you feel a person in the position described in your role *should* behave. Assuming the personality of another person is a stage skill but it is a distinct disadvantage in role playing. A good role player need not be an actor.

## Use of the Book as a Training Manual

*Role-Playing Materials.*    All role-playing materials and instructions are contained in the handbook. Since most of the contents of the book concern the class members and the instructor to a similar degree, it has been unnecessary to prepare separate books for the instructor and the students. For serious study, it is desirable that each person have his own copy of the book, not only to furnish him with needed introductory and concluding sections, but also to facilitate the role-playing process.

*Collection of Data.*    Although sample tables and questions are provided to aid in the compilation of data resulting from the role play, the amount of data collected should be limited by the size of the group and the interest generated.

*Recommended Sequence.*    Since the cases selected for this volume are diversified, taken together they sample a wide range of human relations principles. Unless the objective of a training program is selective or specialized, it is suggested that the cases be used in the order in which they appear. If time is not available for using all the cases, the selection still can be made in recommended order.

*Previous Experience.*    No special training is required of the instructor or of the participants. If the trainer has had previous experience with role playing, it is suggested that he refrain from explaining it. Groups accept and get the feeling for role playing with minimum indoctrination. As a matter of fact, too much talk about role playing often frightens participants. The only preliminaries necessary are (1) those explanations required to cover the company viewpoint or policy on training and (2) a warm-up period during which each participant rises, introduces himself, tells a little about his background, and briefly describes his present position. Even when participants know each other, a little discussion of the latter two items may serve a valuable purpose.

*Size of Group.*    The size of the group may range from ten to fifty persons. The ideal size for single-group role playing is around twelve to fifteen; for multiple role playing it is between twenty-five and fifty. However, the skill of a leader and the type of room facilities are influencing factors. When these are adequate, interest can be maintained in individual-group role playing with classes as large as a hundred persons; and in multiple role playing, successful and spirited participation has been achieved with an audience of 650 executives.

*Differences in Rank.*    It is generally not good practice for a company to mix persons of different rank in a training class. Face-saving problems may be created by status differences, and the greater the spread in rank, the more difficult this problem becomes. However, this problem is not serious in small companies where each supervisor knows all the management personnel and they react to each other's personalities rather than to their positions. The extent of the problem of mixing rank will, of course, depend on the attitudes of the higher officials and the skills of the trainer. When in doubt, it is best to play safe and avoid the situation.

*Mixing Departments.*    The mixing of supervisors from different jobs, departments, and divisions is highly recommended. It permits the attainment of such training by-products for supervisors as:
1. Discovery that others have difficulties and problems similar to their own.
2. A fuller knowledge of the way work in other units relates to their own.
3. The acquisition of friends in several departments.

These by-products improve communication, help in the development of a broader view of company functions, and ease the process of lateral transfers. There is no need to separate men and women supervisors since both can take the role of either sex in role playing, or role names may be changed to fit the sex of the role player.

*The Classroom.*    The room need be no larger than is required to accommodate the group. It is unnecessary to supply extra space for discussion groups since, even in multiple role playing, the noise of adjacent groups tends to stimulate the role play rather than to distract from it.

It is best if chairs or movable seats are furnished so that members can form groups of varying size with comfort and ease. However, auditoriums with fixed seats can be used by having persons in one row turn around to discuss with persons sitting behind them. Inadequate facilities are not a good reason to avoid role playing.

*Furnishings.*  Necessary furnishings are a table and a few chairs that can be moved to the front of the room when required. A card table and chairs will serve this need. Also needed for multiple role playing are newsprint and two large easels. Trainers should use these visual aids as much as possible. The use of newsprint slows down discussion, supplies a more permanent record of the group's thinking, and requires that the ideas be stated efficiently and briefly.

*Class Assignments.*  The question of previous preparation for each case should be left to the instructor. He may wish to make reading assignments in order to give the group a background of related principles. However, this is not a requirement for the use of the cases.

In developing the procedure, it has been assumed that the case has not been assigned ahead of time. However, the instructor should read over the material so that he will be familiar with the procedure and the points in the discussion. But he should not try to be prepared to supply the answers to problems raised. His function is to assist the group in executing the role playing and to direct the discussions.

The last three cases in the book have rather complex role assignments. In these instances, it is suggested that the role players study their roles in advance. These instructions are supplied in the cases.

## Use of the Book by a Small Group Without a Trainer

A teacher or trainer may be available only when an educational institution or a company develops or sponsors a human relations or organization development program. Since this training is of relatively recent origin, it may not be available to all persons who wish it.

The instructions in this section are intended for those whose interests in human relations go beyond the available facilities in their company or community. Dealing effectively with people and obtaining satisfaction from these relationships may be goals not only for supervisors and executives in business and industry, but also for ministers, teachers, parents, social workers, doctors, nurses, committee chairmen, and community leaders. The aspects of drama and the conflicts stimulated by the case situations can be lively and entertaining. The fact that there are important practical gains should not detract from the sociability of the procedure.

Since the case material is placed in an industrial setting, time should be spent at the end of each role play to apply its principles to related problems in the experiences of the group members. If the case under consideration deals with a problem of "fairness," for example, each person in the group may describe a similar problem in his own experience. The fact that different occupational groups have similar or identical human relations problems will serve to enrich and facilitate their understanding of each other's situation.

The procedures described are adequate for groups having no teacher or trainer. Since the instructions are directed to various participants and role players as well as to the instructor, it is only necessary that someone in the group coordinate the activity. On some occasions, cases set up for multiple role playing may have to be limited to one or two groups. In order to obtain more examples of solutions, the role players may wish to exchange roles and repeat the role-playing process. This usually results in a different solution and has a distinct value in itself. One gains a fuller appreciation of the part a person's position plays in determining his outlook and behavior if one can view the same conflict from different points of reference.

## Use of the Cases for Individual Self-Development

The special merits of discussion and role playing for training in human relations already have been enumerated. Since discussions require groups, one person studying by himself to improve his ability to relate to people would be denied the values of discussion. For some time, the authors have been interested in developing a method whereby an individual might gain some of the training values inherent in a discussion.

It is hoped that the present case book will partially satisfy this need. To achieve the benefits, however, the volume must be used according to the instructions. If the individual reader wishes to derive the values of both role playing and discussion from this volume, he must set a block of one to two hours aside for each case and carry out the assignments that follow. Using shortcuts, scanning the materials ahead of time, or using the book to fill short intervals of leisure will not accomplish the objective.

Since all cases are divided into similar sections, the procedure outlined herein will apply to all of them. Once the individual reader gets into the spirit of the method, he will be able to visualize some of the interaction between group members.

The first section, Focusing the Problem, will cause no difficulty, since it is a straightforward presentation of the problem and requires only careful reading. The second section sets the stage for role playing. One should attempt to visualize the setting and individuals involved. When the instructions call for a reading of background materials and instructions, the reader should study these as do regular role players. He should then return to Section II and proceed with any further steps.

The reader should assume that he is to play the role of the leader in *group* cases and of the interviewer in cases dealing with an *individual*. He should then study his specific role carefully and prepare himself for the conference or the interview. The roles for other participants should not be read at this time. (As the leader or interviewer, he would not know what was on another person's mind until it was revealed in a discussion.)

After studying his role, the reader should write out his opening remarks in detail. Any changes should be made only as corrective statements in the form of additions; he should not delete anything. As is the case with the spoken word, the imaginary role player must be required to cope with his previously expressed remarks.

When the introductory statement has been completed, the reader should read it aloud and then imagine the reactions he would get from typical group members or interviewees, as the case may be. A few sample reactions should be noted on a pad, each followed with the response he would give. The brief exchanges should be evaluated by noting whether the imagined reactions he obtained were of a constructive nature and whether he handled the reactions satisfactorily.

Another important phase of human interaction is the acceptance of a line of action. The reader should write out a plan or solution that he feels will be acceptable to the group or the interviewee. Reasons why the plan or solution should be adopted may be noted in the margin so that they can be checked later against the role instructions.

One of the other roles should now be studied. The reader should assume that he has taken this role and then re-read his previous introductory remarks from this new vantage point. In group cases, he should repeat this procedure with a few of the roles to get a feeling for the other side of the situation. He may then imagine the kind of discussion that would occur. After several imagined exchanges, he should examine the solution carefully from the viewpoint of the subordinates.

In case of any differences of opinion, the reader should construct a modified solution, indicating any concessions or changes he would make and the things he hopes to gain by them. When he feels that he has a good, reworked solution, he should read any remaining roles, including the Instructions for Observers if such is included in the case.

The reader is now ready to turn to the exercises concerned with the results and their analyses, devoting time particularly to questions relating to leadership or interviewing skills. These will serve as a guide to the types of mistakes he is likely to make and the types of skills he already possesses. He should compare himself with several other supervisors or executives he knows and imagine what each would have done. This process of thinking through the consequences of alternative procedures should be done carefully and thoroughly, without hurry. A chart or outline would be a useful visual aid.

When the reader is satisfied with his analysis and evaluation, he should carefully study the last section, Comments and Implications. He should note any differences between his analysis and that of the authors, because similar issues may arise in later cases.

Once the last section has been carefully digested, the whole case should be re-read from start to finish in order to discover minor but significant details that may have been overlooked.

# DESCRIPTIVE CHART

| Case | Procedure in Role Playing | Type of Problem | Participants Needed |
|------|---------------------------|-----------------|---------------------|
| 1. | Multiple | Group | 6 per group |
| 2. | Multiple | Individual | 2 per group |
| 3. | Multiple | Group | 7 per group |
| 4. | Multiple | Individual | 3 per group |
| 5. | Multiple | Group | 4 per group |
| 6. | Multiple | Individual | 3 per group |
| 7. | Multiple and Single | Group | 6 per group |
| 8. | Multiple | Group | 7 per group |
| 9. | Single | Group | 13 role players |
| 10. | Single (skit completion) | Individual | 6 role players |
| 11. | Single | Group | 7 role players |
| 12. | Multiple | Individual | 3 per group |
| 13. | Single (dramatized) | Individual | 3 role players |
| 14. | Single | Indiviual | 2 role players |
| 15. | Single | Individual | 2 role players |
| 16. | Single | Individual | 2 role players |
| 17. | Single | Group | 8 role players |
| 18. | Single | Individual | 2 role players |
| 19. | Single | Individual | 2 role players |
| 20. | Single | Group | 4 role players |

# 1

# *The New Truck Dilemma*

## FOCUSING THE PROBLEM

Whenever people are involved in a joint activity, the question of fair treatment becomes an important issue about which opinions differ. Although a supervisor may try to be fair, he soon realizes that no amount of effort on his part to do the right thing is appreciated by everyone. Consequently, he often welcomes rules and company practices, because they promise to protect him from the charge of playing favorites. These same rules and formalized procedures may be regarded by employees as arbitrary, inconvenient, and a way of disregarding individual differences in needs; yet employees prefer them to favoritism, which they believe will occur if supervisory judgments prevail. Management sees rules and formalized procedures as necessary evils that interfere with flexibility and personalized practices. However, these procedures also serve as guides and protections from complaints and permit the supervisor to let the blame fall on the rule. Thus, the rule can be attacked by both parties to a dispute.

It is necessary to clarify the issues involved in a dispute over fairness. Disagreement on issues of fairness may be unavoidable because choices and preferences are, by their very nature, self-centered. It is apparent that if all members of a group had an equal desire for an object, regardless of whether each had an equal claim to it, there would be a struggle since each would try to get it for himself. An outsider might, however, work out a just solution by dividing it equally between members of the group. When an object can be shared or divided, opportunities for finding fair solutions exist, providing that each member respects the claims of others. When, however, needs and claims differ among

21

group members and an object cannot be shared, the difficulties mount.

Some of the more common fairness issues include the following situations:

- How can vacations be scheduled more fairly?
- Who gets time off during hunting seasons?
- What is a fair division of overtime?
- Who should do a disagreeable job?
- Which unit should try out the new chairs?
- Which group should get more space as a result of a move to new quarters?
- How can office space be allocated so that some are not left with less space or less elegant furnishings than others?

Frequently, supervisors are unaware of the many factors that play a part in a dispute about fairness. As the previous list of problems shows, prestige is an issue, and when social recognition is part of the problem of fairness, the emotional involvement is strong.

The incident in this case hinges on the issuing of a new truck to one member of a crew of workers, each of whom uses a truck in his work. The foreman finds himself in a situation in which he must make a wise and fair decision. Since the replacement of trucks has been infrequent, the importance of making the right decision is apparent to the foreman.

The multiple role-playing procedure is used in this case because it is desirable to obtain solutions from a number of groups.

## MULTIPLE ROLE-PLAYING PROCEDURE

### Preparation

1. The participants form groups of six persons each. If the last group has only five persons, they may assume that one of them (George) is home because of illness. Less than five persons may act as observers of role-playing groups.
2. All participants read the General Instructions for Role Players. This data may be consulted during the role play. The instructor may wish to post on newsprint the facts about the repairmen and their trucks.
3. Each group selects one member to play the foreman, Walt Marshall.
4. Other group members play George, Bill, John, Charlie, and Hank. If a group has only five persons, the foreman reads George's role and assumes that he has talked to George on the telephone.
5. The member of each group playing the foreman studies his role

sheet. When he has read it, he stands up to indicate to the instructor that he is ready to role play.

6. Crew members study their role sheets. They avoid reading other roles or discussing the roles with each other.

7. The observers (if any) read their instructions in preparation for their observation of the role play.

8. Each crew member writes his role name on a slip of paper which he wears as a name tag so that other members know who he is.

9. The crew members assume they are in the foreman's office waiting for him.

10. When all participants who are playing the part of the foreman have indicated by standing that they are ready to begin role playing, the instructor asks them to sit down. This signals that the foremen have entered their offices to begin the discussions.

11. Crew members greet the foreman on his arrival and the role play begins.


## Process

1. Groups need between twenty-five and thirty minutes for role playing. Those who have not finished at the end of twenty-eight minutes are given a two-minute warning signal.

2. During the role play, the instructor lists on newsprint the appropriate headings for the recording of solutions and other results from the groups. Sample Table 1 illustrates the types of headings and the method for recording data that may be used. The first letter of each crew member's name is arranged in a column. One column is needed for each group. Arrows may be used to indicate any exchange in trucks. (These should be added later.) An arrow from the left pointing to a name indicates the man who got the new truck, while other arrows (to the right of names) indicate who got his truck, etc. For example, in Group 3, John receives the new truck while Charlie gets John's truck, and Charlie's truck is to be discarded. (This is not a typical solution.)

3. In addition to making arrangements for recording the exchange in trucks, the instructor should plan space for other data. Suggested headings are given below:

   a. "Repairs" indicates whose truck, if any, will be fixed up in any way.

   b. "Number of Exchanges" serves to record the number of men who benefit by the fact that a new truck is introduced into the crew.

In Group 3, shown in the sample table, both John and Charlie receive different trucks as a result of the solution.
c. The heading "Foreman Satisfied" is used to indicate whether the foreman is satisfied or not with the solution reached in the discussion.
d. A fourth heading, "Dissatisfied Drivers," is used to record the initials of the men who are not satisfied with the outcome.

## Collecting Group Data

1. The foreman for each group reports (a) the decision for his group, by indicating the name of the man who gets the new truck, the disposition that is made of his truck, etc.; (b) whose truck, if any, is to be repaired; and (c) whether or not he is satisfied with the outcome.
2. The instructor diagrams the solution as the foreman reports it, and fills in lines (a), (b), and (c) of the table.
3. The crew criticizes the foreman's report if they see fit, and all who are dissatisfied give their reasons—to be reported on line (d) of the table.
4. Observers, if used, briefly report on the discussion process each observed, commenting especially on (a) how the foreman presented the problem, (b) how the crew responded in the discussion, and (c) any helpful or interfering things the foreman did.
5. The process is repeated until all groups have reported. If more than twelve groups participate, it may be necessary to limit complete reports to ten groups and request the remaining groups to confine their reports to the presentation of their solutions.

## General Discussion

All participants then discuss such topics as the following:
1. In what ways are the solutions alike or different?
2. Which of the several solutions is best? (The percentage of satisfied individuals is determined.)
3. What factors influenced differences of opinion on the "best" solution?
4. Could a foreman have made a fair decision on this problem? How many members in a group could he please?
5. What sets of values enter into the question of fairness? (The arguments used by various individuals are listed on newsprint.)
6. Could a company write a rule for the fair way to distribute the new trucks?

7. What solutions would be unacceptable to management? Were any such solutions suggested by groups and, if so, could they have been prevented?

8. Can the problem of fairness be settled by a discussion with the crew without the foreman attempting to influence the outcome? (Arguments for and against this position are listed in separate columns.)

9. In the opinion of each crew member, what did he like most about the foreman's conduct of the meeting, and what did he like least about it? (The instructor may make a two-column listing of these behaviors. Key words should be used to characterize a behavior item and check marks may be made to register duplicate contributions. Discuss various interpretations of the two lists.)

10. What other problems are basically like the new truck problem? (The instructor lists these on newsprint. In cases of disagreement, differences in opinion are indicated by means of a modifying phrase.)

## General Instructions for Role Players[9]

You work for the telephone company and one of you is the foreman while the others are repairmen. The job of a repairman is to fix phones that are out of order, and it requires knowledge and diagnostic skills as well as muscular skills. Repairmen must climb telephone poles, work with small tools, and meet customers. The foreman of a crew is usually an ex-repairman; this happens to be true in this case. He has an office at the garage location but spends a good deal of time making the rounds, visiting the places where the men are working. Each repairman works alone and ordinarily does several jobs in a day. The foreman gives help and instruction as needed.

The repairmen drive to various locations in the city to do repair work. Each of them drives a small truck and takes pride in its appearance. The repairmen have possessive feelings about their trucks and like to keep them in good running order. Naturally, they like to have new trucks, because new trucks give them a feeling of pride.

Here are some facts about the repairmen and their trucks.

|  | Years With Company | Type of Truck Used |
|---|---|---|
| George | 17 | 2-year-old Ford |
| Bill | 11 | 5-year-old Dodge |
| John | 10 | 4-year-old Ford |
| Charlie | 5 | 3-year-old Ford |
| Hank | 3 | 5-year-old Chevrolet |

Most of the men do all their driving in the city, but John and Charlie cover the jobs in the suburbs.

In playing your part, accept the facts as given and assume the attitude supplied in your specific role. From this point on, let your feelings develop in accordance with the events that occur during the role play. When facts or events arise that are not covered by the roles, make up things that are consistent with the way it might be in a real-life situation.

---

[9]Role instructions are taken from an article by N. R. F. Maier and L. F. Zerfoss, "MRP: A Technique for Training Large Groups of Supervisors and Its Potential Use in Social Research," *Human Relations*, 1952, 5, 180–181. Permission to reproduce the roles has been granted by the Plenum Publishing Company, London, England.

## Role Sheet: Walt Marshall, Foreman

You are the foreman of a crew of repairmen, each of whom drives a small service truck to and from his various jobs. Every so often, you get a new truck to exchange for an old one and you have the problem of deciding which of your men should have the new truck. Often there are hard feelings because each man seems to feel he is entitled to the new truck, so you have a tough time being fair. As a matter of fact, it usually turns out that whatever you decide, most of the men consider it wrong. You now have to face the same issue again because a new Chevrolet truck has just been allocated to you for distribution.

In order to handle this problem, you have decided to put the question to the men themselves. You will tell them about the new truck and ask them what is the fairest way to distribute the trucks. Do not take a position yourself because you want to do what the men think is fair.

## Role Sheet: George, Repairman

When a new Chevrolet truck becomes available, you think you should get it because you have the most seniority and don't like your present truck. Your own car is a Chevrolet and you prefer a Chevrolet truck such as you drove before you got the Ford.

-----------------------------------------------------------------------

## Role Sheet: Bill, Repairman

You think you deserve a new truck; it certainly is your turn. Your present truck is old, and since the more senior man has a fairly new truck, you should get the next one. You have taken excellent care of your present Dodge and have kept it looking like new. A man deserves to be rewarded if he treats a company truck like his own.

## Role Sheet: John, Repairman

You have to do more driving than most of the other men because you work in the suburbs. You have a fairly old truck and you think you should have the new one because you do so much driving.

--------------------------------------------------------------------

## Role Sheet: Charlie, Repairman

The heater in your present truck is inadequate. Since Hank backed into the door of your truck, it has never been repaired correctly. The door lets in too much cold air and you attribute your frequent colds to this. You want to have a warm truck since you have a good deal of driving to do. As long as it has good tires and brakes and is comfortable, you don't care about its make.

## Role Sheet: Hank, Repairman

You have the worst truck in the crew. It is five years old and had been in a bad wreck before you got it. It has never been good, and you have put up with it for three years. It's about time you got a good truck to drive and it seems only fair that the next one should be yours. You have had only one accident. That was when you sprung the door of Charlie's truck as he opened it when you were backing out of the garage. You hope the new truck is a Ford, since you prefer to drive that make.

## Observer Instruction Sheet

Using the following items as a guide, note what the foreman does and how the crew reacts.

1. How did the foreman present the problem?
   a. In presenting the problem, did he display the attitude of asking for help?
   b. Did he present all the facts?
   c. Was his presentation of the problem brief and to the point?
   d. Did he avoid suggesting a solution?
2. What things occurred in the discussion?
   a. Did all group members participate?
   b. Was there free exchange of feelings between group members?
   c. Did the group use social pressure to influence any of its members?
   d. On which member of the crew was social pressure used?
   e. Was the foreman permissive?
   f. Did the foreman avoid taking sides or favoring any person?
   g. What were the points of disagreement in the group?
3. What did the foreman do to help solve the problem?
   a. Did he ask questions to help the group explore ideas?
   b. Did he accept all ideas equally?
   c. Did he avoid hurrying the group to develop a solution?
   d. Did he avoid favoring any solution?
   e. Who supplied the final solution?
   f. What did the foreman do, if anything, to get a consensus on the final solution?

## Sample Table 1. Results of New Truck Problem

| | Group 1 | Group 2 | Group 3 | Group 4 | Group 5 |
|---|---|---|---|---|---|
| Group Solution Reached | G<br>B<br>J<br>C<br>H | G<br>B<br>J<br>C<br>H | G<br>B<br>J<br>C<br>H | G<br>B<br>J<br>C<br>H | G<br>B<br>J<br>C<br>H |
| a. Repairs | C | *No* | C | C, J, H | B |
| b. Number of Exchanges | 1 | 4 | 2 | 1 | 2 |
| c. Foreman Satisfied | *Yes* | *Yes* | *No* | *No* | *Yes* |
| d. Dissatisfied Drivers | G, B, J | 0 | G,H | G | J,C |

## COMMENTS AND IMPLICATIONS

This case usually results in an experience of success for the participants. Because most persons who play the part of the foreman have no preconceived solution in mind, they do little talking and are content to sit back and listen. The importance of this state of mind in the foreman can be demonstrated dramatically by asking a person who is to play the foreman to commit himself ahead of time on a solution that he considers to be fair. Such foremen have a difficult time and are inclined to think that the crew is unreasonable. When, however, the crew members realize that their foreman wants to do what they consider fair, there is a free expression of viewpoints. It soon becomes apparent that the opinions of the crew conflict; the noise level in the room rises during this stage. Often the foreman is overwhelmed by the arguing and wishes he had not consulted the group. Fortunately, however, because he usually does not know what to do, he does not interfere too much.

After all members have stated their position, certain members of the group perceive that the conflict is leading nowhere and begin to search for ways to resolve it. Respect for the rights of others becomes more apparent and constructive suggestions are proposed. The sound level now declines considerably. A solution gradually emerges as differences are resolved and concessions are made.

It is important that the foreman refrain from taking sides or agreeing with certain persons; in so doing, he tends only to antagonize others. Rather, he must continue to be patient and regard the conflict as a problem to be solved. Since most groups reach a decision that leaves few or none dissatisfied, it is apparent that the opportunity to express conflicting opinions can lead to a resolution of conflict. In fact, the airing of different views in a freely led discussion is an essential process in the reaching of an agreement. No amount of explaining by a foreman can accomplish this end.

For those crew members who remain dissatisfied, the cause is frequently something that happened during the discussion. Often, the foreman took sides against them, other members attacked them and the foreman failed to protect them, or the foreman ignored the ideas they expressed.

Less than completely satisfactory solutions are caused by a tendency (1) to solve the problem before each member has aired his views fully, and (2) to settle on the first constructive suggestion offered. The foreman can use his status to see that these things do not occur. It is often wise for the foreman to say, "Before we settle on that plan, let's take a look at some other possibilities." It is perhaps too much to expect that all crew members in all groups will be satisfied. Certain employees will create problems. However, as in real life, they usually number less than 10 percent of the total.

Since the issue in this case centers on the question of fairness, and since fairness is a personal matter, the crucial issue is one of employee *acceptance*. The group's decision is perhaps the best way to obtain maximum acceptance, but this does not mean that the foreman should not be concerned with the solution process. He is needed to conduct the discussion and to see that every member has a right to express himself. A point of special interest is the fact that George, the senior man, gets the new truck about half the time—but he gets it more often when he is considerate of others than when he is demanding. Seniority, it seems, is respected, but the senior member's conduct can lower this respect. Since each crew member gets the new truck on occasion, it becomes apparent that the manner in which the men conduct themselves in the discussion is one determinant of the outcome. Although the facts furnished by the role instructions are important, it must not be assumed that they alone should or do determine the solution.

The question of the objective *quality* of the solution does play some part in this case, but the results indicate that it is not a serious problem.

A poor solution is one in which a relatively good truck is discarded. It may be noted from the results obtained that most—if not all—crews reach the decision to discard Hank's truck. This solution conforms with the foreman's view and is therefore acceptable to management. Even though the foreman may not have suggested this solution, it seems that the crew may be depended on to do the right thing. Thus, the fear that a qualitatively poor solution may occur if the crew members make the decision is unrealistic.

It is possible also to argue that solutions that give several people a different truck are superior to those that give a different truck to only one or two. Participants, however, challenge this point and regard it as a matter of preference.

The frequent tendency to repair Charlie's truck is of special interest. Usually the foreman agrees early in the discussion to repair Charlie's truck. Sometimes Charlie does not even keep the truck that is to be repaired. The fact that Charlie exaggerates the condition of his truck because he wants the new one tends to be overlooked. The foreman gives in because he feels that the complaint is a reasonable one and, furthermore, that the request is an inexpensive one—particularly when he finds that everyone else, at this stage of the discussion, is asking for a new truck. It is a common error to take early complaints too seriously.

Of course, trucks should be kept in repair, but what constitutes proper repair sometimes is debatable.

How to distribute the new truck is a typical example of the problem of fairness. The values and issues raised in this case are similar to those raised whenever it is impossible to treat all persons alike. If a group decides the matter, the issue is resolved in terms of needs and values existing in the group at that time. Fair solutions must be tailor-made solutions, and no formula can be written that will take all variables into proper consideration. In order to be fair, all persons concerned must be made aware of the needs of others, and participants must discover that fairness cannot be achieved by judging others.

# 2

# *The Frustrated Supervisor*

## FOCUSING THE PROBLEM

Conflicts and misunderstandings between people frequently develop because of frustration. Disappointment, pressure of work, irritating behavior of other persons, and frequent or unwanted interruptions are a few factors that may give rise to temporary frustration. Most often, frustration of this sort is characterized by a sudden or marked change in behavior which may be triggered by a seemingly trivial incident. When this occurs, the behavior seems out of proportion to the incident itself and may become the cause of serious misunderstandings. Other persons may be aware only of the incident that triggered the behavior and the frustrated person himself often regards the incident as the cause of his disturbance, sometimes seeing the incident in its worst light in order to justify his behavior.

If a condition is temporary, it can be dealt with most effectively by providing a harmless outlet for the frustration. An attitude of understanding and permissiveness, to facilitate the expression of feelings, is the main consideration in furnishing relief. However, such treatment of temporarily frustrated persons may cause adverse reactions in other persons; the exaggerated nature and unreasonableness of such behavior tends to produce anger and frustration reactions in others. Therefore, practice in dealing with temporary frustration is highly desirable as a way to develop new approaches and skills as well as confidence in their usefulness.

In dealing with a frustrated individual, one must allow him to feel free to express himself. One must not be misled by confusing an incident that sets off frustrated behavior with the basic cause of the frustration. What the individual says and feels are the results of tension and do not reveal his true attitudes or his ability to analyze or think clearly.

The present case concerns a first-line supervisor who has trouble with one of his employees. The employee goes to the division supervisor, bypassing his own boss. The incident creates a situation in which the division supervisor feels called upon to talk to the first-line supervisor since the problem must be solved in order to avoid other incidents. This case gives the person playing the part of the division supervisor a good opportunity to practice his skills in diagnosing a situation, drawing out the feelings of another person, and solving a human relations problem between two other people. The fact that three levels of authority are involved does not make the problem easier.

This case involves a number of policy issues, over which there is likely to be considerable difference of opinion. By using the multiple role-playing procedure, differences in attitudes of the groups can be explored. Multiple role playing also gives everyone an opportunity to practice his skills in dealing with a disturbed person. Since the face-to-face aspects of this case are not difficult, most persons should enjoy a success experience.

## MULTIPLE ROLE-PLAYING PROCEDURE

### Preparation

1. Each member of the class pairs up with a person next to him; one member of each pair plays Janice Wells, the other plays Bill Jackson.
2. Participants read the role sheets for their characters.
3. The members of the pairs are advised not to discuss their roles with each other, but to imagine their positions and get in the mood of the problem.
4. When the Bill Jacksons are ready to begin role playing, they stand to indicate their readiness to meet with Wells. The instructor gives the signal for Bill Jackson to enter Janice Wells's office.

### Process

1. When Bill Jackson approaches Janice Wells, Wells greets Jackson and invites him to sit down.
2. All groups role play simultaneously.
3. Between fifteen and twenty minutes is usually sufficient time for the interview to be completed. The instructor terminates any uncom-

pleted interviews after twenty minutes. A warning of one minute is given.
4. During the role-playing process, the instructor prepares headings for the tabulations he will make on newsprint during the general report from the role players. The reports from the persons playing Janice Wells require three columns with the headings: (a) Jackson's trouble; (b) action to be taken; and (c) assistance offered. The reports from the Bill Jacksons require the form shown in Sample Table 2.

## General Report and Analysis

1. The participants who played Janice Wells, in turn, report (a) what they found Bill Jackson's trouble to be; (b) what action, if any, they think Jackson should take; and (c) the kind of help, if any, they think they should give him. These reports are listed in three columns on the board. The instructor tabulates briefly each new item and places a check mark after duplicate suggestions. (When possible, the Wells reporting should indicate whether her opinion agrees with a report given by a previous Wells. This will reduce the number of entries.)
2. When all the Wells players have reported, the instructor briefly summarizes the results.
3. The responses from the Jacksons may be obtained quickly by having the Jacksons indicate, with a show of hands, their reactions to the following questions:
   a. How many feel no better toward Blake since talking to Wells?
   b. How many feel better toward Blake now?
   c. How many want Blake back in their units?
   d. How many intend to apologize to Blake?
   e. How many feel better about their next-door neighbor?
   f. How many will apologize to their neighbor?
   g. How many feel criticized by Wells?
   The instructor enters the appropriate number in line 1 of the table (see Sample Table 2).
4. The Bill Jacksons consider the manner in which Wells dealt with them. She might have scolded or lectured; given advice; listened, but with some advice thrown in; or listened and responded to feelings so effectively that Jackson found himself telling everything. These four classifications are shown on lines 2, 3, 4, and 5 of the sample table. The instructor determines the number of times each type of interview occurred in connection with each of the kinds of feelings listed for Jackson and writes the appropriate number in each of the columns.

5. Whether or not Wells intended to, she may have caused Bill Jackson to think that she was against him, on his side, or neutral. Lines 6, 7, and 8 allow space to record these feelings under the various column headings.
6. Table 2 is discussed and conclusions are formulated on the procedure used by Wells that seemed to attain the most worthwhile objectives.

## Discussion Within Pairs

1. Each Bill Jackson tells his Wells what he liked most about the way he was treated in the interview.
2. Next, Bill Jackson tells Wells what he liked least about the treatment he received in the interview and why he reacted as he did.
3. The members of each pair privately discuss the situational factors, e.g., differences in rank, Blake's bypassing Jackson, work pressure, Jackson's expectation of criticism, etc., that lead to possible misunderstandings between Wells and Jackson.

## Discussion Issues

1. Is Jackson ready to deal with Joe Blake without embarrassment? Should Wells have covered this problem in the interview? Discuss.
2. A former Wells plays the part of Joe Blake. The Bill Jacksons who believe that Blake is entitled to an apology are given an opportunity to do so. Blake indicates what he likes or dislikes about each apology, without bothering to respond to the apologizer. The group discusses and evaluates several kinds of apologies.
3. How does Jackson feel about his neighbor? Is this important? Discuss.
4. How should higher supervisors deal with employees who bypass their immediate supervisors? Discuss.

*Note:* Class members and role players will raise many questions. These should be discussed, but the instructor should avoid supplying answers.

## Generalization of Case

1. Develop a list of situations that participants have experienced or observed that are basically like the case presented.
2. Discuss differences of opinion. Revise the list as indicated by the discussion.

## Role Sheet: Janice Wells,
## Division Supervisor[10]

You are the supervisor of a division employing seventy-five men and women and six first-line supervisors. You like your job and the supervisors and employees who work for you, and you feel that they cooperate with you in every way.

This morning, you noticed that one of your first-line supervisors, Bill Jackson, was rather late in getting to work. Since Bill is very conscientious and was working on a rush job, you wondered what happened. Bill is thoroughly dependable; when something delays him, he always tries to phone you. For this reason, you were concerned. You were about to call his home when one of Bill's men, a young fellow named Joe Blake, came in. Joe is a good-natured kid, just out of high school, but this morning he was obviously angry and said that he was not going to work for Bill another minute and was going to quit unless you got him another assignment. Evidently Bill had come in, started to work, and then lost his temper completely when young Joe didn't do something right.

Although Bill occasionally has his bad moods, it is unlike him to lose his temper this way. This latest rush job may have put him under too much pressure but, even so, his outburst this morning seems difficult to explain. You think that something must be seriously wrong; if you can get Bill to talk about whatever it is that is bothering him, you may get the situation straightened out. In any case, you are determined not to get into an argument with Bill or to criticize him in any way. Instead, you are going to try to get him to talk about his troubles, listen to what he has to say, and indicate that you understand how he feels about things. If Bill seems more angry than Joe's mistake reasonably justifies, you will suppose that there is something more behind all this and that Bill would feel a lot better if he got it off his chest. However, if Bill is thoroughly angry with Joe, you may suggest that Joe be transferred or fired in order to demonstrate that you have not taken Joe's side in the matter.

You talked with Joe for several minutes; after he told his side of the story, he felt better and was ready to go back to his job. You have just phoned Bill and asked him to drop around when he has a chance. Bill said he'd come right over and is walking toward your office now.

---

[10]Role instructions are reprinted from a case in N. R. F. Maier, *Principles of Human Relations,* New York: John Wiley, 1952, 423–425.

## Role Sheet: Bill Jackson,
## First-Line Supervisor

You have just come to work after a series of the most humiliating and irritating experiences you have ever had. Last night, your next-door neighbor, Sam Jones, had a wild, drunken party at his house and it kept you awake most of the night. Jones is a blustering, disagreeable man who has no consideration for others, so when you called him at about 3:00 a.m. and asked him to be less noisy, he was abusive and insulting. Things quieted down later on, but when you finally got some rest, you overslept.

Since you were in the midst of a rush job at the company, you skipped breakfast to hurry to work and, as you were leaving the house, you noticed that someone had driven a car across one corner of your lawn and had torn out several feet of your new hedge. You were sure that Jones or one of the drunks at his party had done it, so you ran right over to Jones's house, determined to have it out with him. He not only denied everything but practically threw you out and threatened to knock your teeth out if you didn't shut up and behave yourself—and you know that he is big enough to do it.

When you came to work, more than an hour late, your nerves were so ragged that you were actually shaking. Everything conceivable had gone wrong. The last straw was when you discovered that Joe Blake, a young high school recruit, had made a mistake that delayed you several hours on your rush job (or at least it would have if you hadn't caught it in time). Naturally, you chewed him out for his carelessness. Blake said he wouldn't take that kind of abuse from anyone and walked out on you. You noticed that he went in to see your supervisor, Janice Wells. Obviously, he is in there accusing you of being rough on him. Well, you don't like that kind of attitude in a young squirt either, and if he has gone in there squawking, you'll make him wish he'd never been born. You have had all you can stand and the boss had better not get tough with you, because she'll have one hell of a time getting the job done without you. Ms. Wells had that snivelling brat in there talking to her for quite a while before she phoned you to come in. Gabbing when there's work to be done—that's certainly a hell of a way to run things. You are on your way to Ms. Wells' office now and have no intention of wasting time on words.

(Try to get into the spirit of this case and feel some of the emotions that would ordinarily be present.)

## Sample Table 2.  Bill Jackson's Report
### (Use Table for Recording Class Data)

| | 1<br>Feel No Better Toward Blake | 2<br>Feel Better About Blake | 3<br>Want Blake in Unit | 4<br>Intend to Apologize to Blake | 5<br>Feel Better About Neighbor | 6<br>Will Apologize to Neighbor | 7<br>Feel Criticized by Wells |
|---|---|---|---|---|---|---|---|
| 1. Number of Jacksons | | | | | | | |
| 2. Wells Scolded or Lectured | | | | | | | |
| 3. Wells Gave Advice | | | | | | | |
| 4. Wells Listened and Advised | | | | | | | |
| 5. Wells Listened and Got Jackson to Tell Everything | | | | | | | |
| 6. Wells Took Sides with Blake | | | | | | | |
| 7. Wells Took Sides with Jackson | | | | | | | |
| 8. Wells Remained Neutral | | | | | | | |
| 9. Wells Brought Up Problem of How to Talk to Blake | | | | | | | |

## COMMENTS AND IMPLICATIONS

A good method of helping to relieve the frustration tension of others is to be a good listener. A good listener can refrain from becoming involved, thus avoiding hostile behaviors and arguments, which only contribute to a need to "save face" and to further frustration on the part of the speaker.

However, *listening* is not easily done. A speaker expects the person to whom he is talking to express his opinions. It is more important, however, to encourage the troubled person to talk about his *own* feelings. In responding to these feelings by nodding, a listener appears to be asking the speaker to tell him more; by showing that he understands, he creates a *permissive* relationship, which is essential for dealing with feelings.

A number of specific aspects of this case raise problems that often are present in real-life situations involving status, company policy, and pride. These factors must be dealt with realistically and put into proper perspective with the counseling type of interview. Some of these problems are examined below, but the suggestions made may not apply to all conditions.

Persons playing the part of Janice Wells may feel that they had an unusually sensitive person to comfort. This sensitivity is partly due to Jackson's feeling guilty for what he has done but, to a greater degree, it is due to his fear that Wells may be critical of him. Since he was asked to come see Wells right after Joe Blake had been there, it is not surprising that Jackson should be in this mental state. In going to see Wells, young Blake went over Jackson's head. This behavior represents an attack on Jackson's status as a supervisor and, under such circumstances, one should expect him to be hypersensitive.

To cope with this condition, it is important that Wells put Jackson at ease as quickly as possible. She must indicate that (1) Blake has been to see her and seemed very upset; (2) since Blake was Jackson's employee, Jackson should know about this visit; (3) the consequence of Blake's behavior is Jackson's problem, but that she (Wells) wants Jackson to know that she is willing to help in any way she can; and (4) she is willing to discuss the matter if Jackson so desires.

If Wells, by her manner, makes Jackson feel that he need not defend himself, Jackson will not only feel better towards Blake, but he will be able to face the situation as it was before Wells became involved. As long as Jackson has to be on the defensive with his superior, he cannot cope with his initial problem.

Once Jackson discovers Wells to be uncritical and understanding about his situation, he can speak freely. He may volunteer to tell about more than the incident with Blake, but if he fails to do this, Wells should realize that there is more to the story. An office error that is discovered before it causes real damage may be serious, but it does not upset a person to the extent that Jackson's behavior indicated. This is the clue for Wells to proffer a question such as "Was there anything else that happened?" in order to encourage Jackson to tell more.

If Wells responds to Jackson's feelings about pressure or lateness or no breakfast by saying, "I can see that upsets you very much," she can help Jackson to relax enough to tell still more about his feelings and state of mind. By being sensitive to little hints of other difficulties and by responding with such phrases as "You felt sure that one of the neighbor's guests had damaged your hedge and shown no respect for property rights," Wells can make it easy for Jackson to talk about the upsetting events. Too often, people are made to feel that they must justify their conduct and, as a result, they hide their true feelings and talk about the situation by greatly exaggerating the problem. Respect for their feelings makes exaggeration unnecessary.

It is through this expression of true feelings that tensions resulting from frustrations are released. Once these interfering emotions are reduced through expression, the original problem can be faced in a problem-solving state of mind.

For Jackson, training Blake and getting along with his neighbor are two challenging problems. The most immediate problem Jackson faces concerns the way he will talk to Joe Blake when he returns to the job. He may want to apologize, yet he fears that Blake will think he has won a victory. Thus, he is caught in a face-saving situation. Although this fear may be more imagined than real, it must be removed because it will influence Jackson's behavior. This is where Wells can be of help—by seeing to it that Jackson's problem is discussed. Together they can work out what Wells should say to Blake in order for Blake to recognize that the problem is back in Jackson's hands and that Wells considers Jackson to be competent to deal with it.

With this fear about Blake removed, Jackson can make a full apology. A partial apology such as "I was wrong, but you must be more careful about your mistakes" usually will not be accepted by Blake—and his failure to accept the apology will reinstate the conflict. A full apology such as "I had no business talking to you the way I did; I had a tough night and lost my temper and I'm really sorry about it" usually will stimulate Blake to apologize for his clerical mistake, his sensitivity, his running to Wells, or some combination of these. Generosity shown by one person stimulates it in another—this is a safe generalization and applies not only in this instance but in many others.

A frequent type of behavior shown by enlightened supervisors who play the part of Wells is to be sympathetic with Jackson and to indicate that they too have made mistakes. It is comforting to know that others err, but time is better spent if the upset person expresses his feelings rather than is comforted by descriptions of someone else's errors. This, too, is a safe generalization.

# 3

# *The Truck Seating Order*

## FOCUSING THE PROBLEM

In every company, there is a formal structure (the company's organizational chart) necessitated by the fact that positions in the company vary in importance and influence. That problems may arise whenever decisions breach this established hierarchy is fairly well understood by management. Any department head will hesitate to put a superintendent in an office that was previously occupied by a general foreman, even if it is a practical move on the basis of convenience and accessibility.

It is also known that status accompanies a job grade, e.g., machine operators will ask truckers to go out for sandwiches, but truckers will not expect operators to do the same. Now and then a problem arises because someone rebels and does not accept the social organization, but the basis of such a problem is usually understood and respected by the supervisors concerned.

When status is associated with a series of jobs in which pay rates or job grades are equal, management is often less understanding. For example, a manager in the telephone company who moved a tandem board operator to a long distance operator's position was surprised when he had a variety of reactions. The tandem operator hesitated, the other long distance operators did not understand the move, and the information operators talked about a walkout. He had overlooked the fact that there was an informal organization within the group of telephone operators that gave differential status in ascending order: tandem operator, information operator, local operator, and long distance operator.

Informal organizations *within* a homogeneous group sometimes go undetected by outsiders. Occasionally, even the insiders may be unaware of them until a problem disturbs the status quo. The tendency for social structuring is so basic that, in a very short period of time, even a group of animals will develop some sort of hierarchy. In a chicken yard, for example, a pecking order is soon established so that each chicken has a different status position. Chicken A can peck all other chickens; chicken B can peck all except A; chicken C can peck all except A and B; and the lowest chicken in the hierarchy is pecked by all but pecks none. Although the arrangement may be reached after a certain amount of strife, in an established group of chickens the existence of the pecking order could easily escape detection. Only when a new chick is introduced into the group does evidence of the social structuring come to light.

In small work groups, the presence of an undetected social structure could conceivably interfere with management directives and lead to misunderstanding. Whether social organization effectively satisfies the needs of group members, protects against their loss of freedom, or violates the democratic right of individuals are social values about which members may differ. The fact remains that an informal social organization can be created by the mere existence of a group of people having different preferences. Popularity, seniority, extent of knowledge, ability to relate to people, impartiality, etc., all may be factors that affect interpersonal relations and, as a consequence, have an influence on social organization and social values.

The case of the truck seating order introduces a situation in which behavior is governed by factors not apparent on the surface. The multiple role-playing procedure is used because it is desirable to have participants understand that outcomes of conferences are influenced by the way this problem is discussed. The solution agreed upon may vary from one crew to another, even though the facts established in the instructions are the same for all groups.

## MULTIPLE ROLE-PLAYING PROCEDURE

### Preparation

1. The class divides itself into subgroups of seven persons. Extra individuals serve as observers. (In the event that only one group of role players can be formed with six persons left over, a second group may be formed by assuming that Jack is home because of illness. His role

should be read by the person who plays the part of the foreman and the information treated as knowledge based on a telephone conversation with Jack. If only five persons remain, it is suggested that the instructor play one of the roles.)

2. All participants read the General Instructions individually. While the class is doing this, the instructor writes on newsprint the names of the foreman and the six crew members, indicating the years of service of each man and who serves as the work leader, the truck driver, and the substitute driver. Figure 2 is also drawn on the board, so that the seating arrangement in the truck will be apparent.

3. Each subgroup selects a person to serve as the foreman, Bert Jones. He takes a seat a short distance from the group and remains there until the instructor signals him to join his group.

4. If room facilities permit, the six workers in the crew seat themselves in a pattern duplicating the arrangement of the truck seating. For example, three may sit on each side of a table, or they may arrange three pairs of chairs facing forward. Each person then assumes the role of the crew member indicated by the seating arrangement and reads the instructions for that role only.

5. Observers have two sets of instructions: one concentrating on the behavior of the conference leader (the foreman, Bert Jones), and the other concentrating on the group process. If two or more persons observe a single group, the observational task is divided: half of them observe the leader's activities, the other half observe the group's interactions. Observers take seats to the right and left of the group they observe; they should be close enough to hear but remain as unobtrusive as possible.

6. When all arrangements are completed, the instructor alerts the foremen to be prepared to return to their groups. The crew members assume they are in Jones's office waiting for the scheduled meeting. All role instructions, except those used by the observers, are put aside and remain out of reach during the role play.

## Process

1. At the instructor's signal, the foreman joins the group, taking a seat to face Gus and George. This indicates that he has entered his office. Crew members should be in character and respond to his entrance.

2. All groups role play simultaneously.

3. Approximately twenty minutes is adequate for most groups to reach a solution.

4. All groups are given a chance to finish, but if one seems to be having

a particularly difficult time, the instructor tells the foreman to do the best he can in the next two minutes.

5. Newsprint is prepared for recording the results while the groups are engaged in role playing. Sample Table 3 shows the column headings that are used.

## Tabulating Results

1. The column with the heading "Solution" (Sample Table 3) is used by the instructor to enter a brief description of the solution reached by each of the groups. If the group reporting has one or more observers for the conference leader, one of them reports the solution. If no such observer is present, the foreman reports the solution. The instructor asks the men if the report accurately describes their understanding of the solution. If the group was unable to reach a solution in the time allowed, the phrase "no solution" is entered in the column for that particular group.

2. The column with the heading "Dissatisfied Men" is used to indicate the names of any dissatisfied crew members. The observers of the group interaction, with the assistance of the foreman, report who they think appears unhappy with the outcome. This report is checked to see if it corresponds with the role players' feelings of dissatisfaction. In cases of discrepancies, the differences in opinions are entered in the table by underlining the name of the man whose feelings were not understood. A little time is then spent in determining why the observer or foreman obtained an inaccurate impression of a man's feelings.

3. The column with the heading "Quality" is used to evaluate each group's solution. The role of Bert Jones contains a statement to the effect that his boss, Mr. Stevens, requested that the tailgate be operated by one of the men in the cab. The question is whether Mr. Stevens will be satisfied with the solution. Observers, foremen, and workers indicate their opinions by answering "yes," "no," or "questionable." The instructor records the results in the left side of the column. He then polls the opinions of other members of the class who participated in other groups and, in this manner, obtains the opinions of "outsiders." These are placed in the right half of the column.

4. Observers of the leader report briefly on the conference leadership functions that seemed to influence the success of the discussion. The instructor briefly notes these items in the column "Leader Behavior." In the event that no observers are used, members of the group comment on the leader's behavior.

5. Observers of the group interaction briefly report the types of conflict and alliances they observed, especially those related to George. The instructor makes brief notes in the last column, "Group Process."
6. If the number of groups is two or less, the observers and/or the foremen of the groups suggest some alternate solutions, so that four or five solutions are discussed. These solutions are tallied and the workers of the group concerned indicate whether they are satisfied. The solutions are also evaluated from the point of view of quality.

## Discussion of Results

1. The table of data is examined to determine why the solutions differed or why they came out the same way. Differences in leader behavior or group processes are examined carefully. (Participants may wish to copy the results in Sample Table 3.)
2. Persons reporting dissatisfactions describe the nature of their dissatisfactions.
3. Evaluations by "insiders" and "outsiders" under the column heading "Quality" are compared. If there are differences, a little time is spent discussing the reasons.
4. Dissatisfaction is then related to the questionable quality of the solutions.
5. If foremen or observers supplied solutions, were these solutions less acceptable?

## General Discussion

1. The request of Bert Jones undoubtedly created both favorable and unfavorable reactions. A discussion is used to develop a list of the disturbing issues raised by the request.
2. Most or all of the participants are probably satisfied with the solution of their group. Each participant describes the specific nature of the satisfaction he obtained from the discussion or the solution. This satisfaction may be as minor as having helped someone preserve his pride or as great as having presented the accepted plan to the group. Each person considers carefully if he can fine a specific item that caused his general satisfaction with the outcome.
3. Some time is then spent discussing the extent to which management should inconvenience itself in order to respect an informal social organization. Agreement on this matter is not sought; rather, the purpose is to discuss the extent of difference in the thinking of group members.

4. The participants explore their own experiences for examples of status problems they have encountered. A few of these are discussed and related to the present case.

## General Instructions

You are seven men who work for a utility. Six of you make up one of several crews whose job it is to maintain power lines; the seventh is your foreman, Bert Jones. Jones is in charge of three crews like yours, so when you are out on a job, you work under the supervision of your senior man, who acts as work leader. Your job statistics are as follows:

> George—17 years of service, work leader.
> Bill—12 years of service.
> Joe—10 years of service.
> Gus—9 years of service, driver of truck.
> Charlie—5 years of service.
> Jack—3 years of service, substitute driver.

Each morning you meet in the garage at the truck you use to ride to and from job locations, which change from day to day. The senior man sits in front with the driver while the rest of you sit on benches behind the cab of the truck. (This seating arrangement is shown in Figure 2.) Since the driver is responsible for the truck and the safety of the crew while riding to and from work, he and his substitute are selected on the basis of special tests. For greater safety—and also to keep tools from sliding out and getting lost—each truck is equipped with a tailgate that is hinged on the bottom edge and held shut with chain fasteners. In order to keep the chains out of the way—and also for greater safety and simplicity of construction—the fasteners are on the outside of the truck, out of reach from the inside.

It has always been customary for the man with the least seniority to have the duty of closing and fastening the heavy tailgate after everyone else is seated and then climbing over it into the back of the truck. When the destination is reached, he then jumps out to unfasten and lower the tailgate so that the other men can get out more easily.

You are all in Jones's office this morning for a meeting before you go out on the job. He has these meetings regularly.

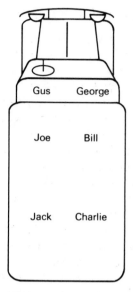

Figure 2. Truck Seating Arrangement.

## Role Sheet: Bert Jones, Foreman

Since you are foreman of three crews, you seldom go out on a job except in emergencies or on inspection trips. However, you meet your crews in the garage in the morning to give out the job assignments to the work leaders. You have noticed that when the trucks leave the garage, each man takes a particular seat. In Crew A, for example, George, the work leader with 17 years of service, sits in the cab with Gus, who is the regular driver and who qualified for the job by passing a driving test. Gus has 9 years of service. The other four men in the crew sit in back. Bill tried out for the driver's position but failed to pass the test. Jack has qualified on the driver's test and, as substitute driver, takes over when Gus is away. However, as low-seniority man, Jack always operates the tailgate, even when he drives.

There have never been any complaints from your crew that this arrangement is in any way unsatisfactory. As a matter of fact, you had never given the seating order any particular thought until the other day when your boss, Mr. Stevens, called you in and asked you to have one of the men who sits in the front seat open the tailgate in the future. Apparently, men in other crews have recently sprained their ankles and sustained other injuries when they jumped out to unfasten the chain. There have never been any injuries of that nature in your crew, but the idea makes good sense to you, so you have decided to meet with each of your crews to discuss it. This morning, you are meeting with Crew A and are about to enter your office where the meeting is to be held.

## Role Sheet: George

As work leader and senior man in your group, you always ride in front with the driver. You like to direct the driver to the particular job location for the day and you have to be comfortable to plan things. You rode in the back on the benches for years before you became top man in seniority and you have earned your right to the front seat. All through the company, the senior man has first choice in seating. This is one of the few remaining recognitions a man gets for his length of service. A few years back, some young college recruit tried to grab the front seat and you and the driver had to throw him out. You got him transferred the next week for picking a fight. Jack, who has the least seniority, has younger legs than you and he has always kept his place.

-----------------------------------------------------------------------

## Role Sheet: Bill

With twelve years of service, you are next to George in seniority. You have always ridden in back of the truck, except when George was sick or on vacation. Your regular seat is the one just behind the cab on the right side. It is smoother riding there because you don't sit over the rear wheels. When George gets promoted or transferred, you will inherit the front-seat privilege. You tried out on the driving test but did not get a high enough score, so the only way you can get the right to the front seat is to wait it out. As things are, the man with least seniority should sit in the back so he is handy for opening and closing the tailgate.

## Role Sheet: Joe

You joined the company ten years ago, when the present type of truck was first bought, so you had your turn handling the tailgate for a year until Gus was hired and took over the job. In those days, the trucks were even higher and it was much more difficult to climb in and to jump out of the truck. You hurt your feet and ankles a few times but never complained about it. You think the present arrangement is fair; being behind the cab on the left, you are out of the wind. But George should not be quite so fussy about always insisting on having the front seat. Even when one of the men is not feeling well, George will not offer to let him sit in front. After all, the whole crew works together and that ought to call for a little give and take. This rigid seating arrangement strikes you as childish.

------------------------------------------------------------------------

## Role Sheet: Gus

You had the job of handling the tailgate for four years before Charlie was hired, and you got sick of it. You feel there is a lot to be said for having the man who sits in front handle the tailgate, but since you are the driver, it is only fair that someone else should do it. After all, you passed the driver's test and are the official driver. Since you are working while the others just sit, you are entitled to some consideration.

## Role Sheet: Charlie

You had the job of opening and closing the tailgate for two years before Jack was hired. You think the fairest way to handle the matter is for the man who sits in the front seat to open and close the tailgate. You never complained when you had the job because each man ought to take his turn like everyone else, but it doesn't seem fair that the newest man should do it all the time. There ought to be some way of balancing out the menial work and the privileges so the newest man is not always the flunky.

--------------------------------------------------------------------

## Role Sheet: Jack

You have been low-seniority man on the crew since you joined the company three years ago. You didn't mind the job of opening and closing the tailgate at first, but you are tired of being treated as a flunky. You passed the driving test a year ago and are now the substitute driver who takes over when Gus is not on the job. When you do this, you still have to operate the tailgate. Some of the older men have more right to the front seat than you do and you wouldn't particularly want the seat anyway if it meant that you had to handle the tailgate. But just the same, one of the men who sits in the front seat should be willing to operate the tailgate. You have never injured yourself climbing into the truck or jumping out, but you have hurt your feet and ankles a few times when you accidentally came down hard on your heels. There is danger, too, if you jump out of the truck before you are sure that the driver has stopped completely. But if you try to play it safe and wait until you are sure, George yells, "Snap out of it!"

# Instructions for Observers of
# Conference Leader

One aspect of a conference is the conduct of the discussion leader, who in this instance is the foreman, Bert Jones. Jot down notes on the things he does that serve the constructive functions given below:

1. Clarifying the problem.
2. Assisting in resolving conflicts.
3. Getting all men to participate equally.
4. Preventing hurt feelings or protecting a member who is attacked by others.

If the foreman takes sides with any of the men or shows a preference for a particular solution, he is likely to create friction. Note whether he arouses unfavorable reactions and determine the cause.

Carefully note the solution agreed upon, since you may be asked to report it to the class.

Use supportive listening skills —

used you messages —
,, I messages —
what egostate did he use from
most often
    P.——
    A.——
    C.——

## Instructions for Observers of
## Group Interaction

An important aspect of any conference is the reaction and interaction of the members. Take notes in order to be prepared to answer the following questions:

1. After the leader presented the problem, which crew member resisted the change most strongly and which was most in favor of the change? Can you see a status factor that accounts for this difference of opinion?
2. To what extent were the arguments based on feelings and emotions, rather than on logical reasoning?
3. What were the choices open to George, the work leader? Which one did he settle for, and why? How would you characterize George's problem?
4. Was social pressure used to influence certain members one way or the other? If so, where did it come from and toward whom was it directed? What effect did it have?
5. Did the crew divide into subgroups? If so, how did they line up?
6. Were there any changes in alliances during the discussion? Note some examples.
7. Which, if any, of the members are dissatisfied with the solution?

8. Did the group play any games? . .

    Yes ___        No ___        Not sure ___

    if so, what were they  P___  R___  V___
    a/what Rules were played
9. what ego state did the
    group behave from most often

    P___        A ___        C ___

Sample Table 3. Results from Discussion on Seating Change
(Use Table for Recording Class Data)

| Group | Solution | Dissatisfied Men | Quality Insiders | Outsiders | Leader Behavior | Group Process |
|---|---|---|---|---|---|---|
| A | Jack in front seat with George and Gus. | George Gus Bill | 5 yes 1 no | 6 yes 2 question- able 8 no | Didn't under- stand. Impatient. Gave good reasons for change. | George was stubborn and disliked Jack. Bill wouldn't talk at the end. |

## COMMENTS AND IMPLICATIONS

The present case is based on an actual situation. The complications it caused surprised management personnel because the existence of a seating order was unknown to them. Every one of the trucks had a seating order and the new ruling disrupted relationships in each one until a new order was established.

A change in status symbols disrupts the best-established persons the most. This is true in community relations as well as in offices and work crews. George happens to be that person in the case under consideration. He has the preferred seat, but Mr. Steven's suggestion requires that he either perform the most menial task in the group or give up his status position in the truck. Since almost anyone in the group would be willing to perform the menial task if the status seat went with it, George's resistance may not be understood by everyone.

Jack, the low-status man, stands to gain the most by the order. This, too, may be hard to take and consequently requires the intermediate-status members to make a choice between supporting the person with more status or the person with less status.

These conflicting loyalties are usually ironed out in group discussion and are influenced not only by the issues in the situation but also by the conduct of the individuals involved. If Jack shows a grasping type of behavior, he may find himself without support.

In some instances, George gives up his seat, and one of the other members of the crew performs the menial task and gains the front seat. In other cases, George accepts the menial task; he does this with satisfaction if operating the tailgate is changed into a prestige duty. For example, group discussion may make it a safety precaution and the duty of the work leader. Sometimes George will agree to a trial period only. This probationary period may serve to test the group's reaction. If Jack tells him to hurry or if someone makes a wisecrack, the problem may be reopened.

Other solutions put Gus on the spot. If George's status is respected, group members may suggest that Gus perform the menial task. If he resists, Jack, the substitute driver, may indicate his willingness to both drive and take care of the tailgate. Usually someone will rescue Gus, but this, too, will depend on the respect that Gus as a personality can command.

The fact that most groups successfully solve this problem suggests the value of group discussion and group decision as a procedure a foreman may use to solve such complex problems. Since so many of the factors influencing the social structure of a group are unknown by a supervisor, he cannot succeed alone. However, the group approach resolves a pattern of conflicting forces that might escape measurement and evaluation.

Actually, a good deal of the success in group problem solving depends on the foreman's failure to have a ready solution. Because he is caught unaware, he lets the group talk it out. If he took sides or showed a preference for a particular solution, there would be less satisfaction.

Status problems are often discovered where we least expect them. In some offices, there is a problem with room temperature. Windows are opened by some and closed by others. People do not like to shift positions in a room so that temperature variations will correspond with temperature preferences. Often, preferred temperature spots are not at preferred locations—locations which have acquired status values. The suggestion that people dress according to the temperature they prefer may also raise a controversy, since those who adapt to the room conditions feel they are accepting a lower status in the group.

Status problems are often involved in the following types of circumstances: when employees are asked to work outside their job classification; when there are variations in conditions of work or in types of desks and chairs occupied by members of a work unit; when a different person is designated as a source of information and assistance for new employees; when the foreman chooses who will introduce a new employee into a unit; and when a new group member takes it upon himself to transmit complaints to the boss. Whenever a whole group is disturbed by a ruling or by what seems, on the surface, to be an improvement, it is worthwhile to examine the social organization.

It should not be supposed that status resulting from informal organization is undesirable. It is usually found that most persons who role play a member of the crew in this case obtain certain satisfactions—in many instances, these must be of a social nature. Group organization contributes to security and a feeling of belonging. A person gains this feeling most effectively when he fits a particular niche in a group. Persons who enter a new work group remain insecure and anxious until they find their places. Often they quit because they do not feel accepted. The question is not whether to encourage or discourage informal organization in work groups, but rather how to recognize it, respect it, and deal with it so as to maximize potential satisfactions.

# 4

# *A Problem with Old-Timers*

## FOCUSING THE PROBLEM

When individuals disagree, they frequently present facts to support their respective arguments with the expectation that when the other person has learned the facts of the situation, he will be won over to the desired point of view. In some instances, this approach may be effective —as when one party to the disagreement lacks certain essential information. More often, however, disagreements are based not merely on different factual information but on attitude differences. In this event, the presentation of facts as a means of argument is inefficient at best and may actually cause the attitude of the other person to become more rigid than before.

Most of the techniques used in persuasion are intellectual approaches in that they appeal to facts and logic. Each party to a dispute presents his side, attempts to find fault with the other's position, and may even attempt to prevent the other from speaking. Discussions are more polite in that there is respectful listening, but the emphasis still is on clarifying one's own position. Frequently the "yes-but" approach is used: one person accepts the point made by the opposition but counters with a better point of his own. What is called "selling" falls into the same category: the seller is busy giving his side while the other person looks for weaknesses and, hence, is concerned with opposite interests.

The failure of factual argument to resolve disagreement based on attitudes becomes more understandable when it is realized that one of the important ways in which attitudes influence behavior is to cause individuals to use only facts that are consistent with their attitudes. Facts inconsistent with their attitudes are either ignored or reinterpreted. Thus, regardless of the facts of the situation, persons who differ in attitude are prone to misunderstand each other and the facts of the case become irrelevant. When this occurs, communication becomes faulty.

The following role-playing case is specifically designed to demonstrate how attitude differences lead to conflict and reduced communication. The case is based on a situation in industry and concerns attitudes regarding the relative desirability of employing "old" and "young" persons in an office. Two persons are involved in the actual interview: one is a personnel director who sees the problem of "old" employees from his position and personal experience; the other is an office manager who is production oriented and sees the problem differently. When they discuss the issue of employment and placement, they are likely to disagree. The manner in which the facts of the case influence the behavior of the participants, the kinds of human relations skills practiced by each, and the satisfactions created in various pairs of role players will furnish interesting comparisons.

The multiple role-playing procedure is described for this case because it allows a comparison of results and the collection of relevant data. If the case is used with a highly trained group of persons, single-group role playing may be used to test the more advanced skills.

## MULTIPLE ROLE-PLAYING PROCEDURE

### Preparation

1. The class divides into groups of three. When a class is not divisible by three, one or two pairs may role play without an observer.
2. One person in each group accepts the role of Mr. Jones, the second plays Mr. Smith, and the third becomes the observer.
3. The Background Material for all Participants is then read by everyone. It is desirable to have the instructor read this material aloud slowly so that participants may become thoroughly familiar with the situation.
4. When the situation is clarified, the individual roles are studied. Those playing Mr. Smith leave the room to study their roles. The observers and the Joneses remain in the room. The observers read the Instructions for Observers, and the Joneses read their roles. (Participants are requested to read only their roles and not to communicate with each other.)
5. When the observers and the Joneses have finished studying their parts, the Joneses tell their observers what they plan to accomplish

in the interview to follow. Then the observers stand to indicate that they are ready.

6. The instructor asks the Smiths to return. At his signal, they join their groups and assume they have entered Mr. Jones's office to keep the scheduled appointment. Mr. Jones stands and greets Mr. Smith.

## Process

1. This case is not intended to be carried to the point of completion. It is a difficult interview and should be terminated when no new factors or approaches are introduced into the discussion.
2. Usually a period of ten minutes is sufficient to clarify the type of approach used by the interviewer.
3. The instructor prepares table headings on newsprint as shown in Sample Table 4, while groups are role playing. Sample Table 5 is also prepared but is not displayed until the discussion period.
4. The instructor gives the signal to terminate all role plays simultaneously, regardless of the different stages they may have reached.

## Observers' Reports

1. The degree of progress made by Jones in converting Smith is evaluated by the observer for each group. (If no observer is present, the report is made by Smith.) Letter grades A, B, C, D, and F may be used to indicate a range of progress from "excellent" to "failure." The instructor writes the letter grade in the proper place on the newsprint (see Sample Table 4).
2. The type of approach used by Jones is described by the observer for each group. If possible, the following categories are used to classify the approach: logical argument, the "yes-but" discussion, the selling method, friendly persuasion, and listening with understanding in order to solve a problem of mutual interest. This observation is indicated on the table. (If no observer is present, Smith supplies this information.)
3. The observer for each group gives his opinion of whether future relations will be better, worse, or about the same as a result of the interview. (If no observer is present, Jones and Smith give their observations.)

## Discussion of Observers' Reports

1. The Smiths discuss the ways in which they agree or disagree with their observers' reports. Each Smith then assigns a grade of A, B, C,

D, or F to indicate his observer's abilities to judge his feelings and methods. These letter grades are entered in the table. (Omit if no observer is present.)

2. The Joneses then discuss the observers' reports from their viewpoints and likewise assign them letter grades. (Omit if no observer is present.)

3. Table 4 is discussed to determine if the degree of progress is related to the method used. It is possible that all interviews erred in the same direction—that of each participant telling his side.

## Determining Whether Facts Selected Reflect Attitudes

1. The facts as classified in the observers' instructions are listed on the newsprint (see Sample Table 5). The instructor polls the observers to determine whether each fact was first mentioned by Jones or Smith. He writes the number of Joneses mentioning a given fact in the first column and indicates the number of Smiths who presented that fact in the second column.

2. When the polling is completed, the totals are filled in. The totals of the Smiths for unfavorable vs. favorable facts indicate the degree to which they selected facts to support their attitudes, as do the totals of the Joneses. These totals for Smith and Jones may be expressed as ratios.

3. The degree to which each participant selected facts favorable to his position indicates the extent to which he was selling or arguing. If the Joneses show a lesser discrepancy between their totals of favorable and unfavorable facts, we can credit them with being less defensive and with being good listeners. Listening is what the interviewer should do.

4. The grand total gives the combined number of facts mentioned by the Joneses and Smiths. It is desirable that this total be less for the Joneses than for the Smiths because the interviewer is supposed to get the interviewee to talk. In effect, the grand total reflects the amount that each talked.

5. Time is allowed to discuss the tabulated data, to introduce additional observations, and to exchange different opinions on the best way to conduct this interview.

## Background Material for All Participants[11]

In a commercial office employing a large number of women, there was a period when business was slack and very few people were hired. Following this period, business improved and there was a good deal of expansion. Thus, during the past five years, many new women have been hired. As a result, there are ninety women who have worked for the company ten or more years, fifteen who have been with the company from five to nine years and who were hired during the slack period, and 450 who have less than five years of service. This hiring pattern has created a unique situation in the office. There is a fair-sized group of old-timers and a large group of newcomers, with an age difference of at least five years between the youngest of the old-timers and the oldest newcomer. These two groups do not get along well with each other. The younger group often refers to the older employees as "old biddies" and "sour pusses," while the latter refer to the younger women as "dumb bunnies" and "young hussies." The office force has recognized the problem and commonly differentiates between the two groups as "the old-timers" and "the kids."

Mr. Jones is in charge of the personnel office and, for the past fifteen years, has done all the hiring and placing of employees. All transfers, changes in pay rates, etc., must be cleared through him. He is in a staff position and his office was set up to service the line organization.

Mr. Smith is the manager of one of four large divisions within the company. There are four supervisors who report to him and his position in the organization is comparable in rank to that of Mr. Jones. Since Smith and Jones report to different vice-presidents, neither has authority over the other. Smith and Jones know each other only through their business relationship. Most of their contact with each other has been by telephone.

Jones has asked Smith to see him to discuss a problem in connection with the old-timers. Smith is about to enter Jones's office.

---

[11]Role instructions are taken from a case in N. R. F. Maier, *Principles of Human Relations*, New York: John Wiley, 1952, 103–104.

## Role Sheet: Mr. Jones, Personnel Office

You have a persistent problem with Mr. Smith, the manager of a large office group in the company. He objects to older employees and refuses to accept them as transfers. He also gives poor ratings to older women and tries to get you to find other places for them. As far as you can tell, he is prejudiced.

You believe that the older women make good, stable employees. You find them more conscientious, more dependable, more business-like, and generally more capable. You can't understand Smith's position and therefore have decided to talk to him to see if you can't convince him to take his share of the older women and to give them a better deal.

You have asked Smith to come to your office because it is designed to be used for interviewing and therefore allows more privacy than does Smith's office. It is just about time for Smith to arrive.

The following are some things you know about the behavior of older women as compared to younger women. (Naturally, you keep records and keep in touch with what goes on around the place.)

- They adapt slowly to new jobs.
- They know the company setup.
- They know how to do a greater variety of jobs in the company.
- They object more to changes in methods.
- They are less sociable.
- They have the same production rate.
- They are less willing to do unpleasant jobs.
- They are tardy less often.
- They spend more time in the restroom.
- They have a lower absentee rate.

Do not try to memorize these points. Just consider them as background information such as you would be familiar with in a real-life situation.

When you have finished studying your role, tell your observer your objective in this interview and how you plan to conduct it. If you have no observer, note these points on a slip of paper.

## Role Sheet: Mr. Smith, Office Manager

You have had considerable trouble with Mr. Jones in the personnel office. He is not cooperating with you on the kind of employees you want and does not help you by obtaining new jobs for those you want to get rid of. Mostly, the issue centers on problems concerning older women. You refuse to accept women over forty years of age and you try to transfer your older women whenever you can. You like a young force. You have had dealings with all types of employees and you and the four supervisors who report to you all agree that younger employees are preferable. You do not like to deal with old-timers and see no reason why you should have to. However, if the company wants to keep them, let those who like them take them into their units. As far as you are concerned, they are not worth the pay they get. They are inefficient, undependable, and slow. (Before attempting to play this role, try to feel dislike for older employees. Remember, you have had some headaches with them.)

You have an appointment with Mr. Jones; he has asked to see you to discuss your views about older employees. You are a busy person and are tired of discussing problems the personnel staff dreams up. As you see it, the personnel department is supposed to assist the line organization—but they seem to talk more than they assist.

Here are some things you know about the behavior of old-timers, compared to younger employees:

- Their absentee rate is lower.
- They spend more time in the restroom.
- They are tardy less often.
- They are less willing to do unpleasant jobs.
- They have the same production rate.
- They are less sociable.
- They object more to changes in methods.
- They know how to do a greater variety of jobs in the company.
- They know the company setup.
- They adapt slowly to new jobs.

Do not try to memorize these points; just consider them to be background information such as you would be familiar with in a real-life situation.

## Instructions for Observers

In their roles, Smith and Jones are given the same facts concerning old-timers. However, the men disagree as soon as they begin their discussion because they have been given different attitudes. Smith's role is designed to induce an unfavorable attitude toward older women and the role for Jones is designed to create a favorable attitude. Observe the extent to which the participants use the facts that are consistent with their own attitudes and how they deal with those facts that are inconsistent with their attitudes. Since the purpose of this case is to illustrate how persons with different attitudes may disagree even when they both have the same facts, the role play may be terminated when it has become apparent that the two men treat facts differently. The instructor may check with you to determine whether or not your pair of role players has ceased introducing additional facts.

The facts supplied the role players are given below. For your convenience, they are divided into three groups: those favorable to old-timers, those unfavorable to them, and those that are neutral or that may be interpreted either way. While observing the role play, place the initial "S" or "J" before a fact to indicate whether Smith or Jones was the first to bring it into the conversation.

FACTS ABOUT OLD-TIMERS

*Favorable*

\_\_\_\_ Lower absentee rate

\_\_\_\_ Less tardiness

\_\_\_\_ Know how to do a greater variety of jobs

\_\_\_\_ Know company setup

*Unfavorable*

\_\_\_\_ Spend more time in restrooms

\_\_\_\_ Less willing to do unpleasant jobs

\_\_\_\_ Object more to changes in methods

\_\_\_\_ Adapt slowly to new jobs

*Neutral*

\_\_\_\_ Same production rate

\_\_\_\_ Less sociable

Mr. Jones has been instructed to tell you what he plans to accomplish in his interview with Smith. Ask him also to indicate the approach he plans to use. Make a note of these points, but do not give him any assistance.

Sample Table 4.  Summary of Progress in Interview Concerning
Old-Timers
(Use Table for Recording Class Data)

| Group Number | Observer's Rating of Progress | Observer's Description of Approach | Observer's Estimation of Future Relations of Jones and Smith | Smith's Judgment of Observer's Report. (Letter Grade) | Jones's Judgment of Observer's Report (Letter Grade) |
|---|---|---|---|---|---|
|  |  |  |  |  |  |

## Sample Table 5. How Attitudes Select Facts
(Use Table for Recording Class Data)

|  |  | No. of Joneses | No. of Smiths |
|---|---|---|---|
| *Facts Favorable to Old-Timers* |  |  |  |
| 1. Lower Absentee Rate |  | _____ | _____ |
| 2. Less Tardiness |  | _____ | _____ |
| 3. Know Greater Variety of Jobs |  | _____ | _____ |
| 4. Know Company Setup |  | _____ | _____ |
|  | Total | _____ | |
| *Facts Unfavorable to Old-Timers* |  |  |  |
| 1. Spend More Time in Restrooms |  | _____ | _____ |
| 2. Less Willing to do Unpleasant Jobs |  | _____ | _____ |
| 3. Object More to Changes in Methods |  | _____ | _____ |
| 4. Adapt Slowly to New Jobs |  | _____ | _____ |
|  | Total | _____ | |
| *Neutral Facts* |  |  |  |
| 1. Same Production |  | _____ | _____ |
| 2. Less Sociable |  | _____ | _____ |
|  | Total | _____ | |
|  | Grand Total | _____ | |

## COMMENTS AND IMPLICATIONS

Arguments, "yes-but" discussions, and "selling" approaches differ in the degree of courtesy shown by the two participants, but they are alike in that a person using them is presenting *his* views to the other person. He is trying to get the other person to see and accept *his* way of looking at a subject as the correct one. Instead, however, he often encourages the other person to defend his own viewpoint more vigorously. Thus, in our case, we saw that Jones's attempts to make Smith accept older employees were often met with increased hostility.

Since these approaches are ineffective, we must look in a different direction for an effective procedure. For example, instead of trying to get Smith to agree with him, suppose Jones tries to understand Smith's position. This means that he would have to take an approach almost opposite to the one usually taken—to try to understand rather than to explain. In order for Jones to learn Smith's viewpoint he must listen; this means he must get Smith to talk freely. In order to get the real facts, Jones must not challenge any statements, since critical behavior will force Smith to resort to presenting reasons or facts that he considers acceptable to Jones and which are not the real basis of Smith's viewpoint.

In order to create a free discussion climate, Jones might express an interest in Smith's view because Smith's office has firsthand experience with the work of various groups of employees. He can indicate that old-timers are a problem for the company and that he would like to have Smith evaluate their behavior. After a few preliminary reactions, he can proceed to make a list of the undesirable behaviors. This gives Smith an opportunity to tell all the bad things he knows about older employees without being challenged. Jones should accept all points and patiently wait while Smith lists as many items as he can. If Smith is not challenged, he is likely to bring up some personal feelings and experiences that reveal the source of his biases against older employees. Since these are probably not good reasons, Smith undoubtedly would not have revealed them in an argument.

When this list is completed, Jones may ask Smith whether the old-timers have any good points. If Smith indicates that there are a few, Jones should list them also. Ordinarily, Smith will be glad to give good points because the opportunity to talk about the bad points will have made him more generous. If both points of view have been contributed by Smith, it is obvious that he accepts them as relevant; once this is accomplished, problem-solving behavior can begin. The problem for discussion may be expressed in terms of the best way the company can accommodate the strengths and weaknesses of older women. This leads to a consideration of their abilities, the types of jobs available in a department, the number of older women in the company, the best way to mix women with different lengths of service, and many other issues that may be of interest and concern to both Jones and Smith.

We call the above approach to an interview the "two-column method" because it is designed to permit one party to express both sides of an issue, one after the other. The side favored by the interviewee is expressed first. This method is useful whenever there is a disagreement on facts that are in the nature of common knowledge. When a situation or controversy is fluid and the actual problem is difficult to locate, the two-column method is useful for clearing the ground and indicating the problem-issue for discussion.

Attitude holders not only organize facts and thereby determine their meaning, but they select facts as well. This means that discussions about facts are irrelevant to the opinions held. The two-column approach to a problem eliminates the dispute over facts and meanings by having all of them come from one source. When this occurs, there is at least some basis for cooperative problem solving. The method is not a cure-all, but it can be useful to separate facts from a controversy and to face more squarely the real problem—the difference in attitude. Once some respect and understanding of an attitude is expressed by the interviewer, the interviewee feels less need to protect his attitude. Thus, an attitude that is not defended can often be changed.

# 5

# *The Change of Work Procedure*

## FOCUSING THE PROBLEM

It is frequently necessary for industry to adapt its operations to new market demands and engineering advances in production methods. The changes involved usually entail the solving of a variety of problems. New patterns of consumer needs must be anticipated, decisions must be made about the utilization of new or existing equipment and procedures, job grades and pay rates may be altered, and employees must be trained in new skills and methods. Despite the rapidity and magnitude of the changes, satisfactory and even ingenious solutions to the technical and engineering problems are often found.

However, changes in operations and methods are seldom confined to the technical aspects of production; they may also require alterations in the work of the employees. When this is true, the new methods not only must be workable and efficient from an objective standpoint, they also must be acceptable to the employees concerned.

This added factor of acceptance makes the problems of introducing changes different in certain important ways from purely technical problems of evaluating new equipment or procedures. For one thing, the quality of a solution and its acceptability are different characteristics and do not necessarily co-exist. Furthermore, while management can control solution quality by reserving decision making to itself, acceptance is inherently voluntary with the employees and is not subject to the will of management. Failure to obtain employees' acceptance of changes that affect them increases many of the problems of management. In some instances, resistance is expressed directly in the form of grievances about rates and earnings, resignations, work stoppages, and open hostility toward management. In other instances, the resistance may be shown in such indirect ways as restriction of output, waste, low-quality workmanship, slow learning of the new methods, excessive absenteeism, and the like.

Management's concern with these negative reactions to change is of comparatively recent origin, but it has led to the development of various methods of dealing with the problem. One of the most widely used is that of "selling" the employees on the advantages of the change. Facts and arguments are presented, the expectation being that once employees have the same facts and information as management, they will adopt a similarly favorable view of change. To the extent that resistance to new methods is based on a lack of correct information, this procedure has merit. However, this deficiency is seldom the case. Instead, resistance nearly always involves feelings of insecurity, distrust of management's motives, and anxiety for the future. Facts and arguments provide small comfort when skills are made obsolete, and they have little or no effect on unfavorable attitudes.

The limited success of the "selling" approach has necessitated the development of other methods. One of these is a procedure by which supervisors consult with employees concerning proposed changes and other problems. The mechanics of what is known as consultative management vary from one company to another; however, the essential feature is that an attempt is made to learn the ideas and feelings of the employees, with management reserving the right to accept or reject the employees' contributions as it sees fit.

Insofar as ways for obtaining acceptance are concerned, the two methods are very different: the "selling" approach emphasizes the presentation of management's point of view, whereas the consultative approach is designed to obtain employees' opinions. In this sense, the latter method is a step in the direction of consideration for the welfare of employees. The two methods are alike in that both reserve the decision-making function for management—the intent being to protect the quality of the decision.

Management's insistence on protecting solution quality by retaining decision power raises the question of whether solution quality is always the prime consideration, or whether there may be circumstances in which a high-quality solution that fails to gain acceptance is less efficient than a solution of less quality that has the support of the employees concerned. The problem is whether both quality and acceptance can be achieved with a single procedure.

There is no formula that will be effective for all instances of resistance to change. The suggestion of change in a work situation sets in motion a series of reactions and, unless one knows what they are, the handling of the matter is likely to be inappropriate. Persons involved in a new plan wonder what effect it will have on their incomes, their future, their working environment, and their group status. They know how they are doing under present conditions but a change means new and, consequently, strange conditions. The person who initiates a change may or may not be on the side of the persons who must adopt the change. The reaction to change cannot be separated from the reaction to the person or group that initiates the change.

It is apparent that resistance to change is not mere inertia but, rather, a response to a threat. If changes could be made without threatening someone, they could be discussed in an intellectual manner and facts would be welcomed; but as long as the threat is present, facts serve to reinforce the threat.

In order to deal with problems of change, the first step is to learn the nature of the resistance. In the present case, many forces are operating: some in the direction of change, some opposed to it. The supervisor in charge will want to use the constructive forces to improve conditions as much as possible. The kind of discussion he stimulates may introduce new negative or new positive forces so that the outcome may, in part, be determined by the discussion he initiates.

The case is set up for multiple role playing so that the maximum number of persons can participate as leaders in a lively discussion. The persons playing the part of workers will profit by experiencing the meaning of change.

## MULTIPLE ROLE-PLAYING PROCEDURE

### Preparation

1. The participants form groups of four persons each. Those remaining may function as observers.
2. One member of each group plays the foreman, Gus Thompson. The other three individuals in each group play the crew members: Jack, Steve, and Walt.
3. When all members have received their role sheets, the instructor reads the General Information for All Participants aloud.
4. The role players than study their individual roles in preparation for the small group discussions. Participants read only their own roles.

5. The Gus Thompsons stand beside their groups when they have finished studying their roles, to signal to the instructor that they are ready to begin.

## Process

1. When all foremen are standing, the instructor helps set the stage for the role play by commenting that the foreman has asked the crew members to meet with him in his office to discuss a problem before starting work. He explains that when the foreman is asked to sit down, it will signal that Gus has entered his office. He hopes that the crew will speak to Gus as he enters.
2. When everyone understands his function, the instructor asks the foremen to sit down. All groups role play simultaneously.
3. During the role play, the instructor prepares a sheet of newsprint with the headings shown in Sample Table 6. This table is used to record the results of the various group discussions.
4. Approximately twenty-five minutes is needed by the average group to reach a decision. At the end of this period, the instructor observes the progress of the groups. If most of them have finished, he gives the remaining groups a two-minute warning signal.

## Collecting Results

1. The foreman of each group reports the solution agreed upon. The instructor enters the solution, in abbreviated form, in the proper column of the table (see Sample Table 6). Care should be taken to include any special or unique features such as rest pauses, partial rotation procedures, arrangements for helping one another, etc.
2. The foreman indicates his degree of satisfaction with the solution; the instructor enters this response in column 2.
3. The members in each crew indicate whether they are satisfied or dissatisfied with the results. The instructor indicates the number satisfied in column 3. Occasionally a member will be mildly inclined in one direction or the other, in which case a question mark is entered to indicate his feelings.
4. Each foreman is asked whether any crew members were unusually stubborn, hostile, or troublesome and, if so, who they were. The initials of these members are written in column 4.
5. The crew members report whether they think production will go up, down, or remain the same as the result of the discussion. When they think there will be a change, they are to agree on a percent increase

or decrease, and the instructor enters this figure in column 5 of the table.

6. The observers (or crew members) report what they feel is the main thing the leader did to help his group reach a decision. The members are to agree on this point so that the instructor can summarize their consensus under column 6.

7. The observers (or crew members) report what the leader did to hinder the discussion. This point is summarized under column 7.

## Classification of Solutions

1. After the results from all groups have been tabulated, the solutions are reviewed briefly in a general group discussion to determine which solutions represent a rejection of changes in the work method. These may be indicated by the letter "R" in the margin.

2. Solutions indicating acceptance of the management solution with minor or no modifications are selected by the group and labeled with the letter "A" in the margin.

3. The remaining solutions are then examined for new features and various concessions, such as rest pauses, partial rotation, more time in one's best work position, ways for the crew members to help one another, trial periods, and so on. These solutions, which represent compromises and the development of new ideas, are indicated in the margin by the letter "C." A short time may be taken to discuss how these various provisions contributed to the satisfaction of the crew members.

4. The solutions are examined to determine which are provisional or of a trial nature. Some time may be spent discussing why foremen made these concessions.

## Evaluation of Methods Used

1. The attitudes of the leaders are discussed in relation to the types of solutions developed. General conclusions are drawn as to what constitutes a helpful, versus an obstructive, leader attitude.

2. Discussion is used to determine the ways in which the airing of feelings and hostilities in the crew influenced the final outcome.

3. On the basis of the tabulated results and the role-playing experience, the group attempts to determine the foreman's part in influencing the outcome of the discussion. Both satisfaction and productivity are considered in relation to the type of solution reached and the foreman's conduct, as described in columns 6 and 7 of Sample Table 6.

4. Column 4 is examined to determine whether certain crew members caused most of the trouble. If different men were troublemakers in the various groups, this suggests that certain events in the discussion, rather than the role instructions, were the cause of their troublesome behavior. In any case, the problem employees report why they acted as they did.

## Analysis of Resistance Forces

1. From the group as a whole, the instructor obtains the various objections to change expressed by the different crew members and lists these on the newsprint. This list usually will include such factors as aversion to boredom, dislike of the time-study man, fear of rate cuts, fear of speedup, fear of running out of work, and the like.
3. Next to the objections, the instructor lists the possible gains or advantages to the crew by changing to the new method. Usually the item of more pay will be mentioned. Other factors, such as time for rest pauses, satisfaction with being in one's best position, etc., may be offered. However, only those aspects actually mentioned in the role-playing discussion are to be accepted.
3. The objections to (forces against) changing work methods and advantages of (forces toward) change are now considered.
4. The list of resistances to the new work method is now examined to determine the items that indicate fear and hostility and those with a more intellectual basis.
5. Ways for reducing fears and negative feelings are discussed. Results from the previous role-playing cases may be considered, if relevant.
6. Participants are invited to describe their personal experiences involving resistance to change.

## General Information for All Participants[12]

In a company manufacturing subassemblies for the automobile industry, the assembly work is done by small groups of employees. Several of these groups are under the supervision of a foreman, Gus Thompson. In one of these groups, Jack, Steve, and Walt work together assembling fuel pumps.

This operation is divided into three jobs or positions: Position 1, Position 2, and Position 3. Supplies for each position are located next to the bench where the man works. The men work side by side and it is possible for them to help each other out if they wish. Since all the jobs are simple and fairly similar, the three employees exchange positions on the line every now and then. This trading of positions was developed by the men themselves. It creates no financial problem because the crew is paid on a team piece-rate basis. In this way, the three members share the production pay equally.

---

[12]Role instructions are taken from a case in N. R. F. Maier, *Principles of Human Relations*, New York: John Wiley, 1952, 154–156.

## Role Sheet: Gus Thompson, Foreman

You are the foreman in a shop and supervise the work of about twenty people. Most of the jobs are piece-rate jobs; some of the employees work in teams and are paid on a team piece-rate basis. In one of the teams, Jack, Walt, and Steve work together. Each one of them does one of the operations for an hour and then they exchange, so that all men perform each of the operations at different times. The men themselves decided to operate this way and you have never given the matter any thought.

Lately, Jim Clark, the methods man, has been around studying conditions in your shop. He timed Jack, Walt, and Steve on each of the operations and came up with the following facts:

Time per Operation (in Minutes)

|       | *Position 1* | *Position 2* | *Position 3* | *Total* |
|-------|------------|------------|------------|--------|
| Jack  | 3          | 4          | 4½         | 11½    |
| Walt  | 3½         | 3½         | 3          | 10     |
| Steve | 5          | 3½         | 4½         | 13     |
|       |            |            |            | 34½    |

He observed that with the men rotating, the average time for all three operations is one-third of the total time or eleven and one-half minutes per complete unit. If, however, Jack worked in Position 1, Steve in Position 2, and Walt in Position 3, the time would be nine and one-half minutes, a reduction of over 17 percent. Such a reduction in time would amount to a savings of more than eighty minutes. In other words, the lost production is about the same as that which would occur if the men loafed for eighty minutes in an eight-hour day. If the time were used for productive effort, production would be increased more than 20 percent.

This makes pretty good sense to you, so you have decided to take up the problem with the team members. You think that they should go along with any change that is made.

## Role Sheet: Jack

You are one of three men on an assembly operation. Walt and Steve are your teammates, and you enjoy working with them. You get paid on a team basis and your wages are entirely satisfactory. Steve isn't quite as fast as Walt and you, but when you feel he is holding things up too much, each of you can help out.

The work is very monotonous. It helps that every hour you all change positions; in this way, you get to do all three operations. You are best on the number 1 position, so when you get in that spot, you turn out some extra work and make the job easier for Steve, who follows you in that position.

You have been on this job for two years and have never run out of work. Apparently your group can make pretty good pay without running out of a job. Lately, however, the company has had some of its experts hanging around. It looks like the company is trying to work out some speedup methods. If they make these jobs any simpler, you won't be able to stand the monotony. Gus Thompson, your foreman, is a decent guy and has never criticized your team's work.

## Role Sheet: Steve

You work with Jack and Walt on an assembly job and get paid on a team piece-rate basis. The three of you work very well together and make a pretty good wage. Jack and Walt like to make a little more than you think is necessary, but you go along with them and work as hard as you can to keep the production up where they want it. They are good guys and sometimes help you out if you fall behind, so you feel it is only fair to try and go along with the pace they set.

The three of you exchange positions every hour. In this way, you get to work all positions. You like Position 2 the best because it is easiest. When you get in Position 1, you can't keep up and then you feel Gus Thompson, the foreman, watching you. Sometimes Walt and Jack slow down when you are on the number 1 spot, and then the foreman seems satisfied.

Lately the methods man has been hanging around watching the job. You wonder what he is up to. Can't they leave guys alone who are doing all right?

## Role Sheet: Walt

You work with Jack and Steve on a job that requires three separate operations. Each of you works on each of the operations by rotating positions every hour. This makes the work more interesting and allows you to help a team member by varying your production speed. It's all right to help out because you get paid on a team piece-rate basis. You could actually earn more if Steve were a faster worker, but he is a nice guy, and you would rather have him in the group than someone else who might do a little bit more.

You find all three positions almost equally desirable. They are all simple and purely routine. The monotony doesn't bother you much becuase you can talk, daydream, and change your pace. By working slow for a while and then fast, you can sort of set your pace to music you hum to yourself. Jack and Steve like the idea of changing jobs and, even though Steve is slow on some positions, the changing around has its good points. You feel you get to a stopping place every time you change positions and this kind of takes the place of a rest pause.

Lately, some kind of efficiency expert has been hanging around. He stands some distance away with a stopwatch in his hand. The company could get more for its money if it put some of those guys to work. You say to yourself, "I'd like to see one of these guys try and tell me how to do this job. I'd sure give him an earful."

If Gus Thompson, your foreman, doesn't get him out of the shop pretty soon, you're going to tell him what you think of his dragging in company spies.

## Instructions for Observers

1. Observe the leader's attitude toward change during the discussion.
   a. Was he partial to the new method?
   b. Did he seem mainly interested in increasing production or in improving the job for the crew?
   c. To what extent was he considerate of the objections raised by the crew? How did he react to their opposition?
   d. Did he defend the new method or argue for its acceptance? What effect did this have on progress in the discussion?

2. Make notes on characteristic aspects of the discussion.
   a. Did arguments develop?
   b. Was any crew member unusually stubborn?
   c. Did the crew members have their say?
   d. Did the leader really listen?
   e. What were the main points of differences?

3. Observe evidences of problem-solving behavior.
   a. What was agreed upon, if anything?
   b. In what respects was there a willingness to make concessions?
   c. What did the leader do to help or hinder a mutually acceptable work method?

Sample Table 6. Group Results on Proposed Change
(Use Table for Recording Class Data)

| Group No. | 1<br>Solution | 2<br>Foreman's<br>Satisfaction | 3<br>Number<br>Satisfied<br>in Crew | 4<br>Problem<br>Employees | 5<br>Future<br>Production | 6<br>Leader Actions<br>that<br>Helped | 7<br>Leader Actions<br>that<br>Hindered |
|---|---|---|---|---|---|---|---|
| 1 | old | low | 3 | W | same | was<br>open | offered<br>no<br>alternatives |
| 2 | new<br>&<br>rest<br>pauses | high | 1 | J | down<br>10% | offered<br>trial<br>period | pushed<br>crew |

## COMMENTS AND IMPLICATIONS

The solutions obtained by various groups usually fall into two categories: those in which the old rotation method will be continued, sometimes with the group members' promise that they will try to increase production if allowed to continue under the old method; and those in which the men accept the plan suggested by the time-study man, usually with the understanding that they can return to the old method if they wish. The foreman ordinarily goes along with either decision, indicating that either he convinces the group to change or the group members convince him that they should not change. Most foremen recognize the importance of gaining acceptance and invariably make the concession of allowing the change to be on a trial basis. The men know they can make or break a solution with this provision. Thus, regardless of the outcome, the discussion usually results in agreement.

Now and then the conflict will not be resolved; then there is dissatisfaction. Often, the men threaten a walkout if the foreman goes ahead with the change or threatens to discharge individuals who refuse to make the change.

Solutions tend to fall into two categories partially because of the way the problem is posed. When the foreman suggests a plan, the men can either accept it or reject it. The problem then becomes a choice between the new and the old way.

However, if the foreman does not suggest a new method but presents the facts obtained by the time-study man and indicates that the men can use the facts in any way they see fit, no one solution is favored by the foreman. As a result, a variety of solutions is possible, each of which not only takes the time-study facts into account but also makes use of the feelings of the men toward their jobs. Examples of such solutions are (1) Jack and Walt exchange jobs, but Steve works permanently at his best position; (2) each man alternates between his two best positions; and (3) the rotation plan is continued, but each man works a longer stretch at his best position.

An experimental study made with this case[13] demonstrated that the selling approach resulted in none of the above three types of solutions, whereas the problem-solving approach yielded 37.5 percent of such solutions, instead of the resistance to change that the selling approach yielded in 50 percent of the groups.

---

[13]N. R. F. Maier, "An Experimental Test of the Effect of Training on Discussion Leadership," *Human Relations*, 1953, 6, 161–173; N. R. F. Maier and E. P. McRay, "Increasing Innovation in Change Situations Through Leadership Skills," *Psychological Reports*, 1972, 31, 343–354.

When groups participate in change, resistance is greatly reduced[14] because people do not fear decisions they make themselves. This means that consultative management does not go far enough toward participation, since involvement that merely allows the voicing of objections falls short of involvement in the solution. However, the consultative approach is better than the selling method because too skillful a selling technique may actually increase fear. Of course, the direct approach of enforcing a change because it is management's prerogative engenders the most fear and hostility.

In handling a discussion on a problem of this sort, it is desirable to differentiate between various forms of resistance. In this particular case, it is probable that the following types of response are supplied as reasons for not changing:

1. Hostility toward the time-study man.
2. Claims of boredom from working at one position.
3. Fear of pay rate cuts.
4. Distrust of management's motives.

These four types of response may be divided into two categories: emotional and factual (or situational). All statements except the one concerning boredom involve attitudes and emotion. To a great extent, these may be imagined or unfounded, but they are not usually subject to change through reason or logical refutation.

Responses having an emotional basis must be expressed by the group and accepted by the leader. He can use such phrases as "I can see that the time-study man bothered you" or "Do the rest of you feel the same way?" or "I am sorry if I did not explain his function to you." The leader can give the group confidence and assurance through such statements as "You understand we do not have to use the time-study man's data" or "An expert's job is to supply information, but we will decide what to do with it." Releasing emotions, accepting feelings, and assuring individuals of status reduce emotional responses, while using arguments and facts increases them—because they threaten. The discussion leader's attitude, understanding, and tolerance will also aid him in being patient and willing to listen, even to unreasonable statements.

Once their hostilities and fears have been expressed, the group members will become interested in facts. They will ask questions and may supply facts of their own. This is the beginning of problem solving.

The objection of boredom may now be seriously considered by the leader. The men may have mentioned it in connection with the other

---

[14]L. Coch and J. R. P. French, Jr., "Overcoming Resistance to Change," *Human Relations*, 1948, *1*, 512–532.

emotional responses, but now it remains as a true obstacle. They see a change as implying boredom since for them, change is synonymous with each man working only his best position. The leader can do a lot to break up this stereotyped response by asking, "Are there any ways of relieving boredom other than by our present method of rotating?" This question separates the old method from its merits for dealing with monotony. Once working the old way is no longer associated with the absence of boredom, it becomes possible to search for a new method that is not boring. The above question helps the men to think of rest pauses, music, partial rotation, and modified rotation as possible alternatives.

The use of exploratory questions is an excellent leadership approach for dealing with sterility in thinking because a group often finds itself in a rut as far as ideas are concerned. It is a device for improving the quality of group thinking, once emotional resistance has been reduced. However, it is not recommended when the group is angry or defensive, since the leader must not influence the direction of thinking on such occasions. Exploratory questions do not direct a group toward certain ideas, but they cause the group to look elsewhere so that progress in ideas can be made.

# 6
# *The Safety-Belt Rule*

## FOCUSING THE PROBLEM

The enforcement of safety practices in industry is a frequent source of misunderstanding and conflict. There are several reasons for this. Probably the most important one is that safety itself is not thought of as a positive goal. Instead of being a source of continuing satisfaction, safety is considered only when an accident has occurred. Moreover, there are often factors that act against safety. Among these are the pressure of work, the fact that safety procedures often interfere with the work, the fact that safety devices can be circumvented, and general hostility toward rules and regimentation. Whether safe work methods will be implemented is often a matter of how these forces are resolved. Obviously, if a particular situation contains more forces against safety than forces for safety, the tendency will be to follow methods that are unsafe.

Once safe methods have been developed and employees have been trained in them, the problem becomes one of motivation. There are two general motivational approaches to the problem of safety in work. One is the use of punitive action to induce fear of following unsafe work methods. This is perhaps the most frequently used system in industry and employs various safety rules with penalties for their violation. Fear motivation, however, has a number of serious shortcomings. For one thing, it places the supervisor in the position of having to spy to detect violations. In addition, fear motivation does not necessarily produce the desired behavior; rather, it tends to highlight the undesired methods and can lead to the learning of incorrect or unsafe methods. Since punitive methods depend on a supervisor's authority and his power to enforce rules, fear motivation tends to weaken or break down when authority is inadequate. In addition, punishment is often frustrating and, as a result, the unsafe behavior may be strengthened rather than corrected. At best, fear can cause workers to avoid methods known to be unsafe—but this avoidance does not necessarily lead to a knowledge of the safe method.

Positive methods of motivation, on the other hand, involve the establishment of desirable, need-satisfying, and attainable goals that result in a rewarding experience for the employee. Such motivation is always constructive in that it encourages safe behavior rather than discourages unsafe behavior. Since positive motivations are rewarding, they do not depend on outside authority or force for their effectiveness. The supervisor is no longer placed in the role of a policeman or spy who must detect violations and punish offenders. Instead, his role becomes a training one in which his duty is to find ways to make safety a satisfying experience. Obtaining the help of subordinates in solving safety problems is one of the best ways to stimulate awareness of hazards and to create acceptable goals.

In the safety-belt case, there are many ways in which the supervisor can deal with the situation that has arisen. Whether he adopts methods that lead to hostile or defensive behavior, or whether he handles the contact with the employee in a way that leads to a satisfactory solution of a mutual problem, will depend on the extent to which he adopts a constructive attitude, and his skill in motivating the employee to adopt positive safety measures.

To encourage skill practice, the multiple role-playing procedure is used.

## MULTIPLE ROLE-PLAYING PROCEDURE

### Preparation

1. The participants form subgroups of three members each. (In order that no persons will be left over, one or two subgroups of two persons may be formed.)
2. One member in each group plays the foreman, one plays the employee, and the third (if present) acts as an observer. (If the same subgroup participates in several cases, role assignments are distributed so that everyone has the opportunity to play a supervisor at one time or another.)
3. All persons turn to the General Instructions and the leader reads them aloud.

4. All players read their role sheets; observers read their instructions. Roles should not be discussed or exchanged.
5. All participants who are to play Jim Welch, the foreman, leave the room to study their roles and remain outside until requested to return by the instructor. When they return, they join their respective employees, ignoring the observers, and proceed to conduct themselves as in a real-life situation.
6. When each participant who is to play an employee has finished reading his part, he stands on a chair to simulate being up a utility pole.
7. Observers prepare to take notes. They do not enter into the discussion in any way.

## Process

1. The instructor gives the signal for the Jim Welches to enter the room and for each to walk toward the telephone pole where his Bill Smith is working.
2. About fifteen minutes is needed to play the roles. When more than half the role players have reached some decision, the instructor gives a two-minute warning signal and asks the remaining pairs to come to a stopping point. (The instructor may check progress with the observers.)
3. During the role play, the instructor prepares a table similar to Sample Table 7.

## Collecting Results

1. Each observer (or foreman) describes in a few words the outcome of the interview. As each subgroup reports, the instructor indicates with a few key words the solution reached and writes these in column 1 of the table he has prepared. (See Sample Table 7.) The report may indicate that sufficient time was not allowed and, in this case, "no solution" may be recorded. Other solutions might be "forgiven," "warned," "scolded," "reduced layoff," and "full layoff."
2. The observer for each group reports how his foreman handled the violation. It may have been ignored, admitted, denied, or hinted about but never established. These reports are entered in column 2. A little time is taken to determine whether each foreman believes a violation occurred in cases where it was denied.
3. Each observer (or the two role players) briefly describes the type of interaction that occurred. The foreman may have done most of the

talking by lecturing, scolding, or pleading; the two may have discussed an equal amount and argued, discussed differences, or tried to solve the problem; or the foreman may have gotten the employee to do most of the talking by listening, asking questions, and trying to understand the employee. The instructor briefly indicates the reports on this point in column 3.
4. Each observer, as well as the role players, reports the kinds of motivations that were used. The instructor can indicate these as plus and minus signs to show positive incentives (praise, participation, recognition, etc.) or negative incentives (threat, danger of falling, family responsibility, etc.) when filling in column 4.
5. Each foreman reports how he feels about his employee. The instructor indicates in column 5 whether the foreman's estimation of the employee increased (+), decreased (−), or remained the same (0).
6. Each employee reports how he feels about his foreman. The instructor summarizes by indicating in column 6 whether the employee's estimation of the foreman increased (+), decreased (−), or remained the same (0).
7. Each employee reports how he feels about his future safety and the instructor summarizes their responses in column 7, to indicate that there will be more (+), less (−), or the same (0) degree of safety.
8. Each employee reports how he feels about his future productivity. The instructor summarizes in column 8 to indicate whether productivity will increase (+), decrease (−), or remain the same (0).

## Discussion of Results

1. The class as a whole attempts to determine the types of approaches that yielded the best results from the point of view of (a) employee morale, (b) safety, and (c) production.
2. Observers pool their views regarding what they consider to be the good and the poor practices they observed. The instructor prepares two columns on the newsprint, one for "good" and one for "poor" practices, and lists the points raised. When the same point is listed in both columns, some time is devoted to discussion of the reasons for the differences. If no agreement results after a brief exchange of views, the item is either left in both columns or removed from both.
3. The group members prepare an outline of the way they think the interview should be handled. The following steps are to be covered:
   a. type of greeting;
   b. what discussion topic or problem should be raised;
   c. how the employee's attitude should be explored;

d. the kinds of motivation that should be used.

If time permits, various suggestions may be tried out on persons who played the part of employees.

4. The class discusses the following practical considerations:

   a.  If the foreman discovers that a violation has occurred, must he invoke the penalty? What are the consequences of his failure to do so?

   b.  If the foreman lays the man off, might a grievance result? Would the company support the foreman if a walkout occurred from the crew's reaction to the layoff?

   c.  The foreman is likely to be caught in the middle if he fails to invoke the penalty, as well as if he invokes the penalty. What is the best way to avoid this situation?

5. The class discusses how the learnings from this case might be applied to other disciplinary problems.

## General Instructions[15]

Jim Welch has been foreman of a repair crew for a telephone company for the past two years. There are twelve men in his crew and they usually work alone or in pairs. The work involves maintenance of telephone lines, replacing worn or damaged equipment, and the like. It is Welch's responsibility to visit his men at their work locations to see how the work is progressing and to give such supervision and assistance as is needed. As supervisor, Welch is also responsible for the safety of his men. This is an important function. Since the men do most of their work atop high utility poles, they are required to use climbers and a safety belt. By setting his climbers securely into the pole and looping his safety belt around the pole or over a crossbar, the repairman leaves his hands free to do the work. In order to make repairs, the men not only have to work fairly rapidly but frequently must shift around on the pole and often have to work in an awkward position. In addition to the danger of falling, there are other hazards—high voltage wires from nearby power lines, wet or slippery poles, adverse weather conditions—which add to the danger. Because of this, the company has very strict safety rules and, as part of the safety program, has instituted such penalties as a three-week layoff for anyone caught violating safety practices.

---

[15]Role instructions are based on a case in N. R. F. Maier, *Principles of Human Relations.* New York: John Wiley, 1952, 106–107.

## Role Sheet: Jim Welch, Foreman

You are the foreman of a repair crew for a telephone company. Your crew consists of twelve men who go out on jobs. They usually work alone or in pairs. As foreman, you spend your time visiting the work locations of your men, checking on progress, and giving such help, training, and instruction as is needed. You are also responsible for the safety of your men. In fact, the company judges you partly on the safety record of your crew. At the present time there is a company safety drive. The slogan is "No job is so important that it cannot be done safely." The company has passed a ruling that anyone found violating a safety practice will be laid off for three weeks.

You have just driven to the place where Bill Smith is working. As you stopped your car some distance away (you cannot drive directly to the work location), you saw Smith working on top of the pole, and you had the distinct impression that he snapped his safety belt. Apparently he was working without using his belt—a safety violation.

Smith is an employee with twenty years of service. He has four children ranging in age from five to twelve. He is a good workman, but quite independent in his thinking. You wish to do what you can to correct his attitudes toward safety. You have ten years' service with the company, but because you have been supervisor of this crew for only two years, you don't know too much about Smith's past record.

## Role Sheet: Bill Smith, Repairman

You are a member of a repair crew for a telephone company. You have been in the company for twenty years and Jim Welch has been your supervisor for the past two. You know the job and think your technical knowledge may be somewhat greater than Welch's—who has worked in the company a total of ten years. You believe he has done a fair job as foreman, but you feel that he supervises too closely.

You usually work alone on repair jobs, except for several visits a week from your supervisor. You are now working on top of a pole and had not bothered to snap your safety belt. You are a careful worker and use the belt when it is necessary, but you find it uncomfortable and in the way, so you frequently don't bother to snap it. You have learned little tricks that give you a rest from the safety belt. One of these is looping your leg over the crossbar and then hooking your foot behind the pole. You have strong legs and find it is easy to support your weight in this manner.

Welch has just driven up, so you quickly snapped your belt. There is an annual safety drive on and the company has threatened to lay off people for safety violations. You can't afford the time off. You have four children and living expenses use up all your earnings. You are quite sure Jim didn't see you snap your safety belt. He is walking toward your pole now. You pretend not to see him, but actually you are observing him closely.

## Observer's Instructions

1. Observe how the foreman opens the discussion. Does he put the employee on the defensive or does he try to put him at ease?
2. The method of the foreman might be to find fault or to try to see the employee's side. His approach will determine whether (a) an argument ensues and both talk a lot, (b) he does most of the talking, (c) he listens to the employee and tries to draw suggestions from him, or (d) they try to solve a problem of mutual interest to both.
3. Take notes on how the violation is raised, if at all. It might be ignored, the foreman might accuse, the foreman might try to draw the answer from the employee, or the employee might admit it, no matter what the foreman does.
4. Does the foreman discover the employee's attitude? Take notes on what he discovers about it. Does he try to change it or try to understand it?
5. Take notes on the ways in which the foreman tries to influence the employee's behavior. Note whether he uses negative motivation by threatening punishment, talking about injury, making emotional appeals about Smith's family, etc.; or whether he uses positive motivation by getting the employee to participate in the program, obtaining suggestions about safety, asking to help in promoting safety among other employees, etc.
6. Make a list of the things the foreman does well or poorly in the interview.
7. Be prepared to describe briefly the decision reached by the foreman. Pay special attention to the manner in which the safety rule is interpreted and applied.

Sample Table 7. Tabulation of Results of Interview
(Use Table for Recording Class Data)

| Group Reporting | 1<br>Solution or Decision | 2<br>Approach to Violation | 3<br>Type of Interaction | 4<br>Motivation Used | 5<br>Foreman's Estimate of Employee | 6<br>Employee's Estimate of Foreman | 7<br>Future Safety | 8<br>Future Production |
|---|---|---|---|---|---|---|---|---|
|  |  |  |  |  |  |  |  |  |

## COMMENTS AND IMPLICATIONS

There are several unsuccessful approaches the foreman may take in the interview. If he accuses the employee of violating the safety rule, he will frequently elicit a denial. On the other hand, if the employee admits the violation, the foreman must decide whether to invoke the penalty. If he does, he leaves himself open to a charge of being too strict and creates bad feelings with the rest of the crew as well as with this employee. If he does not invoke the penalty, he is susceptible to disciplinary action by his own superiors—or the union may involve him in a case of discriminatory practice. In the role play, as is frequently true in actual practice, the foreman usually does not invoke the penalty, but instead brings up the matter of safety violations and gives the employee a lecture on safety. In doing this, he overlooks the fact that the employee has been on the job for twenty years and is well aware of the rules. To give a safety lecture to one who knows the job and the rules is to talk down to him. This is likely to be resented and, even though safety may be improved temporarily, to result in reduced motivation.

Basically, there are three reasons why approaches such as this often fail to improve safety and, instead, contribute to misunderstanding. One is that attention is focused on violations and the unfairness of the penalty; this is not only nonconstructive but often leads to an argument about whether the penalty is too severe or whether a violation actually occurred. This kind of discussion puts both participants on the defensive and new problems are created instead of old problems being solved. Second, such methods fail because they do not promote an understanding of the real reasons for safety violations, but actually prevent it. The third reason for failure is that the methods do not provide positive motivation for safety, but are punitive and rely on fear motivation.

Since the foreman merely suspects that a violation has occurred, the best approach is not to bring up the matter of safety violation at all.

The foreman can learn from his observation that some employees may not always use their safety belts. This is an important discovery; it becomes a crew problem rather than an individual matter. If safety is a group problem, it can be handled best by calling a meeting of the whole crew and asking them for their ideas and suggestions on how to improve safety. The current safety campaign will provide ample justification for such a meeting so that no one will feel accused of a safety violation. Further, this puts the problem to the entire group in constructive terms and, therefore, will elicit cooperative problem-solving behavior with everyone allowed to participate. Social pressure becomes a force working in the direction of safety if the group can plan and assist in the campaign.

An alternative approach that often is fruitful is to hear the employee's side, request his suggestions, recognize his superior knowledge of the job, ask his help in setting an example for younger employees, and inquire if he is willing to help train new personnel in safety. In view of the employee's long service, such a request can be made in complete sincerity.

In the majority of supervisory groups (93 percent) using this role play, the supervisors do not invoke the penalty if the employee admits the violation. It is obviously much more difficult to carry out a penalty than it is to make a rule, because the application of the rule brings one face to face with a particular person. Then the full impact of the rule, and how the penalty creates hardship, must be experienced. Consequently, foremen are reluctant to enforce rules. Many give the person another chance, which leads to nonuniformity of practice; others just fail to "see" the violation, which leads to disrespect for rules. Experimental findings[16] show that when the foreman and the employee have a pleasant conversation (whether or not the violation is discussed), in 82 percent of the cases the employee indicates he would be more safe wearing his belt. When the situation is unpleasant, only 30 percent say they would be more safe.

The whole problem of safety needs to be re-examined from the point of view of the foreman. Rules made by safety departments and higher management may create as many new problems as they solve. New methods of discipline require the involvement of the foreman and he, in turn, can involve his crew. Positive methods of motivation require more imagination and involve more people—but they also are more satisfying and more effective.

---

[16]N. R. F. Maier and L. E. Danielson, "An Evaluation of Two Approaches to Discipline in Industry," *Journal of Applied Psychology,* 1956, *40,* 319–329.

# 7

# *The Use of Office Phones*

## FOCUSING THE PROBLEM

Because decisions usually receive better acceptance when employees are involved in their formulation, the manner in which the supervisor presents a problem to employees is very important. Skill in this area enables supervisors to use employee resources in solving some of the day-to-day problems that frequently plague management.

To pose a problem clearly and successfully, one must identify a particular difficulty or obstacle. Most situations present a number of alternative routes to an objective or goal, but a problem exists because the more obvious paths are blocked. A solution can be reached if a route without an obstacle is found or if a new or better goal that is not obstructed is discovered. Clarification must occur before problem solving can begin. One way of locating an obstacle or finding a new objective is for the supervisor to ask himself why he thinks he has a problem. An obstacle may be found in the group, in the job situation, or even in the supervisor's attitude. When there are several routes or approaches to the solution of a difficult problem, each blocked by a different obstacle, the removal or circumvention of any one of the obstructions is all that is needed. Some obstacles cannot be overcome, others are circumvented with difficulty, and a few are easily eliminated or circumvented. Successful group problem solving is aided when the leader presents a problem in terms of an obstacle that can be surmounted successfully. If this fails, it is desirable to explore alternative objectives.

The general principles described below are useful in assisting the supervisor to formulate a problem for the group. However, it will take considerable practice to make these principles a useful guide; if at first

103

they do not appear practical, the reader should not be discouraged. One may have to violate a principle several times before one appreciates its full worth.

*Principle One.*    A single objective should be identified and presented for discussion. If the supervisor talks about poor quality, poor production, and high accidents as current problems or conditions to be remedied, the group may wonder which is the real problem and where to begin. If the supervisor mentions many deficiencies, group members are likely to think "Things are not that bad—let the boss worry about them." When a discussion leader talks about many things that he wishes to achieve, it usually means that he has a particular solution in mind. His solution may produce several benefits, but a different solution may yield even more and better ones while also attaining what may be called the major objective.

*Principle Two.*    The problem or difficulty should be presented in *situational* rather than *behavioral* terms. If a foreman presents a problem by saying, "You people are having too many accidents; the difficulty is that you don't abide by safety rules, and I'd like to discuss what you want to do about it," he will cause the group to become defensive immediately. They will deny the charge or will countercharge that the rules are no good, but they will show no inclination to approach the safety problem in a constructive manner. A situational approach to a problem in this area would be "What are the hazards on the job that are causing us to have accidents?"

*Principle Three.*    The statement of the problem should not imply a solution. If a supervisor states the problem to be "the excessive amount of tardiness," he implies that the solution is "reduced tardiness." The group may accept or reject his suggestion; they are not free to discover a remedy.

A similar but lesser difficulty is created when the supervisor presents his group with a choice. For example, a problem in a power plant may be presented as "Do you want to clean furnaces the old way or the new way?" Such a question gives the group little opportunity to come to grips with the problem. Rather, the problem solving has been done for the group before the actual meeting, and the supervisor is likely to find that his crew makes a choice he considers wrong. In most instances, there are more than two possibilities and, even when only two exist, much is gained from their being discovered by the crew who must do the job.

*Principle Four.*    The problem should be expressed in terms of a mutual interest. Employees may not be interested in discussing methods for increasing company profits or ways to get the foreman a promotion, but they might be interested in developing their job skills, improving their job placement, increasing the quality of a product, improving service, decreasing accidents, or finding improved work methods. Workers do not expect the company to solve problems related only to employee's interests, and they might distrust the motives of a supervisor who is trying to do favors for his employees. They want a fair give-and-take relationship between themselves and the company, without one taking the advantage of the other. What is perceived as fair, however, may differ—this is the cause of misunderstandings and defensive behavior.

The present case will not be carried to the point of solution, since the main purpose is to discover the effects of different presentations on the outcome of a discussion. A combination of multiple and single-group role playing will be used, in order to provide a variety of reactions to different presentations of the problem and a final opportunity to analyze one presentation in detail.

## MULTIPLE ROLE-PLAYING PROCEDURE

### Preparation

1. All group members read the General Instructions. It is often helpful if the instructor reads this section aloud. At the proper time, the instructor writes on newsprint the name, age, length of service, and marital status of the five clerks as indicated in the General Instructions, so that the information is readily available to the participants during the role play.
2. The members form role-playing groups of six persons each. If five or less members are left, they join role-playing groups to serve as observers.
3. After the role-playing groups have been formed, the instructor designates one person in each group as the supervisor, Marian Telfer. (This imposed assignment will help avoid face-saving problems if discussions fail to yield results.) When all groups have a leader, the roles for the clerks may be adopted by the remaining members of the group.
4. The supervisors for each group study the role of Marian Telfer. When they are ready to begin the role play, they rise and remain standing

until given the signal to sit down. The act of sitting down means that they are entering their offices.

5. Participants who are the clerks in the office study their individual roles. All participants avoid reading any role but their own.
6. All observers familiarize themselves with the Instructions for Observers.
7. The office women assume that they are sitting in Mrs. Telfer's office for a meeting she has called. She is out of the office at the moment, but when she sits down, it will mean that she has entered the office.
8. Role playing will *not* be permitted to continue to the point of completion. In many instances, the discussion may have just begun to get somewhere when the interruption occurs.

## Process

1. When all Marian Telfers are standing and have indicated their readiness to begin, the instructor gives them the signal to sit down and begin the role play. The role playing should be interrupted after five minutes. (This may be a bit difficult because the groups will tend to resist the interruption.)
2. During the role play, the instructor writes the headings for tabulating results on newsprint. (See Sample Table 8.) Separate spaces should be provided to record data from all role-playing groups.

## Results of Multiple Role Playing

1. The observer of the first group (or role players if no observer is present) briefly summarizes the way the leader stated the problem. The instructor enters in column 1 a key word or phrase that characterizes the statement. (See Sample Table 8.) Such expressions as "fairness," "abuses," and "improving efficiency" are examples.
2. The observer then reports whether he thinks the clerks understand the problem and the instructor registers a "yes," "no," or "somewhat" in column 2. The women then indicate how they feel about the supervisor's communication of the problem. The number of clerks who agree with the observer's report is added to column 2 and may be regarded as the rating of the observer's sensitivity. If no observers are used, the number of women indicating "yes," "no," and "somewhat" is tabulated.
3. The observer remarks on the directness of the approach used by Telfer. Such descriptive words as "circled problem," "came to point early," "lots of preliminaries," etc., are entered in column 3.

4. The observer and supervisor present their views on the women's reaction to Telfer's problem. The instructor enters in column 4 the descriptive term that best summarizes the discussion on this point. Such terms as "helpful," "defensive," "hostile," "disinterested," etc., may apply.
5. The observer characterizes the method Telfer used once the problem was stated. Such terms as "permissive," "defensive," "argumentative," "good listener," or a combination of these may be relevant. The appropriate entry is made in column 5.
6. The observer gives his opinion as to (a) whether relationships between Telfer and the employees became better, worse, or remained the same; (b) whether or not an acceptable and reasonable solution would have been reached had no interruption occurred; and (c) whether the group is divided, unified against Telfer, or unified with her. The instructor enters these items as (a), (b), and (c) in column 6.
7. Employees remark on the observer's sensitivity. If the group had no observer, the group's opinion is evaluated.
8. Each group quickly makes a similar report. If more than five groups are used, the remaining groups turn in their reports and the instructor completes the tabulation while groups are preparing to repeat the role play.

## Repetition of Role Playing

1. All groups repeat the role-playing episode from the beginning, with the same Marian Telfer attempting to state the problem to her group again. Role players reread their roles for a refresher, while the Marian Telfers stand waiting for the instructor's cue to begin.
2. The instructor gives the cue for the role playing to begin.
3. After four minutes the instructor interrupts the role play.
4. Each group reports, in turn, whether things went "better," "worse," or "the same."

## Preparation for Single-Group Role Playing

1. The instructor makes up a new group of office employees, using, as much as possible, observers and persons who previously played the part of Marian Telfer.
2. All remaining members assume that they will take the part of Telfer.
3. After each of the five roles has been assigned, the group is asked to leave the room, but to refrain from exchanging information about their roles while outside.

4. Five chairs are arranged in a semicircle in front of the room. These are for the employees to occupy when they return.
5. Marian Telfer's role is read by all persons left in the room. Participants also quickly review the principles for stating a problem for group discussion.
6. After arrangements are completed, the five clerks return and take the prepared seats in the order of Betty, Mary, Linda, Karen, and Susan.

## Modified Group Role-Playing Process

1. The instructor asks a Marian Telfer to state the problem to the group, keeping preliminaries to a bare minimum.
2. After a little interaction, the instructor asks the clerks what they like or do not like about the approach.
3. Another Mrs. Telfer tries an approach under similar conditions.
4. This procedure is continued for one-half hour, with as many Mrs. Telfers testing their skills as possible.

## Discussion of Single-Group Role Playing

1. The most successful statements of the problem are listed. (Three examples are adequate.)
2. The statements are analyzed from the point of view of the four principles discussed in the introduction to this case.

## General Instructions

Marian Telfer is the manager of one office unit in a large insurance company. Her unit serves to make available various kinds of information kept there in large files. Other units in the company call her office for information and data and the office clerks must refer to their records in order to answer these requests. This means that the office has many phone contacts with several other units of the company.

There are five women clerks who report to Telfer. Four of the women are in charge of a particular class of information. All clerks have phones on their desks, but all the phones are on one line. This means that only one person can use the phone at any one time. The fifth woman, with the least service, answers the phone first and notifies the clerk to whom the call is directed, by means of a buzzer system. At the present time, this person happens to be Susan.

The clerks in the unit are:

Betty Northrup—28 years old, 5 years with company, unmarried.
Mary Olsen—23 years old, 5 years with company, married, has three-year-old son.
Linda Wilson—20 years old, 3 years with company, unmarried.
Karen Zimmer—19 years old, 1 year with company, unmarried.
Susan Browning—18 years old, 6 months with company, unmarried.

The peak work load is between 9:00 and 11:00 in the morning and 2:00 and 4:00 in the afternoon. All women are allowed a fifteen-minute relief period both morning and afternoon. These are not scheduled since the group is small and the demands of the work change from day to day.

## Role Sheet: Marian Telfer

You are the supervisor of an office unit in an insurance company. The group you supervise is made up of five women clerks who work at desks. The work involves telephone contacts with company people who require information that the various clerks have in their files. Since all the phones are on one line, the person who answers uses a buzzer signal, and the person requested who has the needed information takes over the call. You never answer the phone unless one of the clerks informs you by buzzer that the call is for you. Ordinarily the woman with the least service answers the phone and then buzzes the one who can handle the call.

A relief period of fifteen minutes, both morning and afternoon, is given to the staff and this is regarded as adequate for the usual personal needs. You have asked them to take their breaks one at a time in order to keep the office covered. When the work is heavy, they frequently skip their breaks.

Your boss has complained that you are hard to reach by phone because the line is always busy. He says that he can reach other units that do the same type of work and he thinks that your group is making too many personal calls. You know that the clerks do call out freely and that they receive quite a number of personal calls, because on several occasions you have picked up your phone and found that the conversation had nothing to do with business. For example, twice during the past week you heard Linda Wilson talking with her boyfriend. You told your boss you would do something about it and you have decided to talk it over with the group first.

Since the load is light from 8:00 to 9:00 a.m., 11:30 a.m. to 1:30 p.m., and 4:00 to 5:00 p.m., you have used these times for discussions, conferences, and interviews with the staff. Because you want your whole crew in today, you set a meeting for 4:00 p.m. It is now time for the meeting and the women have arrived in the office. You plan to take any remaining calls in your office.

The women's general performance ratings are as follows:
1. Betty Northrup—slow, but very conscientious.
2. Mary Olsen—very superior.
3. Linda Wilson—very productive, but she breaks rules.
4. Karen Zimmer—average.
5. Susan Browning—progressing very rapidly.

## Role Sheet: Betty Northrup

You are very conscientious and seldom go out for coffee during the relief period to which you are entitled. Instead, you stay at your desk and work or make personal telephone calls. Some of the girls, especially Mary, receive and make calls on company time, but you do not feel this is right. Lately, Linda has been getting a lot of calls from a new boy-friend.

------------------------------------------------------------------------

## Role Sheet: Mary Olsen

You consider yourself very efficient and perhaps do more work than the others. You have a three-year-old boy whom you leave with your mother while you are at work. She lives just a block from where you live. You frequently call your mother during office hours to check on things, and sometimes she calls you. Now and then, you talk to your little boy. You enjoy your work and stay with the company even though you could make more money elsewhere. You have to have a job where you can be easily reached by phone.

## Role Sheet: Linda Wilson

You like your present job because the hours are good and your boss is not too strict when you are late. You go out nights quite a bit and sometimes oversleep, but you make up for this by skipping your relief period and working faster. You seldom use the phone for personal business as others do, especially Mary. Lately, one of your boyfriends has been pestering you with phone calls. You don't know how he got your number. This has been kind of embarrasing because your boss noticed you talking with him and she obviously didn't approve. This worries you, but what can you do when someone calls you?

--------------------------------------------------------------------------

## Role Sheet: Karen Zimmer

You take your relief periods and go out for coffee in the middle of the morning and again in the afternoon. You stay away for twenty minutes or so and no one has ever criticized you. You enjoy your phone contacts with people in other departments and often extend your calls while doing business with them. However, you never make purely personal calls and rarely receive any. The phones are for company business and you believe that people should realize this.

## Role Sheet: Susan Browning

You are new to the company and like your job. You like to deal with other people and especially enjoy working over the phone. You hope that soon your work will be more interesting. At present you do routine filing, answer the phone just to buzz for one of the others, and help out when they are on relief or busy. The other women seem to have a good deal of fun visiting with people in other units. You are gradually getting acquainted so that now you can kid with some of the people who call, before buzzing one of the other women. You never make personal calls, however. You take a relief period mornings and afternoons and make all your personal calls from the lounge.

## Instructions for Observers

1. Make brief notes on the way in which the leader states the problem. She may state the problem in behavioral terms—the boss has complained, some people are abusing company rules, we need to reduce personal calls—or she may use situational terms—how can we improve service during busy periods? what is a fair way to handle calls? what constitutes a justifiable personal call?
2. Did the office group understand Telfer's statement of the problem?
3. Was the leader's approach direct, or did she hesitate to come to the point?
4. Keep a list of the types of reactions to the way the problem was presented to the group.
5. Observe the conference methods used:
    a. Was the leader permissive and receptive to various ideas and feelings?
    b. Did all the members have their say?
    c. Did Mrs. Telfer show any defensive reactions?
    d. Were there any disagreements between the leader and the group members?
6. Evaluate the approach:
    a. Did relations between the leader and the group improve or deteriorate?
    b. Will the group eventually reach a solution?
    c. Is the group divided or united against the supervisor?

Sample Table 8. Results of Group Role Playing
(Use Table for Recording Class Data)

| Group | 1<br>Statement of<br>Problem | 2<br>Clarity of<br>Problem | 3<br>Directness of<br>Approach | 4<br>Type of<br>Reaction | 5<br>Method<br>Used | 6<br>Evaluation of<br>Success |
|---|---|---|---|---|---|---|
|  |  |  |  |  |  |  |

## COMMENTS AND IMPLICATIONS

The problem used in this case is a difficult one because the employees are doing something that is undesirable from the point of view of management, thus raising the question of discipline. If the supervisor takes an authoritarian approach, she may be met with unified hostility or she may cause her group to divide and, as a result, reduce morale. Usually supervisors are aware of the difficulties of "laying down the law" and frequently postpone facing the problem.

In this situation, the supervisor is asked to confront the group as a whole. Since role players speak more freely than real-life employees, she is assured of a group of sensitive individuals. They may find her remarks to be critical of their behavior even when she had no such intent. A major factor making the employees hypersensitive is the fact that they are guilty of taking advantage of a rather free situation. People who are highly sensitive to criticism or who counterattack vigorously and repeatedly do so because of their own feelings of guilt; the more guilty they are, the more righteous indignation they express. Thus, the timid remarks of a supervisor explaining the issue of the personal use of telephones is likely to be met with silence, hurt feelings, demands that she name people and times, denials, and questions that are designed to put her on the defensive.

It is possible that if she permits the group to talk and refrains from accusing them or becoming defensive, she may bring them around to the point of discussing a better way to budget their personal calls. This presumes that her own attitude is one of understanding and that she is disinclined to use an authoritarian approach.

Examination of Telfer's problem suggests the following possibilities:

1. Some employees use the phone freely for personal calls.
2. Telfer's boss thinks the clerks make too many personal calls.
3. Telfer finds that the younger women use the phones to talk to boyfriends.
4. Telfer has her own ideas of what is fair in the use of company phones.
5. The women are busier at certain hours than at others.
6. There may be a shortage of phones.
7. Service might be analyzed to determine ways to improve it.

It is apparent that if all these points were made to clerks, they would infer that Telfer had a specific solution in mind: stop personal phone calls. This solution, however, is more extreme than Telfer would impose. This approach is critical of behavior, states too many problems, implies a solution, and includes no mutual interest. The immediate countersolution would be "Get more phones."

The problem possibilities may be considered one at a time:

### 1. Some employees are making too many personal calls.

This approach tends to accuse some employees of taking advantage of the company. It is critical of behavior and produces defensive responses. If some employees agree with Telfer, the group is split into factions. Some might have a mutual interest with the boss, but not as members of a group.

### 2. The boss has complained.

The second problem "passes the buck" to Telfer's boss. Telfer must then side either with the women or with her boss, raising the issue "Where does Mrs. Telfer stand?" If she sides with the boss, the problem becomes like the one above; if she sides with the clerks, the solution may be directed toward ways to cover up for Telfer, some of which may be good, others bad, from the point of view of efficiency and service.

### 3. Some clerks are talking to boyfriends.

The third approach to the problem is almost certain to point the finger at particular members of the group. These person may be no more guilty than others, since observed abuses may be no worse than those which go undetected. This way of locating the obstacle in the problem has the following deficiencies: (a) it raises the issue of fair treatment for all employees; (b) it tends to divide the group because of differences in their needs and interests (no mutual interest); and (c) it puts the problem in terms of behavior rather than situation.

### 4. We must do what is fair.

The issue stated here locates the problem in the supervisor's attitude. Even though her attitude may be justified, it is likely that the clerks will interpret her remarks in terms of their own attitudes. If, however, Telfer makes her attitude a problem for discussion, it may be possible to capture a mutual interest as well as to put the problem in situational terms. For example, Telfer might say, "I have an attitude that is out of line with yours and even though I try to change it, I find myself unable to do so. We all have an attitude about the use of company phones for personal reasons and I am frequently critical of you when you use them for your own needs, especially during the busy periods. Can we talk about this problem and see if you can help me get a perspective that will make us all more comfortable?

## 5. *Certain times are busier than others.*

This states a fact about the situation; it almost directly raises the issue of how to even out the work load and the use of phones. This problem is located in the situation, mutual interests are apparent, and the goal is somewhat different from that in the previous problems, but perhaps more inclusive and more worthwhile. The discussion might raise the issue of making personal calls during slack periods, reducing the length of business contacts, and even suggesting changes in procedures that will improve efficiency and increase service quality.

## 6. *There is a shortage of phones.*

This states a goal that might be in the employee's interests but is not in the interest of the company. Increasing the number of phones might actually increase the abuses rather than improve the service. It is possible, however, that if Telfer raised the question of whether or not more phones were needed, employees might, after full discussion, indicate that enough lines were now available if they were used efficiently. This could lead to a correction of the abuses. This success of this approach would be due to the fact that the problem was presented in situational terms.

## 7. *How can we improve service?*

The last problem is stated in terms of a general goal and permits the employees an opportunity to locate the difficulties themselves. If abuses are flagrant, they would be one kind of obstacle that could be removed. However, the employees might see other obstacles as well. Consequently, a series of other problems, perhaps unknown to the supervisor, might be solved. One is more likely to attain this by-product in a real-life situation than in a role play because the former would include richer situational backgrounds from which to draw. The merits of this more inclusive goal are that (a) it permits mutual interests to be explored and discussed, (b) it is a situational problem, and (c) no solutions are implied.

It is apparent that problems stated in situational terms are the most likely to prevent defensive reactions and the most likely to contain a mutual interest. However, interest in problem solving might cause some employees to become critical of others. It is at such times that the leader must protect the individual who is attacked. She can point out that the aim is to solve the problem in a manner suitable to all, that there are bound to be differences in values and viewpoints, and that the purpose of the discussion is to understand and resolve the differences. It may be appropriate for her to say, "No one really wants to hurt someone else, so let's just lay our gripes on the table and treat them as misunderstandings or reasonable differences of opinion." At all times, the leader's job is to keep the discussion situation oriented and to respect differences in needs, values, and attitudes.

# 8

## *Painters and Inspectors*

### FOCUSING THE PROBLEM

Much of the work in organizational settings requires that people work in teams, in the sense that the work of each is in some way dependent on the work of others. This type of relationship between crew members introduces problems that are absent when the work of each person in a group is largely independent of the work of the others. The sociological problems of group work include morale, congeniality, attitudes regarding a good day's work, and fair treatment from the supervisor, all of which indirectly influence productivity. In teamwork one employee can directly influence the work accomplished by his co-workers. At one extreme, a team of workers can perform in a coordinated and supportive manner; at the other extreme, there can be disorganization and interference.

Whether or not jobs should be organized and structured so that teams, rather than independent workers, are utilized depends on the kind of group structure that is developed. A team can be a significant asset if the supervisor knows how to build one. In one case,[17] the daily productivity of six women working independently (in that each did one-sixth of the work that passed on a conveyer) was 25,000 units with 4,116 rejects. The job was then modified so that they worked as a team. The first two women (working on opposite sides and facing each other) did what they wished, the next two did some of the work that the first two left undone, while the last two did the remaining jobs. No attempt was made to equalize the work in the group. The women varied their

---

[17]Based on events observed by N. R. F. Maier in a client's plant.

productivity and the last two usually had little to do. They served more as inspectors and a source of relief. From time to time, in an informal manner, all women exchanged positions. With the new arrangement, it was found that production rose to 30,000 units but, most important, rejects dropped to twenty-six. One day one of the women was late and the supervisor put in a substitute, partly to punish the team member for being late. The production and rejects were so bad during the first hour that the original team had to be reinstated. The poor work was not intentional; the whole team went to pieces with a new woman in the group because there were so many things to explain and so many informal arrangements that she did not like or understand.

The present case deals with a situation in a furniture company in which painters and inspectors work together to produce a finished product. The relationship between them leaves much to be desired. The problem of the foreman is to see if he can transform the two separate groups into a cooperative team. To accomplish this, he must get at the root of the difficulty, a task that may require considerable skill.

The multiple role-playing procedure is recommended, since it is desirable to obtain a variety of solutions.

## MULTIPLE ROLE-PLAYING PROCEDURE

### Preparation

1. The General Instructions and the layout of the job situation in Figure 3 should be available to all members of the class. The instructor may wish to read the General Instructions aloud while the class follows the text.
2. The case requires seven participants. When possible, two or three groups of seven persons are formed. The remaining persons serve as consultants. If one, two, or three persons are left over, they act as one team of consultants; but if four, five, or six persons remain, two groups of consultants are formed and each gives its own report.
3. With Joe Evans, the foreman, as a starting point, role assignments are made in sequence: Mike, Ed, Bill, Jack, Hank, and Charlie. Each person reads only his own role.
4. After the foreman has read his part, he stands and walks a short distance from his group. Each role player writes his role name and job on a piece of paper and wears it as a name tag. Participants and foremen are then able to refer to persons by their proper role names.
5. Consultants read both their instructions and all role instructions.

6. Role players assume that they are in their foreman's office, waiting for him to arrive to conduct the meeting he has called. When everyone is ready, the instructor gives the signal to begin.

## Process

1. Each foreman rejoins his group, to indicate that he has entered his office. He greets the group members and proceeds to conduct the meeting.
2. Consultants meet in another part of the room to study their data and prepare to make their report to the company.
3. Approximately twenty-five minutes is needed to complete this case. Ordinarily, each group requires about the same amount of time, and nearly all groups reach a solution. If one group is slower in settling differences than others, the instructor requests that it hurry.
4. While the groups are role playing, the instructor prepares newsprint, on which to tabulate results, with the suggested headings shown in Sample Table 9.

## Collecting Results

1. The consultants are asked to give their reports first. They indicate what they consider to be the major cause of the difficulty in the crew and describe what they recommend should be done about it. The instructor briefly summarizes the difficulty and the solution reported and enters the key words in columns 1 and 2, respectively. (See Sample Table 9.)
2. The consultants are asked to report on the reception they feel higher management will give their proposal. Such degrees of acceptance as "likely," "probable," "questionable," and "poor" are entered in column 3. (Differences of opinion volunteered by other members of the class are allowed but general discussion of the question is postponed to the discussion period.)
3. Consultants indicate the names of workers whom they think will be dissatisfied. These are entered in column 4.
4. After the consultant groups (if used) have reported, the role-playing groups, in turn, present their analyses of the difficulty, the solution reached, the probable acceptance of higher management, and the names of the men (including the foreman) who are not satisfied. The instructor files these reports in columns 1, 2, 3, and 4.
5. Group members decide whether the foreman was helpful or a source

of interference. If neither word fits, the instructor enters a question mark in column 5, otherwise he enters the appropriate word.

6. A vote is taken to indicate the number of persons in the group (including the foreman) who think team spirit will (a) go up, (b) remain the same, and (c) go down. These numbers are entered in column 6.

7. A vote is taken to indicate the number of persons in the group who think production will (a) go up, (b) remain the same, and (c) go down. These numbers are entered in column 7.

## Discussion Issues

1. The reason for the foreman's effective handling of the problem is discussed. In most instances, the groups will have a success experience and the foreman will conduct a good discussion. Since this degree of skill is not displayed in all role-playing cases, there must be a reason for the successes in this case. Such factors as previous experience, cooperative persons playing the roles, absence of conflict in the case, whether or not the foreman had a solution in mind at the outset, whether or not he was inclined to take sides, etc., should be considered and evaluated.

2. The solutions are examined from the point of view of (a) cost to the company to introduce them, (b) organizational changes in status or wages of either painters or inspectors, (c) change in layout of work or situation, and (d) change in attitude as a result of the discussion.

3. Was there something that all groups agreed to change in the same manner? If so, why was there such agreement on one specific aspect of the problem?

4. What was the main cause of conflict in the group? Persons who played the parts of foremen, painters, inspectors, and consultants give their respective versions of the real source of trouble.

5. Which of the three kinds of changes listed in the second discussion question could not be achieved by consultants? If consultants were used, what difference in approach was in evidence?

6. Discuss why group members might reject solutions offered by consultants. Will one group of role players accept solutions reached by other groups?

7. A solution of high quality might not be reached by the group. What can a leader do to cause his group not to overlook good ideas? Consider such leader actions as (a) suggesting good ideas, (b) pointing out weaknesses of suggestions considered by the group, (c) asking ques-

tions of the group, (d) getting the group to examine several different ideas before settling on any one of them, (e) getting each person to feel free to tell what bothers him, (f) preventing members from speaking their minds, etc.

8. Class members explore problems in life that are suggested by the case study.

## General Instructions

You seven men are all employees of the Home Furniture Company. Four of you, Mike, Ed, Bill, and Jack, are painters; Hank and Charlie are inspectors; Joe Evans is the foreman. The painters and inspectors are all union members.

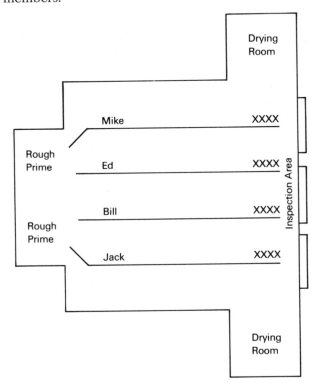

Figure 3. Plant Layout for Finishing Room.

The painters and inspectors are on piece rates which are based on time-study units, so that each job gives a specified number of credit points. The inspectors, however, are graded lower than the painters and earn about 15 percent less per week than the painters.

The appearance of the finished product is naturally quite important. Inasmuch as the paint dries quickly, the pieces must be inspected and the blemishes and bare spots touched up before the finish coat dries. As the job is laid out now, the inspectors spend most of their time applying the rough priming coat. Every half hour they take turns making a tour of inspection, which takes between fifteen and twenty minutes. When the inspector finds a flaw, he calls the painter who applied the finish coat. The painter leaves the job he is working on and corrects the defect. This happens very frequently. As a result, there is bad feeling between the painters and inspectors. The painters have as little to do with the inspectors as possible. Frequently, there are heated arguments over what constitutes a defect; this situation has gradually become worse.

Figure 3 shows the layout of the paint room. The X's at the end of each line represent pieces of furniture awaiting inspection. The inspectors walk from the rough-paint area at the left to the right side of the room whenever they take a tour of inspection.

The foreman, Joe Evans, has called a meeting of the crew in his office this morning.

## Role Sheet: Joe Evans, Foreman

You have been foreman of this finishing crew for three years now and it has always been a tough job because of the needless bickering between the painters and inspectors. They wrangle constantly, and when a blowup occurs and you try to put a stop to it, each party accuses you of taking sides and being unfair. During the past few months, things have become worse. Scarcely a day goes by without a flare-up of some kind, and some of your best men have threatened to quit. Individually all of them seem to be nice fellows, but they just don't get along as a team.

You have called this meeting because you think something must be done about the situation. The painters and inspectors are waiting for you in your office.

------------------------------------------------------------------------

## Role Sheet: Mike Sullivan, Painter

You work toward the rear of the room where the lighting isn't very good. Unless you turn each side of every piece up to the light, it isn't easy to tell whether you have covered the whole area or not. Near the windows where the inspectors work, there's more daylight and that makes it a lot easier to see. If you had light like that, you could do better work with less eyestrain. Besides, when one of the inspectors yells for you, you have to run over and touch up whatever he wants you to fix and that means dropping what you are working on at the time. This constant interruption really bugs you. There must be some way of doing the job that doesn't require constant interruptions. It's the inspector's job to catch the oversights, so it's reasonable that they should have the best light, but how can you make any money on the job when you spend so much time answering the beck and call of the inspector?

## Role Sheet: Ed Jones, Painter

You are sick and tired of all this bickering with the inspectors and you are going to give Joe Evans an earful about it the next chance you get. Why doesn't he take your side once in a while instead of always sticking up for the inspectors? Something has to be done to put the inspectors in their place. All they do is find fault and make a big fuss about a minor defect. You are sick of being criticized and ordered about by them. If they were painters, they would make more mistakes than you do. As you see it, most of the oversights and poor jobs are caused by the inspectors themselves. They call you over to fix a spot you missed and that interruption causes you to overlook something on the job you're working on at the time.

------------------------------------------------------------------------

## Role Sheet: Bill Baker, Painter

You don't like this bickering and quarreling between the painters and the inspectors. The foreman, Joe Evans, is a nice enough fellow and tries to do his best, but when painters and inspectors can't get along, there isn't much he can do about it. You have been keeping out of things as much as possible but it is easy to see that something has to be done. The inspectors are really nice guys but they are on the spot. You find that if you are agreeable with them, they are very helpful. The trouble with the rest of the painters is that they give the inspectors a rough time, so the inspectors fight back. Every time an inspector calls, one of the painters has to drop what he is doing and go over and correct his mistake; that seems to be the real source of the trouble. If the inspector could just wait until a painter came to a stopping place, things would be better—but you can't expect the inspector to stand around and wait. However, there ought to be some way to eliminate the interruptions. You have observed that there seems to be enough touchup work to keep a man busy. Maybe if someone were to do nothing but correct defects, it would eliminate all of the irritating interruptions and the waste of time from the painters' running back and forth.

## Role Sheet: Jack Anderson, Painter

This bickering between painters and inspectors is getting you down. You don't even feel like talking in a civil way to your own friends on the job and lately you have been grouchy with your wife and kids when you get home. No job is worth that. Unless things get straightened out here, you are going to quit. Why should you drop what you are doing and go over and touch up a bare spot just because some damn inspector yells at you? Whenever you tell him you'll fix it up later, the inspector says, "O.K., but I'll have to report it to the boss." These inspectors act as if they had more rank than you do; it's time they were put in their places. They act as if a little oversight is a crime and constantly talk about mistakes and poor workmanship.

---

## Role Sheet: Hank Porter, Inspector

You and Charlie Smith are inspectors and you are both sick of the job. Every time you call a painter over to correct a mistake, he gets belligerent and takes it as a personal insult. Why don't those guys do things right in the first place if they can't take criticism? You have tried pointing out defects in a nice way but, except for Bill Baker, the painters pull their rank and you have to stand around and wait until they feel good and ready to come over to fix up the defect. You've got your job to cover and if you spend too much time standing around, you are likely to get into trouble. Naturally you start getting touchy with them too. Charlie seems to think there's something about the way the job is set up that is causing all this trouble, but you are satisfied that the whole trouble is with the painters, who are stubborn, childish, and abusive, and that the foreman ought to lay down the law.

## Role Sheet: Charlie Smith, Inspector

You and Hank Porter are inspectors. You agree with Hank that it is a poor place to work, with the painters on your neck all day long treating you as flunkies. In some ways, though, you can appreciate how the painters feel when Hank or you interrupt them in the middle of a job. You do a lot of painting around your house and often feel resentful and picked on when your wife interrupts your work to have you run errands or won't let you finish a job because your dinner is getting cold. As you see it, the painters are nice enough fellows; it's the job setup that's wrong. They have their work to do just as you have yours, and yet every time you call one of them over, he has to drop whatever he is doing and touch up the spot he missed. That's the way the job is laid out and it isn't a good way to handle touchup work at all. Sometimes you actually borrow a brush and touch up some minor spots just to keep out of trouble. It saves time too. You'd like the job of just touching up the bad spots and there certainly ought to be a way to handle that, even on a piece-rate basis.

## Instructions for Consultants

The Home Furniture Company has hired you to help them solve a problem in one of the finishing crews. Cooperation between painters and inspectors is poor. There seems to be no particular troublemaker and it has been difficult for the company to place the blame. They feel that you, as an expert on team organization and morale, may be able to study the matter and come up with some practical recommendations.

In approaching this problem, you have made yourself familiar with the job layout and procedure. You also had an assistant interview each man to find out how he feels about the job. When the instructor gives the signal for others to role play, you will work alone or as a member of a team (depending on the number of consultants present in the group) and study the case. Examine the roles of Mike, Ed, Bill, Jack, Hank, and Charlie and assume they are summaries of the interviewer's reports. Also feel free to refer to the plant layout and the General Instructions in analyzing the problem and evaluating ideas.

The company wants a practical solution. Try to come up with a recommendation that the company will accept and that you feel will improve relationships between the men as well as increase their productivity.

Sample Table 9. Analysis of Solutions to Painter-Inspector Case
(Use Table for Recording Class Data)

| Group | 1<br>Major<br>Source<br>of Difficulty | 2<br>Solution<br>Characteristics | 3<br>Probable<br>Acceptance<br>by Higher<br>Management | 4<br>Names of<br>Workers Not<br>Completely<br>Satisfied | 5<br>Did<br>Foreman<br>Help or<br>Interfere | 6<br>Team<br>Spirit | 7<br>Production |
|---|---|---|---|---|---|---|---|
|  |  |  |  |  |  |  |  |

## COMMENTS AND IMPLICATIONS

One of the first things usually agreed upon in discussing this case is to improve the lighting. A painter in the group complains about the light and, since no one has an opposing view, the idea to increase the lighting is accepted. However, it must be recognized that this is a minor factor, and the painter may have made the complaint to justify or to defend himself because he feels criticized or guilty. The general dissatisfaction with conditions is the more basic difficulty, and specific complaints must not be allowed to cloud the issue. Reactions and complaints should be accepted and respected but, generally speaking, action on them should be postponed until the problem has been more thoroughly explored. Job dissatisfaction in this case seems to originate from a conflict or split in the group.

One of the important sources of conflict here is that of status. Painters are superior to inspectors, as evidenced by their pay and by the fact that inspectors aspire to become painters—yet they are placed in a position in which they must appear to take orders from inspectors. This condition makes them hypersensitive; hence, they are inclined to perceive the inspector's report as an attack on their prestige. They defend themselves by verbally abusing inspectors, making excuses (poor light), denying errors, etc., and these responses only cause inspectors to be less diplomatic and perhaps more critical of errors. When the inspectors feel they are misunderstood, they lose their respect for painters and this, in turn, degrades the painters more.

Inspection jobs frequently are of this nature and, in this sense, the case is a typical problem created by low-status persons appearing to give orders to high-status persons. Waiters in restaurants may have similar problems with cooks if they take customer complaints to the cook. Messengers may likewise become the center of a misunderstanding between persons of like or unlike rank. The solution may be as simple as substituting direct communication for the messenger service. In the present case, the inspector has to record the error but the job may be changed so that he does not have to verbally communicate the touchup order to the painter. Some of the solutions reported very likely arrange for a painter to accompany the inspector and make all corrections. It is also possible that a change in attitudes could cause the inspectors' comments to be seen as constructive and helpful by the painters. Group discussion in some instances may supply acceptable ways in which the inspectors can report errors and oversights.

A second source of disturbance in this case is the fact that the job is laid out so that painters have to be interrupted in their work. Interruptions are sources of frustration that frequently are overlooked. Once a person begins work on a task, there is a strong tendency to carry it to completion. Perhaps everyone has been frustrated by interruptions and has reacted with hostility toward the interrupter. Reducing and preventing them may require reorganizing a job. The present arrangement makes it necessary for inspectors to interrupt painters for each error and thereby become the innocent victims of the abuses caused by interruptions. If the job can be reorganized so that painters are not interrupted and the quality of workmanship is not reduced, the bad feeling between painters and inspectors may be corrected. It is also possible that a more efficient method of correcting deficiencies can be invented. Any solution that accomplishes even a part of these objectives would be a distinct improvement.

This case is likely to lead to a successful solution, not because it is simple, but because the foreman has no preferred remedy. He goes into the conference without having made up his mind and, consequently, he is open minded, receptive to ideas, and a good listener. It becomes apparent that a leader can upgrade his conference leadership by simply refraining from thinking a problem through to a solution before he conducts a meeting. His planning should be confined to such functions as (1) finding a way to present the problem without criticizing anyone, (2) determining from his superior the degree of freedom he possesses in the matter, and (3) assuming that there are at least two sides to the problem and that the purpose of the meeting is to locate the sources of misunderstandings.

# 9

# *Unscheduled Coffee Breaks*

## FOCUSING THE PROBLEM

The coffee break is becoming the source of a variety of problems for management. Within the span of a few years, the relief period—initially meant as a privilege for women employees only—has expanded into a coffee-drinking custom that is regarded as a right—not only by non-supervisory employees but by management personnel as well.

Some companies have faced the problem and have allotted the time and the facilities for coffee breaks. Bell signals sometimes are used to control the time, and various units take their breaks on slightly different schedules in order to reduce congestion in elevators and coffee shops or coffee areas. However, most companies have complicating problems. Some of the questions raised are:
1. Should all types of work receive the same consideration in regard to the frequency and length of the break?
2. Should the coffee break represent a rest period and therefore fall near the middle of a work period?
3. If a break interrupts work activity, can employees be permitted to choose the time?
4. Should the company open its cafeteria for coffee?
5. How far should the company go in furnishing vending machines or other coffee facilities?
6. How can one prevent abuses of the coffee privilege?

Some companies have been reluctant to state a policy on the matter. They fear that an announced policy will sanction coffee breaks and thereby cause persons who previously refrained from taking a break to do so regularly. In the absence of an announced policy, work disruptions often occur. Perhaps the most complicating factor is that management itself is not agreed on the coffee issue. It is difficult for supervisors and employees to know just how to conduct themselves when the issue remains vague and explosive, and it is difficult for members of higher management to settle a policy matter when their own attitudes are conflicting and unsettled. Since the issue is not one that must be settled by a given time, there is a tendency to postpone action whenever sharp disagreements arise. In some instances, there may have to be strike threats for coffee breaks in order to bring the matter into the open for a clear-cut decision.

One of the consequences of delaying a decision is its effect on the delegation of authority. The coffee problem may be discussed as an overall company matter, not only at the top management level but perhaps at every management level. As a result, there may be a failure to break down the problem into parts in order to determine the issues that should be solved at each level.

If rank-and-file employees are the worst offenders, the problem arises of how much freedom first-line supervisors should have in setting up a plan that is acceptable to themselves and to the employees. As long as supervisors lack freedom to decide what constitutes a violation, they tend to be arbitrary and inconsistent. Periodically, higher levels feel that things are getting out of hand, so they disturb morale by threatening to take certain actions if things do not improve. Top management personnel are usually fair minded and agree that they want to do the reasonable thing. However, if the discussion is pressed further, they do not agree on what is reasonable. This then becomes a real source of confusion and leads to nonuniform practices within units or departments of the same company.

The present case deals with some aspects of the coffee problem and should reveal a variety of values. Whether or not this is an issue on which a mutual interest between employees and management can be found remains to be seen.

The procedure is set up for single-group role playing, not only because the number of participants is too large for simultaneous group discussions, but also because a more detailed analysis is possible when all observers discuss the same incident.

# SINGLE-GROUP ROLE-PLAYING PROCEDURE

## Preparation

1. Thirteen persons can participate in the role play. (If the class has less than thirteen persons, some participants may combine the individual instructions for two persons.)
2. The instructor selects a class member to play the part of Mr. Johnson, the supervisor.
3. The twelve persons seated nearest the center of the room become the crew members. They count off from one to twelve and remember their numbers, but each retains his own name in the role-playing scene. (In the event that less than twelve persons are available to play the parts of crew members, the counting continues with each person taking a second number until the twelve numbers are used.)
4. Persons who are not role players arrange themselves on the two sides of the crew in order to be able to observe the overall actions. The person assuming the role of Mr. Johnson remains on the sidelines until the action begins.
5. When the room arrangements are completed, everyone reads the General Instructions for the Class.
6. The person playing Mr. Johnson reads his role sheet, crew members read the role sheet for all crew members, and observers read their instructions.
7. Crew members decide among themselves who are especially good friends and go places together. These subgroups of three to five persons may assume that their work territories lie close together.
8. Crew members read the attitude instructions opposite the number they received when they counted from one to twelve during step 3. They adopt the suggested attitude, but should not feel obligated to reveal it to the supervisor unless they consider it relevant and appropriate to the discussion. They should also feel free to reveal any of their opinions or attitudes that develop in the discussion.
9. Observers take notes but do not converse with role players.
10. The instructor makes sure that everyone reads the proper roles or instructions and is prepared for the action. He observes whether the crew members form subgroups and read their personal attitudes as well as the roles for the crew. He also checks that there is a chair in front of the crew for Mr. Johnson and that Mr. Johnson has access to a blackboard or newsprint in case he wishes to use it.

11. When the instructor asks Mr. Johnson to join his crew, everyone should be in character.

## Process

1. The instructor signals for Mr. Johnson to approach his crew and take the seat provided for him.
2. Role playing is allowed to proceed to a solution if progress is being made. In case the supervisor finds himself in serious difficulty, the instructor rescues him by interrupting the role play. The observers (or role players if there are no observers) indicate the reasons for the difficulties and suggest a new approach. After a brief discussion, role playing is resumed. It is permissible to begin over or to resume from any point desired.
3. Role playing, including interruptions, should be limited to forty-five minutes or less, unless interesting new developments occur and the group wishes to continue.

## Analysis and Discussion

1. The class as a whole develops, through discussion, a list of all the attitudes or arguments mentioned by the repairmen during the role play. (The instructor briefly records the items on newsprint.)
2. The list is checked with the twelve attitudes of the repairmen. (The instructor takes each item, one at a time, and determines from the group whether or not it is in the list.)
3. Observers (or the group as a whole) discuss why the list developed contains items not given in the roles or why items supplied in the roles were not brought out in discussion. (Observers reach a conclusion based upon observation, and the role players concerned with the item comment on the accuracy of the observer's analysis.)
4. The observers (or the group as a whole) evaluate the way the supervisor handled each contribution. Descriptive terms such as "accepted," "rejected," "agreed with," "disagreed with," "supplied reasons against," "was sarcastic," "belittled," "ignored," etc., may be written beside each item on the board. These terms are checked with the way the repairmen felt.
5. The discussion is evaluated in terms of whether the crew's feeling toward the company and foreman became worse or better as the discussion progressed.
6. The supervisor, Mr. Johnson, predicts whether his crew will be more careful or less careful about coffee breaks as a result of the

discussion. Each observer then voices his opinion. (If there are many observers, this can be done by a show of hands.) Finally, each member of the crew describes in what manner he will behave differently.

7. In order to demonstrate the difficulties under which Johnson worked, he reads his role to the group.

8. Since this is a difficult problem to handle satisfactorily, a plan for the initial stages of the best approach to the problem is then outlined. This discussion includes (a) locating the problem, (b) deciding on an objective, and (c) methods for confronting the group without producing defensive behavior. (Refer to Case 7 if it has been used by the group.)

9. If time permits, a few of the presentations may be tested by having one person, acting as Mr. Johnson, state the problem to the repairmen, and then letting them report how they respond to his approach. (Six trials should serve the purpose.)

10. Some time is spent relating the problem in the role play to actual problems experienced by class members.

## General Instructions for the Class[18]

Mr. Harold Johnson is the supervisor of one of the repair crews in the American Telephone Company. Repairmen are highly skilled craftsmen and take pride in their ability to diagnose difficulties and do high quality work. They are well paid and most of them regard telephone work as a career.

Mr. Johnson's office is located in a large garage, which is in a central location for the western half of the city. Besides Mr. Johnson's crew, three other repair crews work out of this garage. The building houses the repair trucks and serves as a storage place for the supplies used in making repairs. There are also several tool shops in the building as well as offices and conference rooms.

Each repairman reports to his supervisor's office in the morning in order to pick up his individual assignment. When Mr. Johnson has a general problem to discuss with his crew, he schedules a meeting in the morning before they go out on their calls. These are held in the conference room adjacent to his office. One of these meetings is arranged for this morning and the repairmen are gathered in the conference room awaiting the arrival of Mr. Johnson.

---

[18]Based on case material in N. R. F. Maier, *Principles of Human Relations.* New York: John Wiley, 1952, 127–129.

## Role Sheet: Mr. Johnson, Supervisor

You are a supervisor in a large utility, the American Telephone Company, and are in charge of a crew of twelve repairmen who leave the garage and go to work in different sections of the city. Your supervisor has reported to you that there has been too much time wasted by repair crews stopping at restaurants for coffee in the morning. It seems that groups of them meet at certain places right after leaving the garage and have a morning visit over coffee. This condition seems to apply to all groups who work out of garages, so your group has not been selected as a bad example. However, your boss points out that it has gone too far and the abuse must be stopped. The company is very sensitive about public opinion and wonders what people will think if several company trucks are parked in front of a restaurant.

Employees who work in offices are given a fifteen-minute break both morning and afternoon. No such arrangement has been made for drivers and outside workers, but it is common for them to pause as their work permits. You know they stop for coffee—you did it yourself when you were a repairman. Some supervisors are strict and say that outside workers do not need rest periods. Therefore, the issue of rest breaks has not been clearly defined for these workers. This, you believe is the main difficulty. Your boss told you that he didn't object to a cup of coffee now and then, but he did object to the organized stops and the long visits while company trucks are parked outside a restaurant.

You have called your group together for a meeting and want to go over the issue with them before they go out on their calls. You feel that if an authorized rest period were allowed in the middle of the morning, you would be able to improve the situation. You feel it may be necessary to define rest periods for your group. The production of your crew is slightly, but consistently, above average. You feel that your crew should be given the same consideration as office workers. They are waiting for you now. You have meetings of this kind whenever a general problem has to be discussed and clarified.

## Role Sheet: All Crew Members

You are members of a crew in the telephone company. You do repair work on phones that are out of order and make five to eight repairs per day. All of you leave the garage in the morning and return at night. It is your practice to drive off in groups of three or four and stop at favorite spots for a cup of coffee. When the load isn't too heavy, you may spend as much as a half hour talking. Although the company has never stated its policy on the matter, you assume it is all right. Office workers get fifteen-minute relief periods both morning and afternoon, and they can visit in the company restaurants. Your boss has never raised the question of coffee stops and you are not sure that he knows about them. Some supervisors don't permit their crews to stop for coffee, but the crews do it anyway. The boss has asked you to meet in his office in the garage this morning to discuss a problem. He has these meetings about twice a month.

## Attitudes of Different Members of the Crew

No.  1. You find that if you go directly to your job assignment, you frequently cannot go to work because customers are not ready and you have to wait. If you arrive a bit later, people are more likely to be up and ready for you.

No.  2. You find that coffee in the morning makes you feel more civil toward your customers.

No.  3. You like the coffee at one particular restaurant and do not want to get coffee elsewhere.

No.  4. You find that a visit with the crew keeps you interested in the job.

No.  5. You stop for coffee because everybody else does.

No.  6. You often meet your friends who work for another utility at the restaurant and you like to kid with them.

No.  7. You need a cup of coffee in the morning. Your wife is an invalid and you get the kids off to school in the morning. Then you like to relax with the crew over a cup of coffee.

No.  8. You have stomach ulcers and drink a glass of milk rather than coffee. You carry some milk with you, but if you stop for milk in the morning, your thermos bottle supply holds out longer.

No.  9. Your friend works in the restaurant where you stop and you insist on going to this place, a half mile from the garage.

No. 10. You like the group you stop with and join them at these stops.

No. 11. You believe you can work better if you stop for coffee. It starts the day out right.

No. 12. It is your understanding that coffee privileges are company practice. Office workers have them. Why shouldn't you get your coffee when you want it? You prefer having it early, particularly on cold mornings.

## Instructions for Observers

This problem is difficult because it is not easy to state without producing an unfavorable reaction in the crew members. It will be difficult for the supervisor not to become defensive or not to side with them. Observe especially the following points:

1. How is the problem stated? (Consider the principles of mutual interest, use of situational terms, avoidance of implying or suggesting a solution, and presentation of a single objective—see Case 7.)
2. What causes the crew members to be suspicious or uncooperative? (Take notes on any cause-and-effect relationships.)
3. If the supervisor becomes defensive, what is the first evidence of it?
4. Make a list of the various opinions or attitudes expressed by the crew members, and note how the supervisor deals with each.
5. Make a list of cooperative statements expressed, regardless of whether the supervisor observes them or not.

## COMMENTS AND IMPLICATIONS

This problem is a troublesome one because the objectives are vague and it is difficult to determine Mr. Johnson's responsibility. Three quite different lines of action are open to Mr. Johnson: (1) he may assume that his boss is merely reacting to an incident observed and soon will forget about it; (2) he may take the hint and try to do something without damaging morale; or (3) he may tell the crew of his boss's criticism but take their side—thus protecting himself by "passing the buck." There is no policy on coffee breaks that covers repairmen, but it is known that they make coffee stops; since there is no rule covering the number of company trucks that can be parked together, the supervisor has reason to be confused. He has little basis for assuming that his crew members have been abusing certain freedoms that he has granted them previously.

In many ways, this is a problem in which the cooperation of the crew is desired and in which a disciplinary matter should not be raised. It is Mr. Johnson's boss who gives an unfavorable interpretation to the behavior of the repairmen. Of course, it is quite possible that they have been taking excessive time for coffee, but Mr. Johnson lacks information on this point.

Vague and elusive problems often can be clarified by group discussion; providing clarification rather than correction is the stated purpose of the discussion. A discussion method, which the authors of this volume call the two-column method, seems to be especially suited to clarifying problems of this sort. Using this method in the present case, the supervisor, after the usual preliminaries and niceties, states that the coffee issue for repairmen is a confused matter and neither they nor the company know what is right and proper. This being the case, the supervisor then asks the group members if they would like to clarify the matter in their unit and then come up with a plan that would be satisfactory to the crew as a whole.

Statements of this kind should lead to the establishment of a mutual interest. Once the group favors clarification, the discussion can turn to a listing of the benefits of coffee breaks. The supervisor's role is one of accepting, clarifying, and writing all contributions on the newsprint. He makes sure, too, that the list is complete.

The next step is one of listing any disadvantages of coffee stops to the company as well as to the crew. This list should also be complete; the supervisor's role is the same as above. In a utility where revenue rates are controlled, potential public criticism will undoubtedly appear in this list.

With both lists complete, the problem can be stated as follows: How can we set up a coffee-break plan for ourselves that will retain as many of the benefits and exclude as many of the disadvantages as possible? This statement is in situational terms and does not imply a particular company answer. Thus it satisfies the criteria for good statements of problems (discussed in Case 7).

The two-column method is especially useful when a group is inclined to be defensive. It is important to give persons who may feel attacked ample opportunities to get their viewpoints out in the open and have these accepted as soon as possible. If this is not done, their attitudes will appear as criticisms, objections, and distractions throughout the discussion. The first listing is always the one dealing with the items that concern the group. Once the group members feel that they have been understood, they can examine alternative viewpoints objectively and proceed to engage in constructive problem solving. The two-column method has the additional advantage of creating a situation that makes it easy for the supervisor to listen and to accept the attitudes of the group. While engaged in listing the items, he is forced to listen and must try to understand each item so that he can post it. As a result, he has less time for, and interest in, making evaluative judgments.

There are many vague problems that could be prevented if first-line supervisors had more freedom and if the problems of delegation were clarified. Improper delegation makes supervisors rigid and too concerned with consequences to listen and respect contributions.

The process of delegation is one of downward communication. Beginning with the highest level involved, each supervisory level solves only those aspects that directly concern it and passes as much of the problem down the line as possible.

For example, in dealing with any large or general question, policy and financial aspects of the problem are decided at a top level. Thus decisions about permitting a reasonable coffee break and furnishing a place to drink coffee may be made at this level. The next level might then define "reasonable" by setting up rules for various types of work, making allowances for different distances from the cafeteria and different conditions in various company buildings, etc. At the same time, a staff committee might work with the cafeteria manager to arrange for personnel, extra equipment, etc.

Problems involving uniform practices, employee attitudes, job coverage, and control of time are delegated to levels that are most concerned. The important thing is that each level that delegates a function will be willing to accept the decisions on the problem issues they have delegated. It is this willingness to accept decisions of subordinates that determines the extent and degree of an executive's delegation. It is important that enough of the problem remains for first-line supervisors so that they will have freedom for problem solving beyond mere policing. It should also be added that in passing different aspects of the problem down the line, there is an opportunity for group decisions to be made at each level by the group involved.

Management today is overworked, and one of the skills that must be learned, if this pressure is to be relieved, is that of delegation. Delegating duties and routines is not enough. Only when freedom for certain decisions is delegated and management accepts the decisions of subordinates will responsibility be stimulated and developed. Otherwise, subordinates will try to anticipate the wishes of their superiors in order to prevent criticism or rejection of their recommendations. Instead of solving problems, subordinates will try to please their bosses. To get the full worth of a subordinate's talents, the executive must discover the abilities of his employees and then delegate accordingly. On some matters, a subordinate may not decide as his superior would have wished. His decision may be sometimes better and sometimes worse than would have been the case had the superior been in charge. However, the process of executive development requires that a superior be willing to balance the good with the bad on such occasions; the screening of ideas does not promote responsible problem solving and growth.

This stage of full delegation is a gradual process. At first, only duties are delegated. As a person's knowledge grows, he should be encouraged to participate in an increasing number of matters. Finally, full delegation is given in specified areas and he is held responsible for the results, not for making decisions of which his superior approves.

The areas in which a supervisor has freedom for decision making and problem solving should be made clear to him. Without this understanding, he is inclined to be unimaginative and routine in his management techniques.

# 10

# *The Storm-Window Assignment*

## FOCUSING THE PROBLEM

Ordinarily, job assignments can be made in a fairly matter-of-fact manner. Job descriptions and good employee training methods have clarified the duties and requirements of a given job both for the supervisor and for the individual worker. However, the lack of controversy does not mean that an assignment is accepted wholeheartedly. The job performance of an individual may vary considerably, depending on whether the employee accepts his duties with enthusiasm or with resentment. Jobs can be assigned in such a way that they either give a person a feeling of pride or degrade him.

Many factors contribute to the status of a given job or duty: pay, conditions of work, amount of judgment required, degree of confinement, and the relative job status of neighboring groups. The supervisor can influence these aspects only indirectly. However, a supervisor can control his discussion of job progress and his manner of assigning a particular job, and these have direct effects on an employee's pride in and execution of his job.

The problem of job assignments becomes even more complicated when the members of a crew perform diverse duties and have different jobs from time to time. The foreman must be fair in his assignments and neither expect too much from certain individuals nor underestimate the capability of others. He not only must be sensitive to the abilities of the employees and the complexities of various job assignments, but also must be aware of the prevailing social values of the group and the individual attitudes of the workers. This seems like a lot to ask, but sometimes the effort is rewarded not only by increased employee satisfaction but by the prevention of work stoppages, grievances, and hard feelings.

The present case is purposely designed to be difficult and will challenge the wits of the best supervisors. The background conditions are set up by means of a skit that poses a problem situation. Role playing begins where the skit ends. We call the procedure the skit-completion role-playing method. The single-group role-playing procedure is prescribed because this case is a fairly complex one and emphasis is placed on observing the skills needed for discovering attitudes and feelings in other people. Getting the other person to talk about the real reasons for his actions, rather than giving excuses, demands a high level of skill.

# SINGLE-GROUP ROLE-PLAYING PROCEDURE

## Preparation and Reading of Script

1. Six persons are needed to play the parts in this case. The background for actual role playing is created by the reading of a prepared skit.
2. A table and four chairs are placed in the front of the room to form the setting for the scene in which the script will be read. The chairs may be arranged around the three sides of the table so that the audience can observe the action.
3. Four participants will be the crew members: Jack, Steve, Dave, and Bill. As soon as they are selected, they seat themselves around the table. A fifth person is selected to read the part of Mr. Brown, the foreman in the prepared script. He remains away from the table until the script calls for his entrance.
4. After the crew members are seated around the table, presumably having their lunch, the instructor selects the individual who will be the foreman during the role-playing scene to follow. In order that this foreman will know the names of his crew members, each person at the table writes his name on a piece of paper and displays it in front of him. When these details are finished, this role player leaves the room and studies the role sheet for George Brown. He remains outside the room during the reading of the script.
5. All members of the class not assigned a part act as observers and critics.
6. When the stage is set, the instructor reads aloud the description of the scene. The four crew members prepare to read their lines from

the script. They go through the business of reading the newspaper and finishing lunch.
7. The reading of the script proceeds to the end.
8. After the script has been played through, the person reading the part of Mr. Brown returns to the audience. The crew members, however, retain their places at the table in preparation for the role-playing episode.

## Preparation

1. To introduce the scene, the crew members reread the lines through Part I only, to the point of the foreman's entrance.
2. During the rereading of the script, the instructor checks with the role player who will be playing the part of Mr. Brown (he is still outside the room) to determine whether he understands his role. Mr. Brown is reminded that he is to walk up to Jack, who is seated at the table, and take up the matter he has in mind. How he introduces the job assignment will be left to his discretion. He should be ready for the instructor's signal to enter the room, but he should be out of earshot while the preparations are in progress.
3. At the appropriate point in the role play to follow, Steve, Dave, and Bill should go through the business of returning to their work by returning to their seats in the audience. They remain there until they are called back by the foreman. The foreman may wish to talk with any one of them alone or with all of them together.
4. Observers pay special attention to the crucial skills of the foreman. Knowing the case, they can be sensitive to oversights as well as to his successful or unsuccessful actions and expressions.

## Process

1. After Bill reads the last line of the script in Part I, Steve, Dave, and Bill are instructed to rise and return to their seats in the classroom.
2. The instructor signals for Mr. Brown to enter. Brown approaches Jack, who is seated at the table.
3. All actions and lines are spoken without a script.
4. Role playing continues until some decision is reached. If this decision involves a next step, such as discussing the matter with other persons, this step is role played, too. It is desirable to role play all the steps that would be taken in a real-life situation in order to settle the matter.
5. If Jack is fired or quits, observers should comment on whether the

action was justified. If it is agreed that Jack is not at fault, the foreman should be instructed to learn more about Jack's feelings. The role play is then continued from a point prior to Jack's termination.

6. Occasionally the foreman will look for an out by postponing the decision for a week or so. In such instances, he should either try again (assuming the time has passed) or a different George Brown should attempt to solve the problem. If an observer is used to take the role of Mr. Brown, it should be understood that he has the advantage of knowing the background of the problem. Although this knowledge makes the task easier, many obstacles still remain.

7. If the interview with Jack has been fairly successful, the foreman usually decides that he must take up the storm-window problem with the crew as a whole. In case this does not occur, the instructor should intervene. He can have the role play continue by requesting Mr. Brown to take his problem with Jack to the crew. It is suggested that Mr. Brown call the men back to the table in front of the room for a discussion. Whether or not he includes Jack in the meeting is left for him to decide. He and Jack may talk it over to determine whether it is best for Jack to be present or absent.

## Analysis of Role Play Between Mr. Brown and Jack

1. How soon did the foreman recognize that he was dealing with a problem that involved the other employees? Indicate the ways in which this recognition was reflected in his behavior. The foreman comments on the accuracy of these observations.

2. What significant things did Jack say or do that the foreman failed to respond to or follow up? List the items. Jack supplements the list but confines himself to points he actually expressed in the role play. (Role instructions remains private unless they are brought out in the role playing.)

3. The foreman expresses his opinions on the following questions:
   a. Is Jack more stubborn than most people would be under the same circumstances?
   b. Is Jack a desirable employee?
   c. What are Jack's real reasons for trying to avoid the assignment?
   d. Would Jack put up the storm windows if he were told that failure to do so meant discharge?
   (If several foremen role played parts of the case, each one answers these questions.)

4. The discussion method is used to develop a list of skills used by the foreman in arriving at the correct answers. A list of the skills he might

have used to obtain more valuable information is prepared and discussed.

## Analysis of Role Play with Mr. Brown and Crew Members

1. Why is it better to exclude Jack from a meeting of this kind? Discuss the difference between Brown's role as a referee and as a discussion leader.
2. Did Mr. Brown put the crew members (Steve, Dave, and Bill) on the defensive? How?
3. What did the foreman learn from the group that he did not learn from Jack. List the items.
4. What were the outstanding skills demonstrated by the foreman in conducting the group meeting? Discuss and indicate points of agreement and disagreement
5. If the group failed to cooperate, what were the basic causes of this failure? Only observers participate in developing this list.
6. Crew members voice their opinions of the observers' analyses and make corrections and additions.
7. Did the foreman take Jack's side and thereby assume a stand against the crew members? The foreman, observers, and crew members give their answers in turn.
8. What would the foreman have to do to remain impartial? Participants and observers discuss together.
9. What caused Jack to be in a face-saving situation? Discuss, using Jack as a sounding board to test the accuracy of the observers' analyses.
10. Under what conditions can the foreman find himself in a similar situation in this case?
11. What determines whether or not the crew members find themselves in a face-saving situation? Crew members indicate the way they felt in this regard.

## Role Sheet: George Brown, Foreman

You are a foreman in the plant department in a telephone company and have your headquarters in a small town. The department is located in a two-story frame building, which contains the operation equipment. Your crew is required to maintain the central office equipment, repair lines, install phones, etc. A total of four men report to you and this number is entirely adequate. There is no handyman or janitor in the group because there are practically no upkeep problems. When a door lock needs repairing, someone fixes it when he has a spare moment. Often, you fix little things if the men are busy. However, now and then certain jobs have to be assigned. The accepted practice you have followed is to give these assignments to the man with least seniority. This procedure is followed quite generally in the company and no one has ever questioned it, as far as you know. You put in your share of dirty work when you were new. One of these special jobs that comes up periodically is washing and putting up the storm windows in the fall and taking them down in the spring. There are twelve windows on the first floor and twelve windows on the second. The windows are stored in the basement. There also is a new aluminum ladder that ought to make the job easier.

The time is late October. It is getting chilly, but today is a nice day. It is a good day to put up the storm windows. Jack, Steve, Dave, and Bill have just finished having lunch in the other room. They bring their lunch and have coffee in thermos bottles. You got them a table, and they seem to like eating together. It's time for everybody to get back to work, so it is a good time to assign the job. Steve, Dave, and Bill have just left for work but Jack is still there.

Jack has the least seniority, so you are going to ask him to do the job. Since you have had no replacements for some time, Jack has done this job several years and knows the ropes. He is a nice, cooperative guy.

## The Scene

Telephone crew men work out of a small building that contains central office equipment to serve the community.

Although Jack has been on his job five years, he has the least seniority in his group. Many of the unpleasant jobs around the place fall to him. One of these is washing and putting up the storm windows each year. There are twelve windows on the first floor and twelve on the second. Jack has made no complaint about this assignment.

However, after lunch one day, when he is sitting around with other members of the group, the conversation takes an interesting turn.

## Script: Part I[19]

| | |
|---|---|
| Jack: | Boy, that hot coffee really tastes good. |
| Steve: | Yeah, it's getting chilly outside. Almost had a frost last night. |
| Dave: | Yeah! Time to finish my fall plowing in the garden. |
| Bill: | (*Reading from paper*) Here's a special on storm windows that looks good. It's time to start thinking about them. By the way, Jack, seems to me we ought to be getting them put up here, too, shouldn't we? |
| Steve: | Sure, Jack, get out the cleaner and shine 'em up. |
| Jack: | Aw, quiet—you guys are always on somebody. |
| Dave: | What's the matter, don't you like the job? |
| Bill: | Takes all your brains to do it, doesn't it, Jack? |
| Steve: | That's a real tough job! You have to figure which one to wash first and which end is up. |
| Jack: | Why don't you dry up? |
| Dave: | What's the matter, Jack? Don't you like the job? |
| Bill: | Aw, it can't be that! He's been doing it for years. He must like it. |
| Jack: | You know I don't like it. |
| Steve: | Well, you keep doing it, don't you? |
| Jack: | I'm going to get out of it, though. |
| Dave: | This I gotta see! |
| Bill: | What are you gonna do—jump the seniority list? |
| Jack: | I don't know, but I think it's time somebody else did it. |
| Steve: | Not me! |
| Dave: | You don't hook me on it either. I had my turn. |
| Jack: | For how long? One time, that's all you ever did it. |
| Bill: | And that was enough, too, wasn't it, Dave? |
| Steve: | What's the matter, Jack, can't you take it? |
| Jack: | Sure I can take it. I have for five years. |
| Dave: | Looks like you're gonna make it six years, too. |
| Jack: | Not me—I'm through doing all the dirty work around here. |
| Bill: | What do you mean dirty? You get your hands clean, don't you? |
| Steve: | Who do you think is gonna put 'em up—Brownie himself? |
| Jack: | I don't care who does it, but not me any more. |
| Dave: | Aw, you talk big but you can't make it stick. |
| Bill: | Yeah, Jackie, you're just asking for trouble. |

---

[19]Dialogue taken from N. R. F. Maier, *Principles of Human Relations.* New York: John Wiley, 1952, 114–116.

## Script: Part II

*Mr. Brown, foreman, enters.*

Brown:  Hi, fellas. (*Greetings from the group*) Say, Jack, could I see you a minute? I don't want to break up the lunch session. (*Looks at some papers in his hand.*)

Dave:  Oh no—it's time we were getting back on the job, anyway.

Jack:  Yes, sure, Mr. Brown. (*Picks up paper bag and waxed paper and throws them in basket.*) Anything wrong?

Brown:  No, Jack, not at all. I just wanted to remind you about the storm windows. (*Laugh from group at the table*)

Jack:  What about 'em?

Brown:  It's starting to turn cold, Jack. I think we ought to get 'em up. Don't you think so?

Dave:  This is where we came in, fellows, let's go. (*All but Jack leave*)

Jack:  Yeah, I guess *somebody* ought to put 'em up.

Brown:  Will you take care of that, Jack—anytime this week you can manage it.

Jack:  I wanted to talk to you about that, Mr. Brown. I'd rather not do it this year.

Brown:  Do what—put up the storm windows?

Jack:  Yes, Mr. Brown, I'd rather not do it.

Brown:  Well, Jack, it won't take you any time at all. I'll get you some help to get 'em out when you're ready.

Jack:  It isn't that—I just don't want to do it again. I've had it for five years. It's not fair!

Brown:  Well, now—I know how you feel, Jack. I know it's a chore but somebody has to do it.

Jack:  If you don't mind—count me out this time.

Brown:  But I do mind, Jack. We've got to do what's part of our job. And you're the newest man here. Be reasonable.

Jack:  I've been the "reasonable" goat around here for five years. Let somebody else do it for a change.

Brown:  Now, Jack, the others had their turn.

Jack:  For how long? Dave did it once and so did Bill. I don't think Steve ever had to put 'em up. Why pick on me?

Brown:  Nobody's picking on you. We just have to do our jobs, that's all.

Jack:  Well, it's not part of my job—it's not in my job description.

Brown:  It *is* part of your job, and I think we have a right to expect you to do it.

| | |
|---|---|
| Jack: | Count me out. |
| Brown: | Now, be yourself, Jack. I don't want to be unreasonable about this thing, but after all . . . |
| Jack: | Well, I think I've done my share. |
| Brown: | We can try to work something out on this next year, but suppose you take care of it this time. |
| Jack: | No, Mr. Brown, I just don't feel I ought to do it. |
| Brown: | Jack, I think I'll have to say you've got to do it. |
| Jack: | I'm sorry, but I'm not going to do it this time. |
| Brown: | It's an order. |
| Jack: | Not to me it's not. |
| Brown: | You'll take an order, Jack, or get out. |
| Jack: | You're not firing me. I quit and you can give your dirty job to some of those other guys. I'm through! |

END

## COMMENTS AND IMPLICATIONS

According to Part II of the script, the attempted job assignment ends in a case of insubordination. Most observers regard this outcome as unfortunate because they understand Jack's reason for not wanting to put up the storm windows. Unless one knows the reason for Jack's resistance, he appears to be stubborn and uncooperative. As a consequence, the foreman who role plays the case must be sensitive to the feelings behind Jack's evasive behavior if he is to solve the problem.

The first evidence of Jack's deep-seated problem is the determined stand he takes. He is unresponsive to coaxing and flattery, and he makes his decision quite clear at the outset. Ordinarily a person leaves himself more opportunity to back down or to alter his views. This determined stand should be the foreman's cue not to move too quickly, otherwise he may place himself in a similar situation.

When the foreman asks Jack for reasons, he is likely to get excuses and much time can be wasted in evaluating the merits of the excuses offered. Usually Jack says he has done the job more often than the other men. This makes the assignment unfair and may put Mr. Brown on the defensive. To discuss this point leads nowhere because it is not Jack's reason for refusing the assignment. That this is an excuse may be detected from the fact that Jack repeats himself many times without making it clear to the foreman why he cannot put up the storm windows just once more.

Jack may also talk about the job as if it were beneath him, and again no progress is made if the foreman points out that everyone does some work that he does not like or that is below his level of ability. This excuse, like the one above, fails to convince the foreman that Jack should not do the job. If the foreman learns no more than this about Jack's resistance, he will be inclined to believe that Jack is stubborn but that he will put up the storm windows if he is ordered to do so.

If Jack tells about the kidding he received, the foreman may recognize that he has a group problem. This information adds to the foreman's understanding of Jack because he sees that Jack's status in the group is threatened by the assignment and that he will be kidded even more if he puts up the storm windows now. However, he will find Jack unresponsive to his show of understanding or any remarks about everyone learning how to take a little kidding. Most men will not throw away a good job becuase of such kidding, and although this reason comes close to Jack's true feeling, it lacks the essential ingredient.

Jack cannot put up the storm windows because he told the group he was not going to put them up this year. The others in the crew also have committed themselves—they will have to see Jack get away with it before they believe it. Here we have an emotionally loaded situation. The problem is how to preserve Jack's pride and, to a lesser degree, that of the crew members. If the foreman goes too far in committing himself, he too winds up in a status situation.

In order to get Jack to talk about his problem and his feelings, Mr. Brown must try to understand Jack's position. This means he will have to refrain from judging Jack and, instead, use whatever skills are needed to encourage Jack to talk. Jack has been unwise in maneuvering himself into this position and he will not talk about it too readily. Listening skills and the ability to respond to and reflect Jack's feelings are essential to the foreman's success.

When the foreman recognizes that he has a group problem because he learns about either the kidding or the ego involvement, he will change his approach. He realizes that he must call the group in for a discussion, and his first decision will have to do with whether or not Jack should be present. It is our belief that Jack should not be present at the meeting. He is one faction in the controversy and has already had his say. It is now the foreman's task to discuss the matter with the other faction.

The psychological reason for this decision is that Jack's presence would probably cause the foreman to become a referee in the dispute. Each faction would try to win him over, and the gap between them would gradually be widened. Usually the foreman is sympathetic with Jack by the time he takes the problem to the group, and it is this understanding of Jack that becomes the cause of trouble with the group. If the others see the foreman as being partial to Jack, they will take a defensive position; instead of seeing their contribution to Jack's stubbornness, they will feel hostility toward Jack.

In order to hold a meeting without Jack's attendance, the foreman will want to obtain Jack's permission. To do this he will have to guard Jack's confidence. Jack usually gives his permission readily.

An effective way to introduce the group problem to Steve, Dave, and Bill is for Mr. Brown to state that he has a problem with Jack. He can point out that when he asked Jack to put up the storm windows Jack became very resistant, so much so that it appears he would quit before he would put them up. The foreman can point out that he does not feel he should press the matter further until he talks things over with them.

This type of introduction causes the men to ask questions in order to determine whether Jack has "squealed." When they are satisfied that this is not the case, and realize how seriously Jack has been hurt, they soon supply information regarding the incident that occurred during lunch. If the foreman shows understanding and the discussion focuses on how to save face all around, a cooperative group solution usually emerges. The group must make some concession to Jack for doing the job this particular year, and it should involve Jack's helping the others with the job in order to prevent him from feeling that he has been ostracized.

Once Steve, Dave, and Bill indicate their willingness to cooperate, the foreman must take the solution to Jack and gain his approval. Only then can Jack be brought into the group without risk that the difficulty will be reopened. If Jack fails to accept the group's offer, the foreman can obtain the group's support for dismissal action. Whether or not this becomes necessary depends greatly upon the foreman's skill in handling the matter.

There are many instances where problems of insubordination are unintentionally aggravated by the actions of the supervisor. Such instances frequently occur when a supervisor takes cooperation for granted. There are numerous conditions under which this assumption is unjustified, such as when cooperation implies inferior status or some other form of unequal sacrifice. In most work situations, there are tasks that are assigned to persons of low status in the group and, through this association, they become degrading. In addition, almost every group acquires or develops certain values that form the basis for determining the status of the individual members. A supervisor who is alert and sensitive to the status factors in the situation can avoid many actions that might lead to serious misunderstandings.

Despite a supervisor's best efforts to prevent problems of insubordination, there are times when such problems arise, and when they do, it is necessary to view the employee's rebellion as a new problem that must be given first consideration. This implies an understanding attitude and respect for the employee's feelings. Such conditions will remove the pressure from the employee sufficiently so that he can express his own feelings and gain relief from them, enabling the supervisor to learn the nature of the problem. Once this has been accomplished, there is usually little difficulty in working out a solution together, so that the employee no longer feels compelled to balk.

This case may be regarded as typical of a class of problems that are based on pride and status. Many of the grievances and walkouts that are described as conflicts regarding overtime, disciplinary action, insubordination, safety violations, or discriminatory practices have as their origins the issues named, but become heated and emotional confrontations when someone finds that he is in a situation in which his self-esteem or status within the group is threatened.

# 11

# *The Problem of Overtime*

## FOCUSING THE PROBLEM

It is a common practice in business and industry to give preferential treatment to employees with long service, high job grades, or skills of limited supply. In some instances, such consideration is the result of organized employee pressure for security and recognition and is received by employees with varying degrees of acceptance. In other instances, it represents ways by which management seeks to reward persons with desirable attitudes and to solve its own problems. However, instead of being accepted by employees, such preference may create status problems and dissension.

As a rule, the principle of differentiation among employees is understood and accepted by all concerned and by itself creates no problem. However, the *manner* in which the awards of preferential status are distributed is a frequent source of misunderstanding and conflict. Usually the issues center around fairness and group-membership problems. In order to meet these difficulties, it is customary for management to establish rules and regulations designed to apply equally to all. Formal procedures for insuring impartiality are ways to avoid charges of favoritism, but at the same time, new problems are sometimes created because impartiality and fairness are not the same thing. The former is based on detached intellectual judgments of a legal nature and ignores the needs and feelings of individuals. The latter is based on subjective judgments, which are emotional in nature, and recognizes the unique needs of each individual.

In the New Truck Dilemma (Case 1) the problem was to determine the fair way to share a desirable thing. In the present case, the problem also hinges on fairness, but this time the superior's problem is to find a fair way to share a sacrifice. A group of employees have been working overtime regularly and have set patterns of living on the increased income. If the overtime is reduced, it will be felt as a wage cut and may be taken as such—even though no legal or logical claim for this can be substantiated.

Another special feature of this case is the fact that two classes of people belong to a single group and, as a result, an issue of social status is incorporated. If the group splits into two factions, grade-A workers and grade-B workers, then the issue no longer will center around the real problem. Instead, it may degenerate into a struggle to determine which faction will win. If this happens, reduced cooperation occurs, and the problem of fairness—instead of being solved—becomes the source of a new and persistent problem.

In order to direct everyone's attention to the way these conflicting factors of status, potential group division, and a shared sacrifice develop and influence each other, the single-group role-playing procedure is prescribed. It is important that the various cause-and-effect relationships be analyzed.

## SINGLE-GROUP ROLE-PLAYING PROCEDURE

### Preparation

1. In order to acquaint everyone with the background of the case, the General Instructions for All Participants are read aloud by one member of the class while the others follow the text. The portion at the end in which the names, job grade, and length of service are given is copied on newsprint by the instructor so that it will be visible to everyone.
2. The instructor selects seven participants to role play the case. In a clockwise direction, beginning with the foreman, members assume their roles by taking them in the order listed on the easel. Each person announces who he is and wears a tag bearing that name. The remaining class members become observers.
3. Each participant studies his particular role and does not read any other role.
4. The observers read the Instructions for Observers.
5. While class members are studying their parts, the instructor prepares the setting for the role play. It is suggested that he arrange a table and seven chairs in the front of the room to represent the foreman's

office. The table and one chair will be for the foreman; the other six chairs are placed in a semicircle in front of the desk for the crew members. If no table is available, a chair may be used to designate a desk. The furniture should be arranged to form an arc in front of the room, with the foreman's desk on the left and forward, so that the observers are able to see the faces of most of the role players.

## Process

1. When the participants have finished studying their roles and are ready to begin the role play, the six crew members enter the office. In order to facilitate identification of the role players, they seat themselves in the same order as their names appear on the easel, starting with George Hamill in the chair on the left of the foreman. It is assumed that a meeting has been called in the foreman's office and that he· has not yet arrived.
2. After the crew members are all seated, the participant who plays the part of the foreman, John Willets, enters his office and conducts himself accordingly.
3. The role play will usually take forty minutes. The participants should be allowed to finish whenever possible. However, if the role playing deteriorates into stubborn wrangling and the foreman seems to have lost control of the meeting, the instructor should interrupt the scene. In such instances the participants may wish to discuss the difficulty and offer advice to the foreman. Action can then be resumed with the same foreman or a different one, depending on the decision of the participants and instructor. Role playing should always be terminated before it becomes boring.
4. After the role play has been completed, the instructor moves to the front of the room to conduct the analysis of the role play. The participants remain in their seats in the front of the room to retain their identity in the case.

## Evaluation of Solution Reached

1. The participants, including the foreman, report in turn whether they (a) disapprove, (b) approve with reservations, or (c) fully approve of the solution. They do not give their reasons at this time.
2. The observers compare the degree of acceptance obtained for the group solution with that for a solution that might have been reached by a typical foreman.

3. The quality of the decision is evaluated for (a) its practicality and (b) its degree of detail or completeness. Observers discuss these issues, but the role players remain in character and contribute only to the extent of answering questions regarding their feelings and opinions.
4. Role players report whether or not they agree on what the solution requires of them and what will happen when the solution is put into effect. Any disagreement on detail indicates inadequate communication.

## Analysis of the Conference Process

1. The observers scrutinize the foreman's statement of the problem to see if they can determine what he did or failed to do that caused the workers to assume a problem-solving approach rather than a defensive position. Role players evaluate the observers' comments but are careful to confine their remarks to the initial part of the conference.
2. Should the foreman have mentioned the amount of overtime reduction that he wished to accomplish? After observers have expressed their views, each worker indicates the amount of overtime he would have preferred. These responses may be totaled to determine how much of a reduction would have been acceptable to the group as a whole. How did the goal statement influence the group's views of fairness? Were the goals set by the group more strict than those that might have been imposed by management?
3. Conflicts within a group may arise because of factors that existed before the conference or occurred during the conference. Were there any conflicts that could have been avoided or prevented? All class members participate in locating conflicts within the group.
4. A potential conflict between the two grade-A workers is planted in the roles. What did the leader do or fail to do to prevent this from being a disruptive influence?
5. The group might separate into two factions, with grade-A workers on one side and grade-B workers on the other. What factors caused or prevented this conflict from becoming serious?
6. Observers enumerate the needs and feelings of the various workers that were expressed during the discussion. The participants, in turn, then report (by reading from their roles) the needs and feelings they did not express.
7. Some time is spent in discussing the importance to the foreman of obtaining a knowledge of these needs before attempting to solve a group problem.

8. What part can the conference leader play in bringing the needs of various individuals to the attention of the group? Discuss by illustrating what the foreman did or might have done in this case.

9. Observers report instances in which they feel the foreman took sides for or against some members of the crew. Crew members supplement the observers' reports by telling how they felt about the foreman's biases.

10. Develop a list of things the leader did to upgrade the quality of the solution. Continue the list by adding suggestions about what might have been done.

11. Discuss one or two problems suggested by class members that might be dealt with through group problem solving.

## General Instructions for All Participants

You are a group of six pattern makers who work under the supervision of John Willets. Your work is steady and the pay is good. Each of you has been doing a lot of overtime work during the past six months, for which you get time-and-a-half pay. You are divided into two groups according to skill and wages. Two of you (classified grade-A) have high skill ratings and do the more complex features of the job; your pay is fifty cents an hour higher than that of the others (classified as grade-B workers) who do the more routine type of pattern work.

The job is such that the two highly skilled workers begin a job and the rest carry it to completion. The grade-B workers' overtime is thus dependent on the overtime of the grade-A workers. As a result of the job divisions, the four grade-B workers get less overtime than the grade-A workers. A typical example is an average of eight hours per week overtime for the grade-A workers and an average of six hours overtime for the grade-B workers.

Ordinarily, the arrangment is to give the men in each grade as nearly equal an amount of overtime in a week as possible. If a particular individual turns down overtime in one week, the man next in seniority gets the first chance at the extra overtime. If there is a slackening of work, the man with least seniority takes a reduction first. Since there has been plenty of overtime lately, none of you feel you want any more. As it now works out, each of you usually stays late a few evenings a week and some of you come to work for three or four hours on Saturday morning. You usually alternate the Saturday work, with one grade-A man and two grade-B men taking turns. It is the company's practice to pay for the evening meal when you work overtime at night. The allowance for the meal is $3.00. The company prefers that no one work more than two hours overtime in any one night. Usually, you work until six, take a half hour off for dinner, and then finish work by 7:30 or earlier. The foreman, of course, gets most of the overtime, since he has to stay with the men when they work late and he also comes in every Saturday.

The names of the men, their grade, and their years of experience are as follows:

| | |
|---|---|
| John Willets, foreman | 25 years |
| George Hamill, grade A | 23 years |
| Hank Davis, grade A | 20 years |
| Pat O'Connor, grade B | 12 years |
| Jim Jaffe, grade B | 10 years |
| Walt Jarvis, grade B | 10 years |
| Sam Simpson, grade B | 8 years |

## Role Sheet: John Willets, Foreman

You are the foreman of the crew of pattern makers. For the past six months you have averaged about ten hours overtime, which represents nearly 40 percent extra wages for you. You have been banking this extra money and now have a good savings account. However, your wife complains that all work and no play is wearing you down. You work every Saturday morning and about two hours three nights a week. Although you like to save money, this way of doing it is rough. However, other departments depend on your work, so you have to do this much overtime work to keep up with the needs.

Lately, however, the company has become economy minded. Although business is good, the profits have declined and company officials are worried. It is recognized by management that your unit needs more overtime than others, but the other day your boss told you of a ruling requesting all departments to reduce overtime work. He suggested that all foremen increase the efficiency of their crews so that overtime could be cut at least 10 percent. You told your boss this was a reasonable request. You have called your crew together to discuss the matter of reducing overtime. You think that the foremen may be judged on their crew's efficiency and, therefore, you are more than anxious to meet this request.

## Role Sheet: George Hamill, Grade-A Worker

You and Hank Davis are the two grade-A workers. For the past six months you have been getting at least eight hours overtime a week and this has added about 30 percent to your income. With this extra money, you have made a down payment on a cabin to use for vacations and for hunting and fishing weekends. The cabin is something you have always wanted. If this overtime keeps up, you will be able to take off a little extra time. You wish you could get as much overtime as John Willets, the foreman, and you look forward to becoming a foreman someday. Since you have the most seniority in your group, this is not an idle dream.

Hank Davis takes as much overtime as he can get. He really doesn't need the overtime since his tastes are rather simple. You have tried to get him to turn down more of his overtime and let you at least cover some of his Saturday work this winter, but he won't commit himself. Long hours don't bother you and you would just as soon work as waste your evenings and Saturdays this winter. Your wife is gone a lot (she spends a good deal of time with your two married daughters who live on the other side of town) so you frequently have to eat or prepare your own meals. When you work overtime in the evenings, the company furnishes the meal, saving you trouble and time. Some of the men don't care for so much overtime, so they have been trying to keep up with the job and reduce the overtime. You feel that they are going to spoil things. After all, you do a reasonable day's work, and your overtime efforts give the grade-B boys an opportunity to earn something extra. These days everybody needs an extra source of income.

## Role Sheet: Hank Davis, Grade-A Worker

You and George Hamill are the two grade-A workers. Lately, your wife has been complaining about the fact that you work so much overtime. She also has a job and resents it if you can't spend time with her. Since the two of you make a good income, you prefer not to work overtime. If George weren't such a selfish person, you would give him more overtime. He's always asking you to give up overtime so he can get more, but not long ago when you really wanted a Saturday off, he wouldn't help you out because he wanted to go fishing. It's a one-way deal with George, so you have decided to take your share of overtime so as to keep up with the job. If George would work a little harder, the two of you could keep up with the job by working no more than a couple of evenings a week. Under such circumstances, you would give George all your overtime. You prefer working Saturday mornings if you have to take overtime. This would leave your evenings free so that you and your wife could get out more. You have no children.

## Role Sheet: Pat O'Connor, Grade-B Worker

You have five children ranging from one to ten years in age. With living expenses what they are, you depend on working overtime. The extra six or eight hours a week at time-and-a-half pay that you have been getting lately has increased your income so that things are now running very well. Last month, your wife got the clothes dryer she had been wanting for a long time.

Jim Jaffe has been very decent with you. When overtime needs are less than usual, he turns down some of it so that you can have more. Your main worry is that the overtime won't last. You admit that you have been slowing the job down a bit to insure overtime.

You prefer taking your overtime in the evening. In this way, you get your meal furnished by the company and save travel expenses. It would be ideal if you could always work two hours extra, three or four nights a week.

## Role Sheet: Jim Jaffe, Grade-B Worker

You don't particularly care for overtime, but the company has the custom of dividing it up evenly among the men, so you cooperate to help things out as much as you can. Now and then when you have a good excuse, you turn down some overtime so that Pat can have it. He really needs it.

You are single and enjoy your freedom. You like to have your nights free because you are active in a number of clubs. You don't mind working Saturday mornings now and then, but the evening work has interfered with your other activities and it has gotten you down. Some of the fellows in your group are actually slowing down on the job so as to keep the overtime. It seems unfair that you should be inconvenienced because others want overtime. The trouble with most people is that they are developing standards of living way beyond their class. Of course, some of the fellows like Pat and Sam have heavy responsibilities—but that is no excuse for making everyone work overtime.

## Role Sheet: Walt Jarvis, Grade-B Worker

As does anyone else, you like a chance to earn a little extra money. Since you are doing the same work as Pat, Jim, and Sam, you feel you should have the same amount of overtime they do. Ordinarily John and George get more overtime than the rest of you. They have sort of a controlling position. When they work eight hours overtime, the rest of you have about six hours overtime. If they really did their job, each one of them could keep two of you busy. They are no more entitled to eight hours overtime than you are. If that ratio keeps up, you're going to get the grade-B guys to slow up a bit so that each of you gets eight hours overtime. Why should George and Hank get all the breaks? You know for certain that George is dragging the job out. You are sick of having him say he's doing you and the others a favor by working overtime so that there will be plenty of overtime for you. He sees to it that he gets most of the overtime and he needs it least of all. It's not that you are dependent on overtime. But why shouldn't it be divided fairly? If George and Hank can't do enough to keep up with you, they could let Pat O'Connor help out. He knows just as much as they do and there is no reason why such a sharp distinction should be made between grade-A men and grade-B men. The important thing is to get the job done right.

You are married and have a five-year-old daughter. As you increase your earnings, your wife can always find ways to spend the money. She likes nice things and you are glad to let her spend money when you have it. The extra earnings have made it possible for you to get a color television set and some new furniture.

## Role Sheet: Sam Simpson, Grade-B Worker

The extra overtime has been a big break for you. Your wife had twins two years ago and hasn't been well since. You still are paying off the loan you made to pay the doctor and hospital bills, and you have had a succession of doctor bills since. Now your wife needs an operation. If you knew the overtime would keep up for another six or eight months, you would feel free to have her go ahead with the operation.

Although the overtime work makes it difficult for you to help out at home as much as you would like, you feel that the extra money is more urgent.

The six hours a week overtime that you usually get is entirely satisfactory, but less than that would upset your plans. Since you have the least seniority, you would be the first to be cut if overtime needs fell off. There seems little chance that the other men would let you have extra overtime since there are men with more seniority who take all they can get. So far, you haven't told your troubles to anyone because your tough luck is your problem. However, it would be nice if there weren't such a rigid way of dividing up overtime. Since you have the least seniority, you are not in a good position to suggest a change because the others might consider you a troublemaker.

## Instructions for Observers

1. Did the leader get to the point of the discussion quickly and state the problem clearly? Would you have started the discussion any differently? Make brief notes on your observations.
2. How did the crew members react in the beginning of the discussion? Did anyone show hostility? If so, who was it? Toward whom was the hostility directed? What were some reactions of those to whom it was directed?
3. Was there criticism of the foreman or of the company's way of allocating overtime? If so, how did the foreman react? Did the foreman or any crew member show defensive behavior at any time? What reactions were there to this? Was the leader permissive and accepting of different points of view?
4. To what extent was there a free airing of feelings in the group? What did the leader do to help or hinder this? In what part of the discussion did this occur?
5. What was the solution of the group, if any? If none, what are some of the reasons? What is the extent of agreement on the solution? Did everyone contribute in some way to the solution? Did the discussion allow for improving the solution in the future? In what ways might this method of handling overtime problems be more efficient than a solution developed by the foreman? Which method will result in better human relations?

## COMMENTS AND IMPLICATIONS

In this particular case, the group members often are set to be on the defensive; they will stand together and protect their inefficiency, as well as their overtime, if criticized by the foreman. Even a mild suggestion that increase their efficiency may be interpreted as a demand for a speedup. Before the crew is ready to think constructively, the foreman must explore how they feel about overtime—both the good and the bad features. He must accept and respect these views and look for others because attitudes often represent needs that are not so readily expressed. Often the ideas expressed first in a discussion are excuses or justifications for other opinions. Disagreements in the group should be accepted as problems to solve and the foreman should be careful not to take sides or to push his personal views.

Once the needs and the feelings of the group have been expressed and analyzed, the foreman can talk about a problem of the company—that is, the need to cut costs. He can ask the group members to express their opinions on what would be fair to everyone. His objective should be a solution that will give everybody a more satisfactory experience with the company. If the group does not respond immediately and readily, he should be patient and, above all, avoid becoming defensive. Otherwise, things will go from bad to worse. If the group shows a lack of interest in the problem, the foreman can indicate a solution that will reduce costs without increasing efficiency—e.g., the hiring of an extra man, thereby cutting out forty hours of premium overtime pay.

The crew should set its own goal of how much it can increase efficiency. This goal will be more exacting and strict than management could request or even demand because the crew will not have to fear the consequences—as it would if someone else set the goals. The important thing for the leader to do is to see that, in solving the problem of efficiency, the personal needs of the men will be given a full hearing. Individuals who appear greedy may have to be protected from the force of social pressure, and face-saving opportunities may have to be created for others, but through it all the foreman must play the part of a peace-maker and never act as a judge.

Examples of the way the foreman may prevent critical comments of group members from becoming sources of conflict are as follows:

1. If George talks about taking some of Hank's overtime and if Hank expresses a willingness to give up some, the foreman might restate George's position by saying, "I think George means that he is willing to take any overtime that happens to be left over,

not that he thinks he's entitled to increase his overtime while others take a cut."

2. If Walt criticizes the grade-A workers for trying to create overtime for themselves, the foreman might restate his argument by saying, "Walt seems to feel that we can reduce overtime somewhat. Perhaps if we can see our way clear to get a fair amount of overtime and satisfy our personal needs, we may find ways to take a reduction that will not inconvenience anyone. At least you feel that some saving can be made—is that right, Walt?"

3. If George has indicated that he will not stand for a grade-B worker doing grade-A work, but other workers favor giving Pat some grade-A work, the foreman may smooth things over by stating, "I don't think the others want to upgrade Pat all at once; rather they are suggesting that Pat will be a grade-A worker only when he is temporarily on a grade-A job. Obviously he will need help and training; perhaps together we can work out a schedule for giving him what he needs."

Once the group agrees to take a reduction in overtime and feels that improved effciency can keep production up, the problem of implementation arises. This requires the setting up of a tentative schedule for a trial run. Such a schedule will show each person how the change will affect him. It is at this point that the foreman can see to it that communication has been adequate by concerning the problem-solving process with specific practices rather than generalizations. This is the stage of carrying the discussion from policy to practice. It is important that solutions of this kind remain subject to change. Since the needs of individuals change, the decisions that satisfy needs must also be subject to change. One of the most common faults with solutions to this type of problem is the failure to implement the decision that the group feels it has reached.

This case is of special interest because it shows how the sharing of a hardship tends to be solved on the basis of need rather than on the basis of least seniority. Length of service is more likely to be accepted as a method for distributing privileges than lack of seniority is accepted as a method for distributing hardships. This is one important difference in the way groups behave when they are given the freedom to solve job problems. It is common practice in companies to give the junior man low-status jobs, believing that the crew wants it that way. However, the crew takes this attitude only when it feels the need to defend itself. When the crew participates in decisions about changes, defensive behavior rapidly disappears.

Status is one of the important nonfinancial incentives in a group; many jobs acquire a low-status rating not merely because they are routine, dirty, or simple, but also because they are performed by low-status employees. Jobs performed by senior workers may acquire high status by the same process.

# 12

# *Interviewing the Union Steward*

## FOCUSING THE PROBLEM

It is generally recognized that a knowledge of human relations principles helps a supervisor to deal with his subordinates; the same knowledge also can help him deal with his associates. Since many feel that a company's dealings with the union differ basically from its dealings with an employee, the question arises whether these principles can be applied to working with union representatives. Getting along with the union is a problem of negotiation; this circumstance creates two opposing viewpoints as well as two opposing interests. Success in this kind of relationship seems to require each party to bluff, to exaggerate, and to make demands in excess of what it hopes to get. Many people expect to haggle when bargaining, and some people even think that failure to do so is a sign of naiveté or weakness.

Although the number of persons involved with bargaining issues is small, many management personnel do have face-to-face dealings with union stewards. In cases of conflict, the steward is expected to represent the union member and the supervisor is expected to represent the company. A conflict in viewpoint often results, but there is a possibility that a mutual interest exists and that both parties can gain something that is not at the other's expense.

The purpose of this case is to explore the possibilities for reaching understanding when a conflict between the union and management is imminent. Because solutions to such conflicts frequently create dissatisfaction, grievance procedures have been worked out to prevent the dissatisfaction from leading to strikes or walkouts. The present case can help determine whether legalistic approaches (grievance procedures and legislation) are more effective than human relations approaches (interviewing and conference skills) in industrial relations.

In the present case, an employee was caught smoking ten minutes before quitting time, despite the existence of a "no smoking" rule that is well known to the employees. The foreman imposed the prescribed penalty of a three-day layoff for the infraction. The employee, feeling that he was discriminated against and treated unfairly, reported the incident to his union steward. The steward, after discussing the matter with the employee, thought that he should take the matter up with the foreman. The first interview is thus between the foreman and the steward. Depending on the result of this interview, the foreman or the steward will then interview the employee.

The problem can be role played using a single group, or the entire audience may be allowed to participate. The procedure described here illustrates the multiple role-playing procedure.

## MULTIPLE ROLE-PLAYING PROCEDURE

### Preparation

1. The General Instructions are read silently by all participants while the instructor reads them aloud.
2. The group divides into subgroups of three members each. One member in each group plays the foreman, another becomes the steward, and the third member plays the employee; he also serves as an observer. One or two groups may have a second observer. If one or two persons remain, some groups may re-form so that one or two pairs role play without the employee (Jack).
3. Each player studies his role sheet.
4. Each steward stands when he is ready to begin the role play. When all stewards are standing, the instructor gives the signal to begin. The participant who takes the part of Jack is present during the interview between Burns and Schultz but he serves as an observer and does not participate.

### Process

1. Burns steps toward Schultz to indicate that he has entered the foreman's office to begin their discussion. All groups role play simultaneously.

2. Fifteen to twenty minutes will be needed for the interview between the foreman and the steward. When more than half the pairs have finished or at the end of eighteen minutes, the instructor gives a two-minute warning signal and asks the remaining groups to terminate the interview.
3. During the role play, the easel is prepared with the headings illustrated in Sample Table 10, so that the results can be recorded.

## Collecting Results of Interviews

1. The foremen of all groups describe the solution reached. The solutions reached may be listed in column 1 of Sample Table 10. Each foreman also reports whether he is satisfied with his group's solution. These reports are entered in column 2.
2. The stewards report whether or not they intend to file a formal grievance. (The instructor indicates these responses in column 3 of the table.)
3. The Jack Stevens in each group tells whether or not he is satisfied with the results of the interview between Burns and Schultz. (Indicate these responses in column 4 of the table.)
4. Jack reports whether his amount of smoking on the job will change (column 5) and whether his production will be affected (column 6).
5. Jack then evaluates the steward's performance by indicating whether his estimation of the steward has changed as a result of the interview. (This report is indicated in column 7).

## Analysis of Results

1. It is interesting to note that, in many cases, the foremen rescind the layoff. Discuss reasons given by those foremen who reduced the penalty.
2. If the foreman changes his position, how does he save face? Discuss.
3. The class as a whole discusses what the foreman might gain and what he might lose by sticking to his decision to punish Jack. (The instructor lists all views on newsprint, with gains in one column and losses in another.)
4. Results that maintain good company relationships and also control smoking without a loss in production are most often obtained when the foreman and the union steward approach the problem from the question of how to control smoking. Do the class results support this view?

## Discussion and Evaluation of Various Approaches

1. Discuss the attitude and the approaches the foreman might take in order to make the interview with the steward more constructive. (The stewards participate in this discussion to evaluate how they would react. The instructor accepts all views and summarizes.)
2. Since both parties in the interview are inclined to favor their own viewpoint, how can they get the interview around to solving the problem they are faced with?
3. Jack's objective is to escape punishment. Can each of the participants "give in" on something so that everyone will be able to save his own pride? Evaluate some suggested solutions.
4. Discuss the significance of the fact that many members in the crew smoke despite the "no smoking" rule. (Differences in attitude will emerge, with some blaming the employees and the foreman and others taking a problem-solving attitude. The instructor may wish to use leading questions and probe if necessary to bring out the fact that the prevalence of smoking is a group problem. All viewpoints are to be respected.)
5. How can the problem of smoking-rule violations be presented to the crew so as to lead to problem solving? Can Jack be made an exception without fear that respect for the rule will be lost in the future?
6. If the problem is not solved and a strike eventually is threatened because of the disciplinary action, will members of higher management support the foreman or will they "give in," believing that the incident is not worth the trouble? Discuss.
7. Discuss the prescriptive or authoritarian approach to discipline versus the human relations approach.

## General Instructions

Bill Schultz has been a foreman of a work group in a factory for the past two years. All eighteen of his employees work on individual machines and each has his quota of work to do for a given day. Bill's job is to see that the employees have work to do and that everyone keeps busy.

A company rule prohibits smoking while on the job and it stipulates a three-day layoff for violation of the rule. "No Smoking" signs, stating the penalty, are in view throughout the shop. Smoking is permitted in the restrooms, but employees cannot be away from the job an unreasonable amount of time. There is no obvious fire hazard.

During the past year, employees in other groups have been laid off for smoking and others have been reprimanded for spending too much time in the restrooms. Everyone knows that lots of people steal a smoke now and then. Whether or not a person gets caught and punished for smoking depends greatly on the vigilance of the foreman. Since Bill Schultz took over this group, no one has been disciplined for smoking, although three years ago both Hank and George received a layoff.

If an employee is disciplined by a foreman, he can go to his steward and protest. The usual procedure is for the steward to hear the employee's side because he is responsible for seeing that everyone gets a fair deal. If he feels that an employee has a case, he takes the matter up with the foreman. He can speak to the foreman alone or take the aggrieved person with him. If the foreman and the steward cannot reach an agreement, the steward makes a written complaint. The matter now becomes a formal grievance and is handled in accordance with the procedure prescribed in the union contract. Both management and union prefer to settle disputes before they reach the formal stage.

## Role Sheet: Bill Schultz, Foreman

You have imposed a three-day disciplinary layoff on Jack Stevens, one of your employees, for violating the "no smoking" rule. Both the rule and the penalty for its violation have been in effect for as long as you can remember and are well known by everyone. It is accepted as one of the working rules of the company that anyone caught smoking on the job is subject to a three-day layoff.

Despite all this, you have some reason to believe that at least a few of your employees occasionally smoke on the job. You can't watch everyone all the time; you have other things to do. Besides, you don't want your employees to feel that you are spying on them. Since you have been on the job, there have been no flagrant violations of the rule, so you have felt no need to make a special issue of the matter. There is no obvious fire hazard, but you have been told that insurance costs are higher when smoking is permitted in a shop. You realize that it is your duty to see that discipline and proper respect for company regulations are maintained, regardless of what you personally may think of a rule.

In this instance, you caught the man on the floor with a lighted cigarette in plain view of several other employees, about ten minutes before quitting time. He offered no excuses, admitting that he was familiar with both the rule and the penalty. He protested vigorously, however, when you imposed the three-day layoff, saying that he was going directly to his steward, Joe Burns, about it.

You are in your office now. You notice that Burns is walking across the floor toward your office.

## Role Sheet: Joe Burns, Department Steward

Jack Stevens, who is one of the employees in the work group for which you are the steward, has just told you that his supervisor, Bill Schultz, has given him a three-day disciplinary layoff for violating the "no smoking" rule. You are aware of the rule and you know that Jack is too. Nevertheless, in this case you feel that the penalty is entirely unfair and uncalled for and that it would work a hardship on Jack's family. Most of the other employees take a quick smoke now and then, but Schultz has not been strict in enforcing the rule.

Jack admitted he was smoking, but pointed out that he smokes less than the others. Besides, it was close to quitting time and he had worked fast to get his job finished. Jack has always been thoroughly honest with you and you are convinced that Schultz is merely trying to use Jack as an example to the others instead of handling the case on its merits. Technically, he may have a case. There is a "no smoking" rule. Actually, however, no one seems to know why the rule is necessary. There is no fire hazard. The only possible excuse for it is to keep people busy working. The fact that smoking is permitted in the restrooms is not a true smoking privilege, since employees are disciplined if they spend too much time in the restrooms. Schultz is relatively new on the job and he had better learn that he can't enforce rules just when the mood hits him.

You think that you can handle the matter best by going to see Schultz alone. You are walking toward his office now.

## Role Sheet: Jack Stevens, Machine Operator

Bill Schultz is the foreman of your work group. He has just caught you smoking and has given you a three-day layoff for violation of a "no smoking" rule. You know of the rule and the penalty, but quite a few of the other employees smoke and they haven't been penalized. You actually smoke less than they do. In this type of work, there is no fire hazard; consequently, you don't know why the rule is necessary.

You had worked fast and finished you job ten minutes early, so you had time for a smoke before quitting time. Since the foreman wasn't around, you didn't bother to go to the men's room but just leaned against a post a few feet from your machine.

As soon as Schultz imposed the three-day disciplinary layoff, you went to your steward, Joe Burns, and told him your story. You just can't afford to lose three days' pay. Burns agreed with you that it was unfair and suggested that the foreman may be using you as an example. He said he felt you had a grievance case and that he would go to bat for you. He's on his way to see Schultz now.

### Sample Table 10. Analysis of Interview with Union Steward
(Use Table for Recording Class Data)

| | 1 | 2 | 3 | 4 | 5 | 6 | 7 |
|---|---|---|---|---|---|---|---|
| Group | Solution | Foreman Satisfied | Steward Satisfied | Jack Satisfied | Jack's Smoking | Jack's Production | Jack's Estimation of Steward |
| 1 | Full layoff | Yes | No—Grievance | No | Up, but careful | Down | Same |
| 2 | 1-day layoff | Yes | Yes | Yes | Less | Same | Up |
| 3 | No layoff, Steward will inform all workers he will not support future violators | Yes | Yes | Yes | Less | Up | Up |

## COMMENTS AND IMPLICATIONS

The foreman's dilemma is that he is likely to feel he cannot back down without sacrificing dignity. However, if he insists that his decision stand, he may have a formal grievance to deal with as well as bad relations with his crew. The steward is in a similar position with the employees. He has gone to bat for Jack, and it is hard to back down. Thus, the situation can easily develop into a heated argument in which each tells his side of the story, with neither person seeing the problem in a constructive light. This type of interview goes from bad to worse. If the foreman, instead of arguing the issue with the steward, is willing to listen, accept what the steward has to say, and understand that a problem exists, he may salvage the situation—even though the employee has already been told of the penalty—because a formal grievance has not yet been filed. By giving the steward an opportunity to have his say, the foreman can make it clear that he is willing to be reasonable and do the fair thing; in this way he can improve relations with the steward. If this is accomplished, the steward may be willing to look at the foreman's problem. The foreman can then point out that he does not want to police the job but that he had no other alternative when he caught Jack red-handed.

Once the situation has acquired the elements of mutual acceptance and understanding, it is possible to discuss what can be done. If the foreman gives in by reducing the penalty or giving only a warning, the steward can also give in by indicating that he will support the foreman on the next occasion. The foreman can more readily make an exception to a rule when he has the cooperation of the steward because the fear of being charged with discriminatory practices in the future will be avoided. In this kind of agreement, which results from cooperative problem solving, neither has to fear that the other will claim a victory— always a concern in problems involving status. Any agreement that is reached should later be discussed with the employee by each of them separately.

If the foreman discusses the matter with the employee, he should state the agreement reached with the steward and then encourage the employee to express his feelings freely. As a result of such discussion, the foreman and the employee are likely to understand each other's position more clearly and be willing to deal with the problem in a constructive way.

Since other crew members also smoke, the problem of violating the "no smoking" rule is most properly one for the whole group. The rule was formulated initially to control smoking, not to punish employees. If the problem is presented to the crew for discussion and a group decision, a solution satisfactory to all concerned usually can be developed, provided that the action has the support of the union steward and a reasonable case can be made for the need of a "no smoking" rule on the job. If the group accepts the rule, the problem of enforcement is greatly simplified.

Higher management should also appreciate the problems faced by the foreman. It is relatively easy to institute a rule with penalties attached because this is done in the abstract and particular people are not part of the consideration. However, when a penalty must be applied, a particular person is involved. Punishing a person is an unpleasant duty for most supervisors. Foremen also know that management often will not back them up if the union causes trouble. The foreman therefore finds himself in difficulty if he enforces a rule, and he risks the charge of failing to support management if he does not enforce the rule. Often he resolves the dilemma by pretending not to see the violation, and this is no solution to the problem.

# 13

## *The Personnel Interview*

### FOCUSING THE PROBLEM

Supervisors who are faced with a behavior problem frequently take action that leads to conflict and misunderstanding instead of problem solving. This may be because the supervisor is required to operate within a framework of rules that are arbitrary, unnecessary, or unrealistic. More often, however, needless conflict is due to certain attitudes on the part of the supervisor and a lack of skill in handling people. When the supervisor's approach is to blame the employee for poor behavior, any discussion is likely to result in faultfinding and defensive behavior rather than in a solution to the problem. Under these conditions, both the supervisor and the employee talk themselves into extreme positions, and then neither can yield without losing face.

When conflict rather than problem solving occurs between the supervisor and an employee, a third party—not directly involved in the controversy—is frequently consulted. This may be a shop steward, someone in higher management, a personnel representative, or an arbitrator. Both parties usually will make sincere attempts to resolve their differences before a dispute reaches the stage of a formal grievance or before a valued employee resigns or is discharged. Regardless of who the neutral or third party may be, the success or failure of his efforts to obtain a solution satisfactory to both parties will depend on the attitude and skill with which he handles the situation. It is apparent that both parties to the dispute will try to win him over and that it will be necessary but difficult for him to remain neutral. In the present case, a personnel officer finds himself in a position in which he can perform a function that may be either helpful or harmful to others. Two persons read the

189

script of a conversation between an employee and his supervisor, while the third party is out of the room. Later, this third person interviews the employee and must discover the employee's real problem. Considerable skill is demanded of the interviewer if he is to discern the facts and achieve results that are satisfactory to all concerned.

This case is also used to introduce the dramatized case method for role playing. A prepared script sets the background for the case and establishes a conflict in attitudes.

## DRAMATIZED CASE METHOD

### Preparation

1. Three members of the group are needed to play the roles. Other members participate as observers.
2. One of the role-playing participants acts as Walt Henderson, the employee; the second, as Ken Hardy, the supervisor; and the third, as Robert Welch, the personnel director.
3. After all roles have been assigned, everyone reads the General Instructions.
4. Welch now leaves the room and studies his role. It is important that he refrain from reading the script or other materials. He remains outside the room until preparations for his return are completed.
5. The setting for the role play involving Walt Henderson and Ken Hardy is arranged by placing a table and a chair in the front of the room. The employee, Walt Henderson, then occupies the chair and assumes he has a drawing board in front of him. He and the supervisor, Ken Hardy, should have copies of the script and be prepared to read their parts.
6. Ken Hardy walks to the front of the room and, as he approaches Walt's table, begins reading the script aloud.

### Process

1. When they have finished reading the script, Hardy joins the observers and Walt leaves the room to study the Additional Information for Walt Henderson. Only Walt is to see this material. Robert Welch is now asked to return to the classroom.
2. Observers study their instructions.
3. The table and two chairs are arranged in the front room and become the office furnishings of Robert Welch, Personnel Director.

4. When the setting is completed, Welch seats himself at his desk in front of the room.

5. Walt is cued to come in and go directly to Welch's office. Hardy, the supervisor, remains in the room but assumes he has heard nothing in case he is involved later.

6. Approximately twenty minutes is needed for this interview. Welch should take as much time as he wishes to handle the situation and he should have a free hand to make arrangements for any further actions. He can decide whether to have Hardy come in, whether to talk to him privately, or whether to make arrangements without consulting Hardy. If Welch brings Hardy and Walt face to face and they become involved in a wrangle in which no progress is made, the discussion is terminated.

7. After Welch has completed the interview with Walt, it may be worthwhile to give observers a chance to discuss the progress made before taking the next step, which may be an interview between Hardy and Welch or between Walt and Hardy. This evaluation consists of an exchange of predictions on the outcome.

8. The steps agreed upon are role played. If Hardy is involved, he should forget what he has just overheard.

## Analysis of Welch's Interview with Walt

1. Observers report the extent to which Welch was concerned with (a) the *facts* of Walt's reason for leaving and (b) Walt's *feelings* about the matter. Examples are cited and some agreement is reached regarding Welch's approach to understanding Walt's problem.

2. Observers express their views concerning which of these areas should have been explored more carefully.

3. What occurred in the interview to indicate whether or not Walt actually had a job offer? This point is discussed by observers before Walt supplies the answer.

4. Everyone reports whether or not he believes the interview with Welch influenced Walt's desire to quit the company. These views are expressed in this order: Welch, observers, Walt.

5. In most instances, Welch is sympathetic with Walt and attempts to induce him to stay. Discuss whether Welch conducted himself properly as a personnel representative. (It is understood that his situation was a difficult one and that opinions on this question are controversial.)

## Analysis of Welch's Interview with Ken Hardy

(This analysis may be conducted with or without Walt present.)
1. What did Welch do to prevent Hardy from becoming defensive? What more should he have done?
2. Did Welch take sides with Walt or Hardy, or did he remain neutral? Views on this question are expressed in this order: Welch, observers, Hardy.
3. Should Welch have Walt in the room when he first interviews Hardy?
4. What would be the best approach for Welch to use in order to gain concessions from Hardy? Observers discuss this before Hardy explains what would have worked best for him.

## Evaluation of Solutions

1. The solutions reached in this case are evaluated, not only from the point of view of satisfying Walt and Hardy, but also from the standpoint of company policy and the morale of a work force. The role players remain in character during this evaluation while the observers supply the objective viewpoint.
2. It is quite probable that Walt will want some material concession from Hardy in order to be induced to remain with the company. The observers discuss the inducements that could reasonably have been offered to Walt and attempt to agree on several of them. Hardy then indicates the ones he would have been willing to give Walt. Finally, Walt indicates the ones that would have satisfied him.
3. How can these concessions be made so that Hardy will not lose face?

# General Instructions[20]

Ken Hardy is a supervisor in the engineering drafting department of the Wilson Construction Company. The company employs thirty draftsmen, all of whom work in a large room. Approximately half of them are supervised by Hardy; the remainder report to another supervisor. All engineering work is under the general supervision of the department head, Mr. Johnson. The draftsmen perform assigned duties such as developing and checking written specifications and cost estimates on construction projects. In addition, they use drawing boards and various complex instruments in making detailed drawings for use by the construction foremen on the job.

Walt Henderson is one of the engineering draftsmen who works under Hardy's supervision. Walt has been with the company for eight years. He is regarded as highly competent and is well liked by others. He is married and has a four-year-old daughter.

Like most large businesses, the Wilson Company employs a personnel manager, Robert Welch. Welch is responsible for all hiring and job classifications; he also approves all pay rates and changes in pay. Employees often come to him to discuss company matters and even personal problems. He also interviews all persons who leave the company.

It is now 10 a.m. on Tuesday.

---

[20]Case material is taken from N. R. F. Maier, "Dramatized Case Material as a Springboard for Role Playing," *Group Psychotherapy*, Vol. VI, 1953, J. L. Moreno, M.D., Editor, Beacon House Inc., Beacon, N.Y. Permission to use this material has been granted by the publisher.

## Role Sheet: Robert Welch

You are head of the personnel department of the Wilson Construction Company. Your department does all the hiring and must approve all recommendations for changes in pay rates. You have the authority to turn down recommended increases and to make changes in job classifications and you are in a position to influence personnel policy. Your door is open to employees who want to discuss company matters or their own personal problems. You or your staff interview all employees who leave the company.

Walt Henderson of the drafting department has just called you and wants to see you on what he called "an urgent matter." You've asked him to come right down. To prepare yourself, you looked up Walt's record. He works for Ken Hardy, a drafting department supervisor, whom you regard highly, and Hardy has given him a very good rating. The record shows Walt to be a top-notch draftsman who turns out a lot of work. He has worked with the company eight years, which is about average for the drafting room. Walt Henderson is married and has one four-year-old daughter. He has listed fishing and sailing as his hobbies.

The door opens and Walt walks in. It is now 1 p.m. on Tuesday.

## Script

*Walt Henderson is working at his drafting table as his supervisor, Ken Hardy, comes by.*

Hardy:   How's the work going, Walt?

Walt:   Fine. All caught up.

Hardy:   Even that set of specifications of Joe's that I gave you to check yesterday?

Walt:   Yep. Took it home and worked on it there so I wouldn't be so rushed today.

Hardy:   Well, now I don't want you to have to be taking work home, Walt. I didn't know you were going to do that or I'd have asked Fred to help Joe out on it instead.

Walt:   Oh, that's O.K. I didn't mind doing it. I knew Joe was going to have a rough time getting it all done by noon today, anyway.

Hardy:   What are you working on now?

Walt:   Some plans for that little boat I told you I was going to build.

Hardy:   I see. Think you should be doing that on company time, Walt?

Walt:   Well, I don't know. I've done all my own work and put in three hours of my own time last night to help Joe out. Besides, I don't have my own equipment at home to do this drafting. What's the harm in it?

Hardy:   It just looks bad to be doing something like that on company time. You know that as well as I do.

Walt:   Well, when I have all my work done and more, what does the company expect me to do—twiddle my thumbs?

Hardy:   Now let's not get hasty. We went through all this last year when you got both of us in hot water with Johnson over that garage of yours that you drew up here. Remember?

Walt:   Sure, I remember. And I still don't think it's anybody's business what I work on here so long as my own work is done and I don't bother anybody else.

Hardy:   That may be what you think, but let's get it straight. Nobody's telling you what to do before or after office hours, but when you're here drawing pay you're supposed to be earning it. And I don't want another mess like the one we had about that garage of yours. Understand?

Walt:   Yes, but I don't see why we have to have such rigid rules. Just because Johnson doesn't know how much work I turn out is no reason why you should give in to him.

Hardy:    Look, Walt, I'm not giving in to him. I didn't like the idea of your doing your own work here either, but I decided to let it pass. But when he caught you at it and you didn't have the good judgment to be a bit more careful—well, you've just got the wrong attitude.

Walt:    How can you say that? You know perfectly well I turn out more work for the company than anyone else. Is it my fault if you can't keep me busy?

Hardy:    Walt, I know you're a top-notch draftsman, but a good employee is something more than that.

Walt:    Yeah—a good employee is a yes-man.

Hardy:    Not at all. A good employee works well with others. He's got to follow rules so that he doesn't set a bad precedent. Suppose the others brought their own work down here?

Walt:    Well, make them do their jobs first.

Hardy:    How can I if they say I let you work on your personal things?

Walt:    But I do company work at home and more than make up the time.

Hardy:    Walt, am I supposed to let you choose when and where you do company work? What a mess it would be if I had to keep track of everyone's homework. Anyway we've never asked you to do work at home. When we have more to do than you can handle during working hours, we'll pay you overtime.

Walt:    Ken, I'm not asking for overtime. All I want is to be treated as an honest person. I've never gypped the company out of anything and whenever the company is behind schedule, I've worked like the devil to help out. Now I've got a personal problem and all I'm asking is to borrow some of the facilities. Is that unreasonable?

Hardy:    I can see your side, Walt, but we can't give favors to some and not to others. I've just got to make a rule—and remember you've forced me into it. There will be no more personal work done during company hours. I'll let you finish this job, but that will have to be the end. I am not going to have others say I play favorites. Sorry, but that's it.

                              END

## Additional Information for Walt Henderson

You were disturbed by this conversation, so at noon you called your friend Bill Alden who told you there was an opening in the drafting department of his company (Jones Bros., Inc.). You asked him to check the details. That afternoon Bill's boss, Mr. Hansen, called you and told you he was very anxious to have you come to work for Jones Bros. He told you that he would take you on Bill's recommendation and the salary he quoted was thirty-five dollars a month more than you are getting. From his description, the work seems about the same as you are doing now. When you expressed interest, Hansen asked if you could start next week. That would be next Monday. Since Jones Bros. had another applicant for the job, he asked if you could let him know right away. You asked if you could have until Wednesday morning, so as to have time to talk it over with your wife. Hansen said that would be O.K. He suggested that you give as good an excuse as you can for quitting so suddenly, because he wants to stay on good terms with the Wilson Company.

After this talk, you thought a bit and decided that it would be nice to work in Bill's office. You have often compared companies and although you have sometimes thought of making a change, you could find little difference between them. Since you have eight years with the Wilson Company, you have some seniority and retirement benefits. Now you have a reason for quitting. You know your wife will go along with any decision. The important thing now is to let the company know about your decision. You therefore called Robert Welch in the personnel department and asked to see him on an urgent matter. Welch asked you to come right down.

## Instructions for Observers

1. Walt requested the interview with Welch, but Welch does not know anything about Walt's trouble with Hardy. Naturally, he will explore the problem with Walt. In order to keep track of Welch's approach, make an "X" in your notes for each time he probes for facts, and an "O" for each time he encourages Walt to talk about his feelings.
2. Note the things Walt tells about the Hardy incident and the things he withholds.
3. Walt may talk about another job offer. See if you can tell whether he actually has one. Note whether Welch pursues this point and determines if Walt has an offer and really wants to leave.
4. Does Welch discover what it will take to keep Walt? What more should he have done?
5. Note whether Welch takes sides. This will become particularly apparent if he interviews Hardy.

## COMMENTS AND IMPLICATIONS

Welch usually will be puzzled about why Walt wants to leave and will be skeptical about the initial reason given. If he listens and probes sufficiently to discover the conflict between Walt and Hardy, Welch most often will ask that Hardy be brought into the interview with Walt—on the premise that if he can get facts on both sides of the controversy, he can smooth things over. This will almost inevitably renew the argument between Walt and Hardy and will produce stubborn, hostile, and defensive behavior on the part of Hardy, since he is put in the position of justifying his previous action in disciplining Walt. Furthermore, Walt will usually become sufficiently irritated to quit. The nonconstructive emotional behavior shown will cause Welch to lose control over the situation and the problem will remain unsolved.

However, if Welch creates a permissive interview situation, uses the listening technique, and probes for Walt's feelings, he will probably discover the real reason why Walt is considering quitting. When he gets Walt into a reasonable frame of mind, Walt usually will defer a decision until Welch can take further action by discussing things separately with Hardy. In a similar and separate interview with Hardy, Welch again must be understanding and encourage expression of feeling. If Welch does not take sides, he usually can cause Hardy to be reasonable and to welcome a discussion of alternative solutions to the problem. These may include placing less emphasis on rules; discussing the problem with Johnson to obtain his cooperation; permitting employees to use drafting equipment at lunch break or at night; giving special permission for employees to take instruments home; conducting a group conference with the other draftsmen as to how the problem of personal work should be handled, and so on. The skill displayed by Welch will determine whether Hardy regards Welch as a source of help or a source of interference.

After both Hardy and Walt have been interviewed separately and their hostility has been expressed, they usually are able to adopt a more understanding attitude toward each other. During this stage, Welch can elicit their ideas for constructive approaches to be taken. Some Walts resign, some are given a small raise, and some are content with minor concessions.

The practical considerations of this case are especially interesting because they raise the question of whether or not one can give a good employee special consideration without creating problems with others. Often, the fear that a concession made to one employee will cause a wave of demands from others is more imagined than real. In this case, it is quite possible that most of the other draftsmen did not have Walt's desire to do personal work while on the job. Even if they did, the extent of personal work could be controlled by setting a limit on the privilege.

The talent a company may lose when it attempts to hold strictly to a regulation is important to consider. As is partly true in this case, it is often the feeling of regimentation rather than the actual restriction that creates the rebellion; sometimes it takes only a little flexibility in a rule to ease the dissatisfaction. For example, if employees are regarded as being tardy when the time clock indicates even a minute after the hour, they show resentment because no credit is given if they "punch in" a few minutes early. There might be a zone of five minutes before and after the starting hour that is regarded as "on time." This kind of ruling should cause less feeling of regimentation.

Even if the above possibilities do not solve the problem, the company should *not* consider offering an employee special treatment as a condition of employment if the employee in question is not especially desirable. When, however, a special concession seems desirable from the point of view of both the company and the employee, it may be worth consideration. Often, it is possible to gain the consent of other employees to make an exception for a particular employee. This acceptance of a special case requires group decision. In one office, a woman was given special hours for work because of unusual circumstances in her situation. Her exceptional conditions were respected by all other employees and her new hours turned out to be convenient for everyone concerned. No one else in the office requested similar consideration.

# 14

## The Promotion Interview

### FOCUSING THE PROBLEM

The promotion of an individual in an organization frequently causes a series of reactions and adjustments in a group, which may lead to apprehension, misunderstanding, and lessened cooperation. When one person is selected for promotion, others feel rejected or discredited, fear of change is aroused, expectations and aspirations are threatened, and differences of opinions on the meaning of fairness are raised. Many persons may agree that the choice made is a poor one, although they might not agree on a choice that should have been made. It may be expected that different feelings will be aroused when a group includes persons who want the promotion for themselves, persons who feel that seniority is threatened, persons who are surprised by the choice made and feel that a change in policy is occurring, persons who agree with the choice but feel they must support the group reaction, and persons who fear promotion as well as fear to turn down an opportunity.

In some organizations, attempts have been made to reach at least a partial solution to this problem by establishing certain policies and procedures as a basis for promotion. These include seniority, periodic merit evaluations, job sequences, and the like. While such methods tend to regularize promotion procedures, they do not solve the problem of adverse reactions. Rather, they remove the surprise element and, in a sense, make it possible to ignore feelings in the group because they are less acute.

Some companies attempt to deal with the problem by interviewing candidates. One procedure begins with the selection of a reasonably broad field of candidates; then, prior to the announcement of a promotion, all persons considered are interviewed—with the objective of gaining their acceptance of the choice.

Obviously, the effectiveness of this method for preventing misunderstandings and overcoming undesirable feelings depends considerably on the attitude and skill of the interviewer. In informing all persons who may be considered eligible for promotion that a particular person has been selected, an interviewer must be prepared for various reactions. An important question is whether he should prepare himself to meet all possible objections. In looking for methods that avoid undue disappointment in the individuals not selected and also consider the mixed feelings of the person who is chosen, the interviewer must find ways to obtain acceptance and support of the decision and, at the same time, protect the managerial prerogative.

The following case provides an excellent opportunity to demonstrate the values of certain interview principles and techniques. It also offers the chance to practice the skills necessary for applying the principles effectively.

The single-group role-playing procedure is described for this case in order to give the group members an opportunity to test their sensitivity to the feelings aroused. Since all observers will view the same performance, a detailed discussion and analysis of cause-and-effect relationships in behavior is possible. Persons playing the roles will be the center of attraction, and the person playing the part of the foreman who does the interviewing may anticipate that his performance will be discussed in some detail. It is expected that he will make mistakes; from these the importance of skills becomes apparent. He may be consoled by the fact that no one to date (including the authors) has turned in a perfect performance. It is hoped that he will welcome criticism and discussion of his behavior as a learning experience for everyone.

## SINGLE GROUP ROLE-PLAYING PROCEDURE

### Preparation

1. The Situation and Background Facts are studied by everyone. The instructor may wish to read aloud while the class follows the text.
2. Two role players are needed: one to play the part of Smith, the foreman; the other to play the part of Cole, the skilled worker. It is best if the persons who are to play the parts are designated by the instructor. Two different persons are selected to repeat the role play later, for purposes of comparison and discussion. (The person chosen

to act the part of the foreman should not be a person who feels that he must put on a good demonstration; rather he should be a person who wishes to learn from his own mistakes and is not overly self-conscious. If the group has worked together on other cases, almost anyone will satisfy the above qualifications. The role of Cole is an interesting one, but since the person playing his part is the interviewee, his feelings rather than his skills will be the subject of scrutiny. He should feel free to act naturally.) The remaining class members will act as observers; their task is to discover the cause-and-effect relationships in the events that transpire.
3. While the role players read their role sheets and the observers study their instructions, the instructor prepares the setting for the scene by placing a table and two chairs in front of the room to represent Mr. Smith's office furniture. The table and chairs are placed so that the observers can see the faces of the role players during the scene.
5. When the first pair of participants are ready to begin role playing, the instructor signals Smith to take his place at his desk. Cole enters the office a few moments later and the scene begins.

## Process

1. Role playing in this case is allowed to proceed for approximately fifteen minutes without interruption.
2. Should the role playing result in mutual frustration and bickering with no progress being made, the scene is interrupted. The cause of the difficulty is discussed, but care is taken not to reveal information supplied in the roles. It is Smith's problem to unearth the facts and feelings.

   After discussion, observers give advice on procedure, which the role players may try out. It may be desirable to delete a part of the interview or to start over. The foreman then resumes the interview.
3. If progress is made and no interruption seems necessary, the foreman decides when to terminate the interview.
4. The case is repeated with one or two different pairs of role players. Finally, Smith and Cole may exchange roles to discover the effects of role reversal.

## Observers' Reports and Analyses of Findings After Each Interview

1. The observers report (a) whether they think that Smith feels better

or worse about Cole as a result of the interview, and (b) whether they think that Cole thinks better or worse of Smith.

2.  Each participant reports whether he feels better or worse toward the other person than he did before the interview.
3.  If the interview has created new misunderstandings rather than good communication, the group may wish to consider the value of promotion interviews and the skills necessary to conduct them successfully.
4.  Smith describes why he thinks Cole feels as he does about the promotion. (For the time being, Smith should not be told whether his description is accurate.)
5.  Observers discuss why the interview turned out as it did, being careful not to reveal any facts or insight gained from reading the Instructions for Observers.

## Discussion Following Each Interview

1.  The question of whether a foreman should interview before making a final decision is discussed. Relevant issues include the following: (a) could Smith have made a wiser decision by talking to Cole first? (b) would he have been more open minded if he had discussed the problem before forming an opinion? and (c) would he have been less inclined to distort the facts if he had presented the problem to Cole before rather than after the decision?
2.  The role sheets for Smith and Cole are read aloud to the class by one person who played Smith and one person who played Cole.

## Developing an Interview Plan

1.  Assuming that an interview must be conducted under the conditions of this case, how should Smith present the purpose of the interview to Cole? Prepare a list of possibilities. Some of the approaches might be tested by trying them out on Cole and noting his reactions.
2.  Develop a list of the ways in which Smith can recognize Cole for the contributions he has made to the company.
3.  Suppose Cole makes favorable remarks about Brown. Should Smith respond by thanking him and encouraging a fuller expression of opinion; by defending his decision; or by trying to change the subject?
4.  Suppose Cole makes sly remarks about Adams that differ from Smith's opinion. Should Smith defend Adams, draw Cole out and respect his views, or try to change the subject?

5. At what stage in the interview should Smith tell Cole about his decision?
6. The group should develop an outline of the procedure that it would recommend. (The outline is not to be viewed as the only or best method, but as one that the group regards as a distinct improvement over present industrial practice.)

# Situation and Background Facts[21]

Mr. Smith, a foreman, has been asked to recommend one of his twelve workers for a position of foreman that has just opened up in another part of the plant. He was requested to recommend a person who not only would qualify but had the ability to go higher in the organization. It is the company's practice to hire and promote a certain percentage of workers who have abilities beyond the jobs in which they are placed. Since it is the company's policy to promote from within the ranks, this practice is necessary to insure having good people in top positions.

Smith is a college graduate, has been with the company five years, and has been a foreman for two years. Three men have records that would make them eligible for promotion. They are as follows:

John Adams, a college graduate with three years of service. Adams is bright, has a pleasing personality, seems conscientious, and has been highly cooperative. Smith knows Adams very well and has spent a good deal of time with him. Adams makes a good appearance and is at ease in a group. However, he does not seem to have much in common with his associates on the job.

Walt Brown, a high school graduate with six years of service. Brown is also a very satisfactory employee with a good personality. He is very popular with the men and seems to have their respect. He has a lot of natural intelligence and inventive ability.

Jim Cole, a high school graduate with twelve years of service. Cole is an excellent worker. He trains new employees and actually trained both Adams and Brown when they started with the company. He also successfully takes over the foreman's job when Smith is absent. The employees seem to like Cole and have confidence in him. Although Cole is highly competent, he is not easy to handle. He is sure of himself and sometimes argues about the way a job should be done. He lacks a certain polish and makes mistakes in grammar. He is by no means a problem employee, but, on occasion, he speaks his mind.

Company practice requires its supervisors to interview all employees who have been considered for a particular promotion. Today, Smith will interview Cole.

---

[21]Role instructions are modified from a case in N. R. F. Maier, *Principles of Human Relations.* New York: John Wiley, 1952, 119–121.

## Role Sheet: Mr. Smith, Foreman

After careful consideration, you have decided that John Adams is the person for the job. You were influenced by the fact that you must choose a person with potential; you feel very strongly that people must be found who can eventually fill top jobs. All three men considered would be good foremen, but Adams can go farther, you believe. Adams is a college graduate, and that means something. The fact that Adams graduated from Cornell, your alma mater, did not influence you in this choice. Since he is the only college graduate in your group, you had no other choice.

You recognize that Brown has leadership ability, but not to the degree that Adams possesses it. The strong point in favor of Cole is his seniority, and the fact that there are no real weaknesses to point to. His personality is not bad enough to be used against him, but he does have a way of putting things bluntly. You don't think that he would make a good impression on your superiors.

You have therefore recommended Adams; this recommendation has been accepted but has not been officially announced. You have, however, told Adams about it confidentially—largely because you were so pleased that your recommendation was the one accepted. Before the promotion is announced, you must interview both Cole and Brown. This is company policy.

You have arranged an interview with Cole. Your goal is to get Cole to accept your recommendation. You do not want to create bad feeling in Cole because you must still work with him and, besides, Cole is your best worker.

## Role Sheet: Jim Cole, Skilled Worker

You have heard through the grapevine that a new job is opening up. You feel you have a chance at it, but you aren't confident you will get it since you have been passed up a few times already. Nevertheless, you have, on occasion, taken Smith's place as a foreman and so have some reason to believe you may be considered. However, you do not feel completely qualified for such an assignment. You are happy in your job and like doing work rather than directing it. You take pride in your skill. If a position for supervisory work is opening up, you feel that the best qualified person is Brown. In your book, Brown has everything needed to get ahead in the company. However, you do not think that Brown will get the job because college graduates are favored strongly.

As for Adams, you consider him to be an apple polisher and worse. He hangs around the boss and, you believe, talks about ideas he got from you when he was being trained. Since Adams got in good with the boss, he spends less time with the other workers and no longer is as friendly as before. You think that Adams has changed. Maybe it's natural, since they both went to Cornell. Maybe that is the way to get ahead. You think that promotions have not been fair and that knowing the right people is a factor in getting ahead. But you certainly don't like apple polishers. You also believe that Adams is unpopular in the group, whereas Brown is well liked.

You are about to go to Smith's office for the scheduled interview. You suspect it's about the job. You fear that you may not like the results but are determined not to get into trouble over it. You consider Smith one of the best foremen you have had, even though he isn't very experienced in the company. You don't want to get on the wrong side of Smith but, nevertheless, you have your principles.

## Instructions for Observers

There is a source of misunderstanding in this case in that Smith will assume that Cole wants the promotion himself, and he is likely to attribute to jealousy any objections that Cole raises. Actually, however, Cole has mixed feelings. He thinks that Brown should get a promotion, he likes his present job, and he is strongly opposed to Adams getting a promotion because he regards him as an apple polisher. How he resolves these feelings will depend, in part, on the interview.

As observers, you should take particular pains to make note of any behavior or remarks that bear on the key issues below.

1. What does Cole say that reveals his interest in Brown? Does Smith respond by encouraging further expression, does he disagree, or does he change the subject?
2. What does Cole do that indicates his dislike of Adams? Note all veiled hints in this direction and see if you can discover if and when Smith discovers this attitude.
3. Note all skills Smith uses to get Cole to talk, as well as all things he does that discourage frank expression.
4. If the interview gets better or worse as it progresses, take note of the cause of the change.
5. Be prepared to report on the following:
   a. Does Smith's estimation of Cole go up or down as a result of the interview?
   b. Does Cole's estimation of Smith go up or down as a result of the interview?
   c. What did Smith learn about Cole's attitude?
   d. What recognition did Smith give Cole?
   e. What was said that Cole might take as criticism of his work or his attitude?

Note: In discussing this case it is important not to reveal Cole's attitude as furnished in these instructions. The discussion should be confined to evidence seen in his behavior.

## COMMENTS AND IMPLICATIONS

The interviewer is placed in a difficult situation in this case, partly because we have made a decision for him which he may not personally support and partly because it may not be his practice to make decisions without consulting his employees. The poor judgment shown by Smith in telling Adams about his promotion can be overlooked because Adams has said nothing to Cole and no harm came from this indiscretion. Since real situations often confront supervisors with actions or decisions that are not of their own making and that they must support, it is important for them to learn how to deal with problems that are imposed on them from the outside. Recognizing the difficulties written into the role, let us evaluate how these could best have been met. This does not exclude the need to discuss ways of preventing the problems that occurred in this case.

The case is likely to demonstrate dramatically the importance of discovering the interviewee's viewpoint or attitudes as early as possible. If Smith assumes that Cole wants the job for himself, all of his prepared sales points become sources of irritation instead of favorable influences. This is a basic weakness in the "selling" approach: it presumes a particular need. Smith must draw out Cole and discover how he feels about his own future, how he feels about past promotions, and how he feels about this one. To learn these things, Smith must be willing to accept as reasonable and understandable any opinion Cole expresses. He need not agree with him, but he should try to understand him.

It is reasonable for Smith to accept and appreciate Cole's remarks about Brown, and he can thank him for the information as well as indicate that Brown was considered and will be even more seriously considered in the future because of Cole's high evaluation. He can also thank Cole for information about Adams, indicating that this is a side he may have overlooked, thanking him for drawing his attention to the weakness, and asking for a description of any relevant behavior in the future. He can then ask Cole to remark on any good points he knows about Adams. Usually the opportunity to express freely the bad things about Adams makes Cole feel more generous toward Adams.

Cole should be told at the outset that he was considered for the job and will be considered for others. Recognition that he is a qualified candidate, with no criticism for any weaknesses, should characterize the introductory part of the interview. The actual decision should be stated as the choice that seemed most appropriate for the particular job opening. No defense beyond this is required. Rather, Cole should be given a chance to respond by telling what he thinks. The whole introduction should require only a few sentences. Small talk should be kept to a minimum because Cole wants to know what the interview is about.

If Cole asks why his advice is being sought for something that has already been decided, a number of reasons can honestly be given: (1) Smith is sincerely concerned about how Cole feels; (2) Cole's opinions can influence future promotions; (3) Smith was required to make a recommendation and now that it is accepted, he is concerned with the reactions of the crew; (4) Smith wants Cole to have advance notice because he values his support; and (5) Cole trained Adams and may rightly be concerned with the progress of his trainees. One or two of these reasons may be enough to convince Cole that there is a purpose to the interview.

Little hints of dissatisfaction may be followed up by (1) permitting pauses to be long enough to be uncomfortable; (2) reflecting the feelings expressed, e.g., "You think that we favor college graduates in this company"; (3) showing concern for the opinions Cole expresses; and (4) asking general exploratory questions about Cole's feelings, e.g., "How do you mean that?" Smith must be very sensitive to Cole's feelings and must avoid intellectualizing or asking Cole to justify his opinions.

Cole may need comfort and recognition from time to time. He should derive comfort from the fact that he was considered, from the fact that his views are sought, and from Smith's respect for his feelings. He can be recognized and praised for (1) his ability to substitute as foreman; (2) his job skills; (3) his contribution to training; (4) his faithful service to the company; and (5) the crew's esteem for him. The fact that Adams has said many good things about Cole and his ideas would be welcome information.

Smith should never be defensive about his choice. It may even be advisable, on occasion, for him to state that he is glad to hear an opposing viewpoint. This is not an admission of error; rather, it gives Cole an opportunity to save face and to recognize that there may be two or more sides to the question. Together, they may then discuss ways by which each can benefit from the knowledge and viewpoint of the other.

This interview is representative of interview situations in which there is a difference in rank between the interviewer and the interviewee. On one hand, if care is not taken, the person with less rank sees the person with superior rank as a threat to his own interests. On the other hand, the person with superior rank is inclined to judge the worker and assume that he is biased or uncooperative, unless he carefully explores the subordinate's attitude. Interviews involving differences in rank, therefore, incorporate a source of misunderstanding and complicate the problem of communication. The first step in developing a constructive and cooperative approach is to discover and understand the attitudes that exist. The interviewer should come into an interview with an open mind, perhaps even unprepared, because his preparation may include an assumption that the interviewee holds a particular attitude which, in fact, he does not. It is seldom that an interviewer changes a judgment that he brings into the interview: some persons playing the role of Smith unfortunately persist in believing that Cole really wants the job himself.

Whether or not interviews of this kind should be conducted will obviously depend on the skills of the interviewers. It is apparent that a company policy requiring such interviews could do as much harm as good. One way of approaching the difficult problem is to consider both self-evaluations and peer evaluations. Or all interested parties may be invited to apply for the posted opening and then to submit to tests and interviews. This approach gives persons with seniority an opportunity to suggest others or to turn down an opportunity by not applying. There are many persons who do not want a particular promotion but feel that they have been overlooked if they do not receive an offer. Sometimes they are embarrassed by the remarks of friends who tell them they have been treated unfairly. Saying that they did not want the job seems like "sour grapes." Persons who have seniority still need recognition and reinforcement of their status.

# 15

# *Bill Edwards, House Service Worker*

## FOCUSING THE PROBLEM

Certain objects or events act as incentives for all persons. A raise in pay is one of them. Pride is another factor that motivates people. In the case of The Storm-Window Assignment (Case 10), it is probable that anyone who found himself in Jack's situation would quit his job rather than accept the assignment the foreman wished to give him. A knowledge of the general principles of motivation can contribute greatly to making jobs more attractive—or less unattractive—to employees.

In considering job motivation, however, one must also consider the ways in which people differ. What serves as a strong incentive for one person may leave another unmoved. Even the same person's motivation changes from one day to the next. A poor person works primarily to earn a salary, but a more affluent person often may require approval or recognition in addition to his pay. An assignment that is a reward for one individual may be seen as punishment by another. We often overlook potential ways of motivating people because we do not know their particular needs. The study of motivation requires an understanding of people; a supervisor must be taught to be sensitive to differences between persons if he is to succeed in treating them as individuals. As companies grow larger and supervisory responsibilities increase, there is less time available to learn about each person: one must learn more from the few opportunities one does have.

Learning to know what different employees like and expect from a job is only one side of the picture. One must also discover particular dislikes and their intensity.

Such knowledge about an employee may sound like a large order, and no management could require this degree of attention for each employee. However, there are saving considerations. First, all employees do not require specialized consideration, and many employees are alike in many ways. Thus, the supervisor need merely be sensitive to situations in which personalized considerations are required. Even if he does this, however, he is performing his job at a level beyond the call of duty.

Second, the time spent on any one occasion may yield understanding and insight that will help the supervisor deal more effectively with people in the future. The cost of a misunderstanding often exceeds the time that would have been needed initially to conduct a careful interview.

Third, one of the important rewards for knowing people as individuals is that the supervision and management of employees becomes a more satisfying experience. It is always unpleasant for a supervisor when one of his employees disappoints him. If he knew more about the feelings and needs of the person who is causing a problem, he would be less upset. When one knows why an employee is late for work, one is inclined to be less irritated by his action.

The present case deals with an employee who is asked to take an assignment much like the one in Case 10. The setting and the job are different; the approach indicated may be similar or different. The case is set up for single-group role-playing, but opportunities to involve the observers are provided to further the development of sensitivity and of insight into behavioral problems.

## SINGLE-GROUP ROLE-PLAYING PROCEDURE

### Preparation

1. Two persons are needed to play the roles: one to serve as Henry Spring, the superintendent, the other as Bill Edwards, a handyman. The instructor divides the class in half and selects one role player from each half.
2. The instructor reads the Background Instructions aloud while the class members follow silently.
3. Each role player reads his role sheet. Members in the half of the class from which Henry Spring was selected are to identify with him. They read his role instructions and serve as observers from his point

of view. Members in the half of the class from which Bill Edwards was selected are to read his role instructions and identify with his point of view while serving as observers.

4. Observers are to keep notes on behaviors and statements they consider significant. They also should record the things that the person playing the opposite role does to hurt or irritate them. Observers, however, are not to interrupt the role play.
5. The instructor arranges a table in front of the room.
6. Henry Spring should be in readiness to approach Bill and begin role playing when the instructor signals them to begin.

## Process

1. Bill Edwards starts the business of sanding the table in the front of the room.
2. The instructor gives Henry Spring the signal to approach Bill Edwards.
3. Role playing proceeds until a decision is reached. This may require more than thirty minutes and some help from the observers.
4. If Henry Spring seems to be having difficulty, he is allowed to stop the role play and discuss the problem with the observers who have read his role. Other observers do not enter into this discussion. Spring may accept or reject any advice given. Bill Edwards assumes that he has not heard the discussion. In order to resume role playing, Henry Spring may briefly summarize some aspect of the interview or ask to have any part deleted. He then proceeds with a question or statement of the problem to re-open the interview.
5. If a decision is reached to discharge Bill Edwards, the observers who are familiar with his role are asked if they consider the decision wise. If they feel that the foreman has been insensitive to certain cues or leads dropped by Bill, these oversights are pointed out to Spring.
6. Role playing is resumed in order to give Spring a chance to test the suggestions.
7. When a decision is reached or when no further progress results from discussion during the interruptions, the role play is terminated.
8. If no satisfactory solution is reached, the role play may be repeated with two new participants, one from each half of the class.

## Analysis of the Needs of Bill Edwards

1. Observers who identified with Henry Spring report what they have learned about Bill Edwards' special needs, attitudes, or feelings. (The

instructor tallies the observations on newsprint.) Persons who identified with Bill do not participate.

2. Bill's behavior is evaluated in order to determine whether his needs clarify his apparent stubborness, evasiveness, or reluctance to talk. All class members participate in this evaluation. (Persons who identified with Bill should be careful not to reveal any information about him that Spring failed to discover.)

3. Persons identifying with Bill discuss what Spring did to make Bill tell as much as he did and what Spring did to cause Bill not to tell more.

4. Bill reports how he felt toward Spring and what caused him to feel as he did.

5. Although Bill seemed stubborn and uncooperative, are there any reasons for regarding him as a desirable employee?

6. How might Spring have come to the conclusion that Bill had a special problem even if he did not reveal what it was? List the things that Bill did or said in the interview that could cause his boss to respect his attempts to avoid putting up the storm windows.

7. Compare the listening and questioning methods used in discovering Bill's problem. What might have been learned from each?

## Evaluation of Possible Solutions

1. What are the arguments for and against attempting to force Bill to put up the storm windows?

2. What are the arguments for and against discharging Bill for his conduct in the interview? (When differences in opinion occur, the instructor should determine whether these are due to the special orientations of the observers.)

3. Suppose Bill's special problem is respected by his boss and he is to be excused from working in high places. What new problem is created by this decision?

4. How should the rest of the crew be approached so that they will accept Bill's special treatment? Outline a plan for taking this problem to the crew.

5. If it is necessary to share Bill's secret with the crew, discuss how this should be handled with Bill.

6. Is Bill in need of psychiatric care? What are the arguments for and against his need for treatment?

# Background Instructions[22]

The offices, mills, and shops of the Eastern Paper Company cover a wide area at the edge of a small city. Some of the buildings are old and are now occupied by service departments that have no need for a specialized structure or floor plan. One of these buildings is a two-story wooden structure occupied by the House Service Department, which is managed by Henry Spring. Twelve skilled handymen work for him.

The house service crew is called upon (1) to do maintenance work of a minor nature, such as repairing doors, chairs, chutes, docks, etc.; (2) to do a variety of carpentry jobs, such as installing shelves, making cabinets, and handling minor remodeling projects; (3) to refinish office furniture; and (4) to perform smaller paint jobs, such as painting the building and inside walls of the structure they occupy. Some jobs can be performed in the house service building, but for most jobs the men have to leave the building.

The scene today takes place on the second floor of the house service building. Henry Spring, the superintendent, has a job he wants Bill Edwards to do. Bill is busy sanding a desk top.

Bill has worked for the company for nine months. He is twenty-eight years old, is married, and has two children.

---

[22]Role instructions are modified from N. R. F. Maier, *Principles of Human Relations.* New York: John Wiley, 1952, 116–117.

## Role Sheet: Henry Spring, Superintendent

You are in charge of a crew of men who do house service work, and you try to make assignments fit a man's ability and status. You have a new man, Bill Edwards, who has been with the company for nine months. He is a responsible worker and seems happily married. When you hired him, you couldn't get much information from him about his background. He is not talkative about his past but he is a pleasant fellow, and you want to give him a fair trial. You have been quite pleased with him because he is very handy and has considerable proficiency in cabinet work and furniture refinishing. He also seems to get along fairly well with the other men, but you think he sometimes tries to get others to do his work. The other members of the crew have been with you for four years or more and you think the group has good morale. You have always tried to be fair.

It has always been your practice (and that of the company) to give certain recognitions for seniority. The man with more seniority is given more overtime work if he wants it. Furthermore, undesirable jobs which usually are simple and routine are given to the man with least seniority.

One of the routine jobs is that of washing and putting up storm windows in the small building you occupy. There are twenty-four windows, twelve on the first floor and twelve on the second. This work has always been done by the man with least seniority. Joe Drake did it for four years. You are about to ask Bill to do the job.

## Role Sheet: Bill Edwards, Handyman

You do repair jobs including carpentry, cabinet work, refinishing tables, and painting. You are a good repairman and like carpentry and painting, but you could not go into either of these trades because you are afraid of high places. You had to leave several good jobs for this reason. You figure that in house service work you can avoid high places and still do the type of work you like best. So far, you have not had to do work that brought on your fear. On one occasion, you had a job that required the use of a stepladder. This made you nervous but not panicky, and you were able to cover up.

You are ashamed of this fear and have never mentioned it to your associates. It has been very inconvenient and has greatly interfered with your selection of a vocation. At last, you feel, you have found a job that permits you to use your skills without exposing your fears.

You are happily married and have two children, a boy of two and a girl of four.

You are anxious to get ahead in the company and, so far, you think that the boss approves of your work. You have managed to hide your fear of high places from your boss and hope he never finds out because it might endanger your chances of getting ahead. Abnormal fears aren't things that people understand, and you might be considered neurotic.

## COMMENTS AND IMPLICATIONS

Despite the fact that the job assignment in this instance is like that in Case 10, there is little similarity between the situations. The problems are entirely different because the reluctance to accept the job assignment is different. A supervisor will discover that one cannot generalize regarding personal problems.

If Bill Edwards' fear of high places becomes known, Henry Spring probably will no longer consider him to be uncooperative or insubordinate. Instead, he is likely to feel that Bill's behavior is justified and that he should not be asked to work in high places as long as he does not use his special problem as an excuse to get out of doing his share of the undesirable work. Most people accept a good excuse, although controversy may arise over what constitutes "good." In most instances, such disagreement hinges on inadequate knowledge. Perhaps if we knew a person's *real* reasons, we would be more inclined to accept his behavior as justified. Perhaps all persons have special fears or unique needs and, hence, have personal problems at one time or another; it is an injustice when actions or decisions do not respect these needs.

In role playing this case, however, Henry Spring may not discover Bill's fear of high places. As a consequence, he is likely to be at a loss about what to do. Not infrequently, he feels that Bill Edwards is behaving badly.

A supervisor who is aware of employees' special needs or problems improves his ability to motivate individuals and to be fair in his evaluation of them. Employees are not likely to freely share some of their problems because supervisors, like other people, often judge rather than try to understand their fellow men. When one judges, one usually uses oneself or some "average" person as a standard, and, as a result, a person with an unusual problem is not likely to receive a favorable judgment. Persons with problems learn to hide their traits, actions, or experiences that are judged to be unfavorable and account for their behavior with explanations (excuses) that they think will be accepted. Thus Bill Edwards usually gives a series of excuses and may even demonstrate considerable intellectual agility in telling the supervisor why he should not put up storm windows. He must be evasive without actually being insubordinate, a task that sometimes becomes difficult when the supervisor presses his case.

Before Bill will discuss his fear with the supervisor, he must be convinced that Spring is trying to understand him rather than judge him. Any threat or any talk about what the other men did when they had the least seniority casts the supervisor in the role of a judge.

If, however, the supervisor indicates that he feels sure that Bill has a strong reason for not wanting to put up the storm windows, and if he explains how he can use Bill's ability to better advantage provided he knows the reason for his behavior, he may cause Bill to confide in him. His manner of accepting Bill's attitude thus may determine to a considerable degree the extent to which Bill will share his problem.

The supervisor may also discover Bill's problem by interpreting his behavior. If Bill generally is willing to do menial tasks and yet shies away from tasks that have as their common element "working in high places," he may deduce the difficulty. If he suspects certain illnesses or fear of high places, a few good questions about job choices would settle the matter in his mind. In this way the supervisor can respect Bill's problem, even if Bill never mentions it.

How is one to know when Bill has a good excuse or when he is merely trying to avoid his share of work? The distinction between these two possibilities becomes apparent if Bill says how much he likes the company and the other workers, volunteers to do extra work, and offers to do certain parts of the assigned job. A cooperative and friendly manner is inconsistent with stubbornness, laziness, defensiveness, or selfishness. If the supervisor realizes this, he may conclude that there is more to the problem. If Bill indicates that he will quit before he puts up the storm windows, the supervisor should clearly be alerted because in terms of what he knows, such extreme behavior is inappropriate and, therefore, must have another basis.

If and when the supervisor learns Bill's problem, he still has his own problem to solve—getting the storm windows put up. He must now give the assignment to someone else, but this cannot be done in an arbitrary manner. The group must accept any deviation from the particular assignment pattern they have followed in the past if trouble is to be avoided. It is likely that the crew will respect Bill's problem, especially since they have accepted him and like him. This means that Bill must be willing to have his personal problem discussed by the group. If Bill is reluctant to permit this, one might conclude that he is in need of counseling. Usually, Bill sees the point and consents to let the supervisor take the problem to the rest of the crew for a decision. Invariably, when the crew members are consulted, they decide to give Bill some other job and develop a plan to reassign the job of putting up the storm windows.

Fears of the kind shown by Bill, known as phobias, are not uncommon. They are highly intense, bordering on panic, and are quite unrelated to the degree of danger involved. They are also highly specific, such as the terror of specific animals (snakes, spiders, etc.), small enclosures, or high places. Although many phobias can be cured or relieved, the need for doing so depends on the degree to which they interfere with one's life. Bill seems to have made a good adjustment in general, so he can be a valuable employee even if he does not seek a cure.

Bill Edwards is an example of an individual who requires special treatment and consideration. There are many employees of this kind; some good ones are lost because job routines are too inflexible to allow exceptions.

The method for discovering employees' special needs or problems is generally the same, regardless of the need. Many problems, however, do not require the patience, understanding, and listening skills that Bill's required, since some of them can be readily divulged. The cue for recognizing an individual in need of special consideration is behavior that is out of proportion to the situation. A mother who becomes hysterical when her child is run down by a car is behaving appropriately to the situation, but an employee who becomes hysterical when he cannot have the afternoon off evidences inappropriate behavior. If this occurs, it may be assumed that there is more to the situation than is apparent.

Special privileges can be granted to certain employees only when the company is not inconvenienced and when other employees accept such special treatment as fair. For example, it might be convenient for a company to permit one office clerk to work from 8:30 a.m. to 5:30 p.m. if the regular hours are 8 a.m. to 5 p.m., but the company might be reluctant to do so if other employees, as a result, also wanted to set their own hours. If, however, the other employees agreed to the special arrangement, the company could grant the privilege without the charge of favoritism. In order to obtain this kind of treatment, however, the employee would have to have an acceptable reason and not abuse the privilege. Difficulty getting up in the morning would probably not be considered acceptable; but a widow who had to drop a child off at school might receive special consideration. If Bill Edwards' problem were of his own making, or if he inconvenienced others unfairly, the group might not adjust to his needs; the supervisor would then have to conclude that Bill could not meet the job requirements.

# 16
# *The Personnel Adjustment Problem*

## FOCUSING THE PROBLEM

There are many problems in human relations that are easy to handle in early stages but become progressively more serious if not resolved. However, even supervisors who are well aware of this fact frequently put off taking the necessary action until the seriousness of the situation forces them to do so. In many instances, supervisors are too preoccupied with other problems to be aware of minor problems of employees. In other cases, they lack the sensitivity necessary to detect undercurrents of difficulty. In still other situations, supervisors are aware that certain problems exist but put up with the conditions until they become frustrating; they then take punitive actions that aggravate the difficulty. There are also supervisors who are aware of problems but who are reluctant to take action because they feel that they are lacking in skill and are unsure of their ability to meet problem situations. Frequently, the necessary steps are delayed until a salvage operation is about all that can be attempted.

If certain attitudes and skills prove useful in situations that have been allowed to deteriorate, they should also be highly effective under more favorable circumstances.

The Personnel Adjustment Problem concerns an employee who has been on the job for two months. She was hired as a private secretary on a three-month probationary basis. Her supervisor has not discussed her work or progress with her. However, just prior to leaving for a one-month vacation, the supervisor asked his assistant to do this. Ordinarily, the assistant exercises no supervision over this secretary, although he does act for his superior when the latter is absent.

The case calls for considerable competence in the appropriate attitudes and skills. Because the case creates many opportunities to discuss cause-and-effect relationships, it is recommended that the single-group role-playing procedure be used, so that all persons will observe the same events.

## SINGLE-GROUP ROLE-PLAYING PROCEDURE

### Preparation

1. All group members read the Background Information silently while the instructor reads it aloud.
2. The instructor selects two members to play Virginia Clark and Paul Williams. The remaining members of the group act as observers.
3. The role players study their own roles in preparation for the scene. They do not read the role for the other person. The observers also study their instructions.
4. While all members are preparing for the role play, the instructor reads Section IV, Comments and Implications.
5. The instructor prepares the setting for the role play by arranging a table and two chairs in the front of the room to represent Paul Williams' office. The table and one chair is for Williams and the other chair is for Virginia Clark. The furniture should be placed in such a way that the observers can see the faces of the role players during the scene.

### Process

1. Paul Williams enters his office and sits at the desk. Then Virginia Clark enters, approaches Williams' desk, and the role play begins.
2. About twenty minutes will be needed for the role play. The participants should be permitted to finish except when the interview deteriorates into conflict. If, after fifteen minutes or so, no progress is made, the scene is ended. Frequently, the interviewer will reach a dead end in the interview and want to try it again, or one of the observers may wish to attempt the interview.
3. After the role play has been completed, the instructor leads a discussion of the scene.

4. It is advisable to repeat the role play with one or two new pairs of participants.


## Analysis of Results of Interview

1. What do the observers think of this interview? To what extent did the interaction improve or become worse?
2. How do the observers think Virginia Clark feels about things? Is she bitter and disappointed or does she feel that she has been treated fairly? (The observers support their views with concrete behaviors that they observed. Their sensitivity to Virginia's feelings can then be checked by asking the participant who played Virginia how she felt.)
3. How do the observers think Williams feels about the outcome of the interview? To what extent might he experience frustration or defensiveness? Was Drake's objective accomplished? In what ways, if any, might this have been a success experience for Williams? (The observers again supply evidence from Williams' behavior to support their opinions. These reactions are checked with the participant who played Williams.)
4. Which participant talked the most? How did this influence things?
5. The instructor briefly summarizes the group's opinions on the success or failure of the interview.


## Discussion of Method Used

1. How did Williams begin the interview? What effect did his manner have on subsequent events?
2. How well was the purpose of the interview stated? In what ways did Williams' manner of stating the issue influence Virginia's reactions? Examples are listed.
3. To what extent was Williams permissive? Should there have been more expression of feeling?
4. What did the interviewer learn during the interview? To what extent did he use what he learned to help in problem solving? How could he have done this in a better way?
5. What were Virginia's real feelings about herself and her work?
6. What was her real problem in changing jobs? What did the interviewer do to help or hinder acceptance of the change?

The instructor highlights the points brought out in the discussion and reflects as accurately as possible the views of the group, regardless of whether or not he agrees with them.

## Developing an Interview Plan

1. What should be the attitude of the interviewer in this situation?
2. Should Williams try to justify Drake's actions in any way? (This question will frequently bring out attitude differences. The authors believe he should not defend Drake: first, because Drake is in error and second, because to do so will only generate further resentment in Virginia and serve no constructive purpose. However this does not mean he should criticize Drake in any way. It is best for him to remain neutral.)
3. How can this interview be handled so as to save Virginia's pride? (If the interviewer is friendly, accepts her and encourages her to tell how she feels about her present job, she may be more likely to reveal that she feels inadequate and, therefore, be more willing to accept a transfer.)
4. What things can the interviewer do to get the secretary to accept the change? Could she be prompted to suggest solutions herself? The instructor summarizes and highlights the points discussed.

## General Discussion of Principles and Applications

1. List some of the conclusions drawn from this case.
2. List things that can be done to avoid problems of this sort.
3. Link applications of these principles to other cases.

## Background Information

Virginia Clark is private secretary to Mr. Drake, the personnel director of a large university. She was hired two months ago to replace a woman who had resigned, after two years on the job, to be married. The position is an important one and calls for an individual with (1) poise and competence, (2) the ability to grasp quickly the details of office correspondence and files, and (3) the maturity sufficient to handle appointments and deal with various members of the administration and faculty. In accordance with the personnel policies of the university, Virginia was hired on a three-month probationary basis, with the understanding that if her work proved satisfactory, she would be employed on a permanent basis.

In addition to Virginia, there are three other inexperienced young women in the office. All of them work under the supervision of Paul Williams, the assistant director of personnel. He has had this job for the past six months. Williams is responsible for the day-to-day operations of the personnel office, including (1) interviewing and referring job applicants to the various administrative and clerical vacancies in the university, (2) arranging for transfers, and (3) maintaining personnel records. As assistant personnel director, he acts for Drake in the latter's absence.

Before leaving on a month's vacation, Drake asked Williams to have an interview with Virginia. She is about to enter Williams' office.

## Role Sheet: Virginia Clark

You are private secretary to Mr. Drake, the director of the personnel office of a large university. You were hired two months ago to replace a woman who had held the job very capably for two years. The job is an important one: it involves a detailed knowledge of the office correspondence and filing system, as well as handling appointments, dealing with important members of the university administration and faculty, and performing other duties requiring both poise and capability.

The other girls in the office are also fairly new and inexperienced and none of them can do much to help you in learning the office routine, the location of various documents, and so forth. You are quite overwhelmed by all the details of your new job, and it has taken you some time to become familiar with the office routine. Furthermore, you are very shy and find it hard to get accustomed to all the personal contacts with visitors, job applicants, directors of other offices, and so on. You feel that you are a conscientious and willing worker but that you cannot cope with all your new responsibilities, especially since no one in the office is able to help you.

Mr. Drake, your boss, is a very busy man. He is always nice to you and never criticizes anything you do. However, you sense that he is in some way displeased with you, and you try extra hard to make a good impression on him and please him. You have been trying hard to increase your typing speed, thinking that he realizes that you have not had a great deal of practice.

Although you were hired for a three-month probation period, with the understanding that you would be hired permanently only if your work proved satisfactory, you feel that you have been doing the best you can during the past two months. Your boss has just left on a month's vacation. Since he has never criticized you, you are puzzled as to why his assistant, Mr. Williams, has called you into his office.

## Role Sheet: Paul Williams

You are the assistant director of the personnel office of a large university. You have had this job for six months now and are very anxious to please Mr. Drake, the director of the office—a man whom you admire greatly. During the past two months, Mr. Drake has talked to you several times about the inefficiency and ineptitude of his new secretary, Virginia Clark, and you have heard complaints about her from others in the office and from outside visitors. She is not only very awkward in dealing with people but she is also a very poor stenographer whose work has to be corrected constantly.

Because Mr. Drake is very kindhearted, he has not criticized his secretary's work. He has often asked you to see to it that her work was done over again, without her knowledge, by one of the other, more capable, stenographers. Because Mr. Drake thinks that Virginia is extremely sensitive, he is afraid of the emotional effect criticism might have on her. However, he realizes that a job as important as hers requires efficiency and capability. He has asked you to hire a new secretary for him and to transfer Virginia to one of the other university offices.

You have found a job for Virginia in the registrar's office, where the salary is only slightly lower but the duties involved are much less demanding. You think she would be much happier in this job, but you now have the problem of telling her about this decision. Since you know she will be upset, you have a difficult problem and you want to handle it without either damaging the girl's self-confidence or making yourself and your boss appear arbitrary and unreasonable. She is about to come to your office for an interview.

## Observer's Instructions

Use the following outline as a guide for observing and evaluating the interview.

1. In what ways did the interviewer show a friendly and helpful attitude?
2. How well was the purpose of the interview stated? In what ways did Virginia react? Were her reactions the sort that might be expected?
3. Was Williams on the defensive at any time? If so, why? What effect did this have on the interview? Did he attempt to justify Drake's actions? If so, in what way was this a hindrance?
4. Which one talked the most, the interviewer or the person being interviewed?
5. Was a solution reached? If not, why not? If so, how did it occur?
6. How do you think the secretary feels about this interview? To what extent does she accept the idea of a transfer? In what ways did the interviewer help or hinder her acceptance?
7. What were some of the helpful skills the interviewer used? Which ones might he have used to better advantage?
8. How might future problems of this sort be prevented?

## COMMENTS AND IMPLICATIONS

In this case, the interviewer will usually find himself in serious difficulty early in the discussion. Many possible errors can lead to failure, but probably the most likely one is vagueness in stating the purpose of the interview. This creates suspicion and anxiety in the person being interviewed and produces hostile reactions.

Another common error is for the interviewer to announce bluntly that he has found a different job for the secretary. This is neither an explanation nor a statement of a problem, but a solution that the interviewer is attempting to impose or sell. Since this is an abrupt action that the employee had no part in planning, she will usually see it as a crude attempt at manipulation and will show strong resentment. Further, she will quickly sense that the interviewer is the hatchet man for his superior. At this point, the interviewer himself will usually become defensive and make the situation worse by attempting to justify both his own actions and those of his superior.

However, the interviewer can adopt a permissive and accepting attitude and ask the employee how she feels about her work at this point in the three-month probationary period. This will help the employee speak freely without feeling the need to cover up her deficiencies and feelings of inadequacy. Once she has expressed these feelings, she will usually be more receptive to the idea of transferring to a less demanding job. Under these conditions, it would not be necessary for the interviewer to bring up her unsatisfactory performance in the present job. Should she resist a change, it would be necessary to discuss her performance, but the establishment of a friendly atmosphere will help a great deal. It is not necessary to take final action during this interview because a month of the probationary period still remains. If, however, the interviewer can bring about a satisfactory solution during the interview, it can be to the advantage of everyone concerned.

Problems caused by a supervisor's undue delay in action can arise for a variety of reasons. Often supervisors are forced to focus their attention on work instead of on working conditions. This approach diverts the supervisor from functioning effectively as a representative of management and makes him appear as a judge or critic. If an alert and sensitive supervisor maintains close, friendly contact with his employees, he can anticipate many human relations problems and deal with them before they become serious. He will also create an atmosphere of frankness in which employees do not feel uncomfortable about correcting deficiencies. The difference between an employee's resentment at being corrected and her appreciation for being helped to do better is largely a matter of the attitude and skill of the supervisor; these can be developed through training.

# 17

# The Parasol Assembly Bottleneck

## FOCUSING THE PROBLEM

Officials in business and industry will often go to great lengths to recruit and train promising individuals for management positions, the expectation being that such individuals will deal with problems in an intelligent and effective manner.

Decisions often are made by supervisors as operating heads of various units within the organization. Problems that cut across different functions are customarily solved in formal or informal conferences between the individuals concerned. Frequently staff experts are brought in to contribute technical information or other highly specialized knowledge. These approaches to problem solving raise the question of whether the resources of talent in the company are utilized fully and effectively.

Research findings have demonstrated, for example, that an interacting group obtains insightful and effective solutions to certain problems more readily than a similar number of individuals working independently.[23] The introduction of a leader into a group also has a favorable influence on the quality of problem solving,[24] in that a person

---

[23]Marjorie E. Shaw, "A Comparison of Individuals and Small Groups in the Rational Solution of Complex Problems," *American Journal of Psychology* 1932, *44*, 491–504.

[24]N. R. F. Maier and A. R. Solem, "The Contribution of a Discussion Leader to the Quality of Group Thinking: The Effective Use of Minority Opinions," *Human Relations*, 1952, *5*, 277–288; N. R. F. Maier, *Problem-Solving Discussions and Conferences.* New York: McGraw-Hill, 1963, 20–48, 74–155; N. R. F. Maier, "Assets and Liabilities of Group Problem Solving: The Need for an Integrative Function," *Psychological Review*, 1967, *74*, 239–249.

with the best solution will be given an opportunity to influence the majority of members. In the absence of a leader, this contribution tends to be lost. It has further been shown that a leader who has creative ideas and skills can upgrade the quality of solutions by diverting individuals away from dead-end thinking and causing them to explore new directions in search of a solution.[25] Still other studies indicate the importance of democratic attitudes in the leader's ability to improve the quality of solutions.[26]

These findings suggest that useful methods for achieving high-quality solutions are available to industrial and business management. Although these methods require certain attitudes and skills that are not prevalent in management, they can be developed through training and practice.

The purpose of the Parasol Assembly Case is to demonstrate an effective approach to problem solving and to indicate the attitudes and skills required of the leader. The case furnishes a problem for which there are various solutions, one of which is clearly superior to others.

Although individuals working by themselves rarely develop the superior solution, a group under proper leadership often does. As the skills of the leader improve, the frequency with which groups develop the superior solution further increases.

This case concerns a crew of seven men who work on a circular assembly line. The crew members differ in ability for the job. Since the line is paced by the slowest member, and since production is low, there is a need to improve the situation.

It is recommended that the single-group procedure be used in role playing this case, so that specific skills can be discussed in detail.

## SINGLE-GROUP ROLE-PLAYING PROCEDURE

### Preparation

1. Eight group members are needed to play the roles, one for the foreman and seven for the members of his crew.

[25]N. R. F. Maier, "An Aspect of Human Reasoning," *British Journal of Psychology*, 1933, *24*, 144–155; H. Guetzkow, "An Analysis of the Operation of Set in Problem Solving Behavior," *Journal of General Psychology*, 1951, *45*, 219–244.

[26]A. R. Solem, *The Influence of the Discussion Leader's Attitude on the Outcome of Group Decision Conferences.* Unpublished doctoral thesis, University of Michigan, 1953; A. R. Solem, "An Evaluation of Two Attitudinal Approaches to Delegation," *Journal of Applied Psychology*, 1958, *22*, 36–39.

2. Persons who do not participate as role players either act as observers or play the part of consultants. Approximately four persons are needed as consultants; the number of observers can be unlimited. (If the class is small, the consultant group is eliminated.)
3. All persons read the General Instructions.
4. All participants study their roles carefully, so that it will be unnecessary for them to refer to the written material during the scene. They do not read any role except their own.
5. Observers read the Instructions for Observers.
6. Consultants read the Instructions for Consultants.
7. While group members are studying their materials, the instructor draws on newsprint the diagram of the assembly shown in Figure 4. This diagram helps everyone visualize the work place.
8. The setting for the role play is arranged to represent Benton's office. A table and one chair are for Benton's use and seven chairs for the crew form a horseshoe pattern in front of Benton's desk.
9. The crew members enter Benton's office and seat themselves in the chairs in the same order as shown in the diagram. Name tags will assist the foreman and the role players in calling each other by name.

## Process

1. Consultants move to the end of the room away from the role-playing scene and begin working on their solutions to the problem in accordance with their instructions. The observers are seated where they can readily observe the role play.
2. The foreman enters his office and begins the scene.
3.  Role playing usually takes forty-five minutes. Participants are allowed to finish the scene whenever possible. However, if the discussion breaks down and no progress is made after twenty or thirty minutes, the scene is interrupted. Observers offer the foreman advice on how to proceed. The foreman considers their suggestions and uses any he thinks are helpful. The instructor then deletes any parts of the discussion that led to difficulty and requests the role playing to proceed from any point agreed upon. The foreman can resume the role play by summarizing what he has learned, correcting any misunderstandings, and assuring the group that he is not interested in breaking up the team.
4. In many cases, several interruptions, followed by a discussion of progress, may be needed.
5. Role playing is carried to a natural stopping point. A unanimous

agreement to try something, a majority decision, or a decision imposed by the foreman are typical stopping points.

6. Consultants are asked to return to the class and join the discussion.


## Discussion of Solutions Reached

1. The group's solution is summarized for the benefit of the consultants.
2. Consultants present their solution for comparison.
3. The foreman and workers indicate what they like and dislike about the consultants' solution.
4. Observers comment on basic differences in the solutions. Such factors as complexity, concern for the feelings of the workers, and practical considerations are compared.
5. Even though the consultants were given the viewpoints of the workers, it is unlikely that they expected the faster workers to help out the less capable ones. Compare the solutions in terms of the degree to which more capable workers were required to work according to their abilities.
6. What are some of the problems of gaining acceptance of a solution offered by consultants?


## Analysis of Foreman's Handling of Discussion

1. How did the leader begin the discussion? From his statement of the problem, what would you infer concerning his attitude toward the group? Was his primary interest to increase production or to improve job satisfaction for his crew? Did he have a solution in mind? Observers comment on these issues and all members join in the general evaluation.
2. Did the crew members react constructively to the problem in general, or did they feel pressured by the leader? What did the leader do to produce the reactions shown by the crew?
3. In what ways did Joe make the leader's situation more difficult? Should the leader protect Joe from pressure by other crew members? In what ways would defending or not defending Joe influence the discussion? Role players, especially Joe, contribute their evaluations of the opinions expressed.
4. What did the leader do to help or hinder the crew members in expressing their feelings about the work? To what extent did he accept complaints or criticisms from the crew? (To be helpful the leader should invite and accept comments and criticism. Complaints

will usually involve not having enough to do, being bored, and being paced too fast.)

5. Did the leader learn about George's real feelings on the matter? After observers have discussed this question, George reads his role sheet to the class.

6. To what extent did all crew members share in the discussion? What did the leader do to encourage full participation? What might he have done differently? (Unless the leader draws out silent members, some crew members are likely to dominate the discussion, thus reducing full participation.) After discussing the matter, the persons who talked the least during role play tell why they did not talk more.

7. Where did the solution come from? To what extent was the final solution a group product? In what ways does the solution improve the job for the crew members? What will be the effect on productivity of the crew's participation in reaching the solution? (Good solutions are usually the product of pooled thinking in the group; they improve the job, and production is increased.)

8. In what ways could the foreman capitalize on the complaints and differences of opinion in the crew to improve problem solving? How would the quality of the solution be affected by exploring the various complaints and ideas? What are some things a leader can do to bring out many different approaches to the problem? What advantages would this have?

9. In what ways can we apply the results from this case to our own problems? (This question is explored by the use of a few specific situations contributed by group members.)

## General Instructions[27]

The job is a subassembly situation in which seven men, working in a circle, assemble a part of a car (carburetor or instrument panel, for example). The article enters the circle at one point, and each person adds his pieces and pushes the unit to the next worker who adds his elements. When the unit leaves the circle, it is a completed part. This arrangement is diagramed in Figure 4.

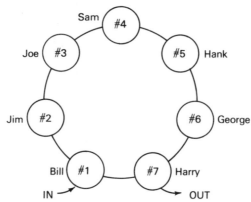

Figure 4. Positions of Men in Parasol Assembly Team.

There are four such "parasol" subassembly stations, each one supervised by a foreman. Station A assembles eighty-five units per day; Station B, eighty per day; Station C, sixty units per day; and Station D, fifty units. Station D previously assembled sixty units per day. The foreman was dissatisfied with the production and reprimanded the group; thereafter, production fell to fifty units.

The assembly work is simple and requires a minimum of training. The aptitude requirement is primarily good finger dexterity. The materials for each assembly position are located in bins that are supplied by material handlers, so that each worker has his essential material at his elbow. The job has been analyzed by time-and-motion experts so that the positions are of equal difficulty. Pay is based on hourly rates.

The total factory production is dependent on receiving the required number of assembled units from these four stations. The produc-

[27]Role instructions are taken from an article by N. R. F. Maier, "The Quality of Group Decision as Influenced by the Discussion Leader," *Human Relations,* 1950, 3, 159–160, 173. Permission to reproduce the roles has been granted by the Plenum Publishing Company, London, England.

tion is now so low that the factory output has had to slow down. The desired quota is 300 parts per shift for the four stations combined.

We are concerned with Station C, producing at the rate of sixty units. The work piles up at the position of Joe Brown (position 3). Foremen on nonproduction jobs are not willing to accept Joe as a transfer. Joe is a man of sixty with thirty years of service in the company. Emphasis on improving production has brought his deficiencies to light.

## Role Sheet: Hal Benton, Foreman

You are the new foreman of Unit C and have been instructed to increase production. A time-and-motion study analysis has shown that the amount of work at each position is practically the same. The number 3 position (Joe's position) is, however, slightly easier than the others in that one less motion is required. Undoubtedly, the previous foreman put Joe there to reduce the bottleneck. You have received training in solving problems by using the crew's participation and you are going to try to work out the problem by this method. You therefore have stopped the production line for a discussion. You understand that Joe is your problem—you cannot pass him off to another foreman. You find Joe a likable person and it is your impression that he gets along well with the other men in the unit.

---

## Role Sheet: Bill, No. 1 Position

You find you can easily do more work but have to slow down because Joe gets behind. In order not to make him feel bad, you hold back. You don't want to get Joe into trouble.

## Role Sheet: Jim, No. 2 Position

You and Bill work closely together and you are usually waiting for your part from Bill. This is more likely to happen in the later part of the day than in the beginning. To keep busy, you often help out Joe, who can't keep up. However, you are careful not to let the foreman catch you helping Joe because he might let Joe go.

-----------------------------------------------------------------------

## Role Sheet: Joe, No. 3 Position

You work hard but just aren't as fast as the others. You know you are holding things up, but no matter how you try, you get behind. The rest of the fellows are fine boys and have more energy than you do at your age.

## Role Sheet: Sam, No. 4 Position

Joe has trouble keeping up, so you sometimes grab Joe's part and finish it for him when the boss isn't looking. Joe is a bit old for the pace and he feels the strain. For you the job is easy and you feel the whole job is slowed down too much because of Joe. You ask yourself why Joe couldn't be given less to do.

---

## Role Sheet: Hank, No. 5 Position

You feel a bit uneasy on this job. There isn't enough to do, so you have to act busy. If only Joe could speed up a bit. Why don't they move him out of the group? Is the company so blind that they can't see where the production trouble is?

## Role Sheet: George, No. 6 Position

You are able to keep up with the pace, but on the last assembly job, you were pressed. Fortunately Joe is slower than you are so he keeps the pressure off you. You are determined that Joe not be moved off the job. Somebody has to protect people from speedup tactics.

---

## Rold Sheet: Harry, No. 7 Position

You get bored doing the same operations over and over. On some jobs, you vary your pace by working fast for a while and then slowly. On this job though, you can't work fast because the parts aren't fed to you fast enough. It gets you down to keep doing exactly the same thing over and over in slow motion. You are considering getting a job some place where they can keep a man busy.

## Observer's Instructions

The foreman's attitude, his skill in sensing feelings and ideas developed in the discussion, and his ability to act on the basis of what he learns will mainly determine the success or failure of the discussion. Be especially alert to how well he adapts to new developments.

1. Observe how the leader begins the discussion and what this indicates about his attitude.
2. Note the favorable and unfavorable reactions from the group members. Take note of what the leader did to cause these reactions. Did the leader get trapped into discussions with individuals or was he able to cause members to interact with one another?
3. Did everyone participate? What did the leader do to help or hinder participation? Did he have to call on crew members in order to elicit their participation or was he able to achieve participation spontaneously?
4. Make a list of what the leader learned about how the men felt about the job. Note the ways he used this information to help in problem solving.
5. On what things did the crew members disagree? What did the foreman do to use the disagreement as a basis for getting at the main problem? What was this main problem?
6. Who suggested the solution? Was the initial idea altered or improved in any way by the discussion? How did the leader help or hinder this interaction?
7. What were some indications that thinking in the group went in circles or got into a rut? How could the leader encourage the crew to try different approaches?
8. Did the leader encourage the search for a list of solution possibilities?

## Instructions for Consultants

You have been asked to solve the bottleneck problem for Hal Benton. In order that you can better understand his situation, read his role instructions. Assume that you have interviewed each of the men and have gained an appreciation of the way they see things. Read the role instructions for the crew members.

In light of the facts of the situation and the attitudes of the crew, prepare a practical solution to the problem. It is hoped that your group can come up with a unanimous decision.

## COMMENTS AND IMPLICATIONS

In this case, the leader's approach in the first few minutes of the discussion will determine whether the situation will become better or worse. Failure is almost certain if the leader displays a complaining or critical attitude toward the crew, or states the problem as one of low production. This will produce defensive reactions and hostility toward the leader. Some crew members will blame Joe for the poor showing of the group and other members will protect him. This splits the crew into two factions and usually leads to a breakdown of the discussion.

However, if the leader has a considerate attitude toward the crew and if he shows an interest in their needs and in making the job run more smoothly, sincere attempts to solve the problem will occur. The leader should maintain a free, permissive atmosphere from the beginning. He must be sensitive to the feelings of the crew members and should demonstrate that his main concern is the problem in the crew, not the inadequate production. Furthermore, he must protect Joe and show that he would like to keep the crew together. He may say that since all people differ in ability, he would like to find a way to adjust the speed of the production line so that it would be satisfying to all crew members. Instead of reacting negatively, the crew members will be more constructive and cooperative and will look for ways to improve the situation. In one way or another, such methods will remove the pressure on Joe. Usually, fast workers find some way to help Joe with his work. This willingness to help Joe is a distinct gain and is something that management could not ask them to do.

However, helping Joe is not sufficient to clear up the bottleneck. His removal threatens the crew as a whole and makes apparent the next-slowest worker—in this case, George. If production increases, George will soon need help; for this reason, he may resist any efforts to help Joe or to get rid of Joe. Clearly, a solution that also deals with George's problem will be better than one that deals only with Joe's.

In order to obtain the best solution, it is necessary for the leader not only to have the proper attitudes toward the crew, but also to demonstrate considerable skill in discussion leadership. If the leader invites a discussion of problems and difficulties and lists these on newsprint, he creates a basis for discussing ways of improving the job. The ability to ask good questions and to encourage crew members to look for new ideas is also an important aspect of the leader's contribution. Helpful questions would concern (1) ways to relieve boredom, (2) methods whereby a work pace can be found that will fit everyone's capabilities, (3) uses that can be made of variety, and (4) how a person's pace changes at different times of the day. Summarizing progress and pointing out differences and agreements also seem to move the discussion into new territory. The leader must encourage full participation and be capable of adapting to new developments in the discussion as they arise. This will lead away from nonconstructive blaming of Joe and produce various ideas for reducing boredom, fitting the pace to individual abilities, keeping the crew together, and so on. Exploring different ways for solving these problems is necessary for obtaining an inventive solution and seeing that its merits are recognized.

An elegant solution, in which all members move to the next position in the circle at regular intervals, e.g., every hour, is sometimes developed. This improves the job in many ways. Boredom is relieved by the change in work (both the activity and the pace) and by the next expected change. Joe is no longer a bottleneck problem because his unfinished work becomes distributed over all the positions on which he works. All crew members can set their own pace; slow workers may create a backlog, whereas fast workers can make up the leftover work in the position they assume. A state of equilibrium is soon reached. The assembly line is no longer paced by the slowest man; instead, it operates at a rate equal to the average pace of the entire crew.

All production lines have some bottlenecks, and in every production line phased by the workers there are solutions that are better than that of getting rid of the slowest worker. Usually, workers handle the problem in their own way: they let the slowest worker set the pace. The elegant solution above applies only to lines having jobs sufficiently alike to make costly training unnecessary.

Typical solutions obtained that improve conditions somewhat include: (1) Jim or Sam or both help Joe as his neighbors, (2) Harry and Joe trade jobs when Joe gets behind, and (3) Hank, Harry, and Joe rotate positions periodically. Although these solutions help the slow worker, they do not make use of all the unused and willing ability available, since there are five workers who do not have enough to do.

Another approach is to make the positions unequal so that each worker's job fits his ability. This type of perfect fit would set the pace achieved at that of the average worker, but then the line would be unbalanced whenever a regular worker was absent and a substitute worker was used.

Even though the elegant solution may not be reached, the above alternatives not only are improvements but they also represent steps toward the elegant solution, providing the leader continues to search for a way to give each worker who is willing to do more a chance to do it. The leader must not push the group into his way of thinking. It is better to accept a solution of lesser quality than to force the group into one of "higher quality" that they may not like. Since the problems of reducing boredom and handling the bottleneck are linked together, both management and the crew stand to gain from any good solution.

# 18

# *The Appraisal Interview*

## FOCUSING THE PROBLEM

When a supervisor conducts appraisal interviews with his subordinates, the results are often ill feelings and misunderstandings rather than improved relations and employee development. The subordinates often feel there is undue emphasis on deficiencies and they become defensive. When the superior, as a result, feels impelled to justify his point of view, he also becomes defensive. As a consequence, the interview frequently creates conflict and new problems rather than solves existing problems.

A common cause of difficulty is the difference in frames of reference between the supervisor and his subordinates. The supervisor's situation tends to make him sensitive to deficiencies in job performance because these create problems for him; he is likely to take adequate performance more or less for granted. The employee, on the other hand, is aware of the little extras he does and is likely to blame poor results on inadequate or unclear assignments, poor training, or someone else's failure to cooperate. Thus, the interview tends to highlight divergent views.

Because difficulties are encountered in interviews of this kind, supervisors are reluctant to conduct them. If a company program requires periodic evaluations, there is a marked tendency among supervisors to avoid mentioning unfavorable points, thereby defeating the purpose of the evaluation. The success or failure of an employee developmental program largely depends on the skill with which employees are interviewed by their superiors.

Because the purpose of this case is to develop sensitivity toward communication problems in this type of interview, the single-group role-playing procedure is recommended. If the objective were to give practice, the multiple role-playing procedure would be desirable.

## SINGLE-GROUP ROLE-PLAYING PROCEDURE

### Preparation

1. Two members from the group are selected, one to role play the supervisor who conducts the appraisal interview and the other to role play the employee interviewed. (It is unwise to use volunteers because, if they fail, they may be embarrassed.)
2. All other members act as observers.
3. All participants read the General Instructions.
4. The participant who will conduct the interview studies the role of George Stanley while the participant who is to be interviewed studies the role of Tom Burke. Both should role play their parts without referring to their role sheets.
5. The observers read the instructions for Observers.
6. The scene is set up: a table in front of the room to represent the interviewer's desk and two chairs arranged by the desk in such a way that the participants can talk to each other comfortably and still have their faces visible to the observers.

### Process

1. When everyone is ready, George Stanley enters his office and sits at his desk. A moment later, Tom Burke enters the office and the scene begins.
2. The amount of time needed to complete the interview will vary, but twenty to thirty minutes usually is adequate. The interview is carried to the point of completion unless an argument develops and no progress is evident after ten or fifteen minutes of conflict.
3. If an interview ends too quickly, alternative approaches suggested by observers may be tested briefly.
4. One or two new pairs of participants may role play in order to permit comparison of different interview styles and their outcomes.
5. A Stanley and a Burke exchange roles and role play the case. Observers read the role instructions for both players.

## Evaluation of Each Interview

(The instructor leads the discussion, which consists of comments by the observers.)

1. Was mutual understanding increased or decreased as a result of the interview? (If the supervisor emphasizes weaknesses, there inevitably will be misunderstanding and hard feelings; if he listens without judging, understanding will be improved.)
2. Did Burke go up or down in Stanley's estimation, as a result of the interview? (If good communication occurs in the interview, Stanley will think more highly of Burke. If an argument arises, Stanley may think less well of him.)
3. Is Burke's opinion of Stanley better or worse as a result of the interview? (If Stanley encourages Burke to make suggestions and considers Burke's ideas, Burke is likely to think better of him. If Stanley rejects Burke's feelings, or is critical of his thinking, Burke will usually think less well of him.)
4. Will Stanley alter his judgment about Burke's performance as a result of the interview? (If Stanley comes to understand Burke's side of the problem, he will probably rate Burke higher in several respects. If misunderstanding arises, his rating of Burke's performance will either remain unchanged or become lower.)
5. Who talked the most, Stanley or Burke? (If Stanley succeeds in drawing out Burke, Burke will do most of the talking.)
6. Will the interview have favorable or unfavorable effects on Burke's future motivation? (If Stanley accepts Burke's feelings and recognizes his performance and ideas, motivation will be helped. If Burke feels his efforts are unappreciated or that his ideas are not accepted, his motivation may be hindered.)
7. How was Burke's motivation influenced (helped or hindered)?

## Discussion

After all interviews have been completed, the instructor leads a discussion of the following:

1. Is it possible for most interviewers to avoid the pitfalls present in this type of situation?
2. How can performance appraisal programs be improved?

## Developing an Interview Plan

1. In starting an interview of this kind, the interviewer should consider (a) preliminary remarks, (b) how and when to state the reason for the

interview, and (c) the use of open-ended or broad questions such as "How are things going?"

2. Discuss in what areas of the work Stanley can give recognition or praise to Burke. (Those aspects of the work that are going well and are not giving difficulty can be discussed at this point.)
3. What are the best ways to get Burke to talk freely about ideas he has or problems or things that give him trouble? (Places in which to use the listening technique and other problem-solving approaches should be determined.)
4. How can the supervisor in such interviews make it clear that he wants to be helpful? Who should bring up the existence of difficulties? How can improvements in the situation be made? What kind of help can be expected?
5. How can the supervisor ask questions without seeming to cross-examine the employee and question his ability?
6. How accurately can employees evaluate their own performance? (Compare self-evaluations of poorly and well-adjusted individuals. Which are most likely to overestimate or underestimate their own performance? Which will tend to cover up deficiencies, and which will be most on the defensive if criticized?)
7. What type of interview situation will make a person feel most free to discuss his shortcomings?
8. What conclusions about the appraisal interview can be drawn from this case? (A list of the contributions made by the group may be written on newsprint.)
9. How can the learnings gained from this case be used in other situations?

## General Instructions[28]

George Stanley is the electrical-section head in the engineering department of the American Construction Company. The work in the department includes designing, drafting, making cost estimates, keeping maps up to date, checking standards and building codes, doing field inspection and follow up, etc. Eight first-line supervisors report to George Stanley. Their duties are partly technical and partly supervisory. The organizational chart for Stanley's section is shown in Figure 5.

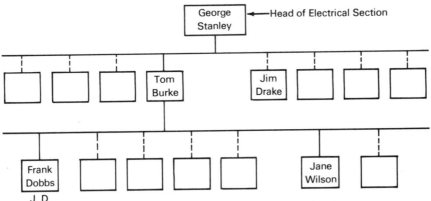

Figure 5. Organizational Chart for Electrical Section.

Company policy requires that each section head interview each of his supervisors once a year. The purpose is to: (1) evaluate the supervisor's performance during the year; (2) give recognition for jobs well done; and (3) correct weaknesses.

The evaluation interviews were introduced because the company believes that employees should know how they stand and that everything should be done to develop management personnel. Today Stanley will conduct an evaluation interview with Tom Burke, one of the supervisors reporting to him.

Tom Burke has a college degree in electrical engineering; in addition to his technical duties—which often take him to the field—he supervises the work of one junior designer, six draftsmen, and two clerks. He is highly paid, as are all the supervisors in this department,

---

[28]Roles and instructions are taken from a laboratory exercise in N. R. F. Maier, *Psychology in Industrial Organizations* (4th ed.). Boston: Houghton Mifflin, 1973, 605–608. Permission to use this material has been granted by Houghton Mifflin Company, publishers.

because of the job's high requirements in technical knowledge. Burke has been with the company for twelve years and has been a supervisor for two years. He is married and has two children. He owns his home and is active in the civic affairs of his community.

## Role Sheet: George Stanley, Section Head

You have evaluated all the supervisors who report to you and during the next two weeks you will interview each of them. You hope to use these interviews constructively. Today you have arranged to interview Tom Burke, one of the eight first-line supervisors who report to you. Burke's file contains the following information and evaluation:

> Twelve years with the company, two years as supervisor, college degree, married, two children. Highly creative and original; exceptionally competent technically.

His unit is very productive and during the two years he has supervised the group, there has been a steady improvement. Within the past six months, you have given him extra work and it has been done on schedule. As far as productivity and dependability are concerned, he is your top supervisor.

His cooperation with other supervisors in the section, however, leaves much to be desired. Before you made him a supervisor, his originality and technical knowledge were available to your whole section. Gradually, he has withdrawn and now acts like a lone wolf. You have asked other supervisors to talk over certain problems with him but they tell you that he offers no suggestions. He tells them he is busy, listens without interest to their problems, kids them, or makes sarcastic remarks, depending on his mood. On one occasion, he caused Jim Drake, one of the supervisors in another unit, to make a mistake that could have been forestalled if Burke had let Drake know the status of certain design changes. It is expected that supervisors will cooperate on matters involving design changes that affect them.

Furthermore, during the past six months, Burke has been unwilling to take two assignments. He said that they were routine and that he preferred more interesting work, and he advised you to give the assignments to other supervisors. To prevent trouble, you followed his suggestion. However, you feel that you cannot give him all the interesting work and that if he persists in this attitude, there will be trouble. You cannot play favorites and still keep up morale in your unit.

Burke's failure to cooperate has you worried for another reason. Although his group is highly productive, there is more turnover among his draftsmen than in other groups. You have heard no complaints yet, but you suspect that he may be treating his group in an arbitrary manner. Certainly if he is demanding with you and other supervisors, he is likely to be even more so with his employees. Apparently the high productivity in his group is not due to high morale, but to his ability to use his employees to do the things for which they are best suited. You do not want to lose good draftsmen. You hope to discuss these matters with Burke in such a way as to recognize his good points and, at the same time, correct some of his weaknesses.

## Role Sheet: Tom Burke, Supervisor

One junior designer, six draftsmen, and two clerks report to you. You feel that you get along fine with your group. You have always been pretty much of an "idea" man and apparently have the knack of passing on your enthusiasm to others in your group. There is a lot of "we" feeling in your unit because it is obvious that your group is the most productive.

You believe in developing your employees and always give them strong recommendations. You think you have gained the reputation of helping your employees grow, because they frequently go out and get much better jobs. Since promotion is necessarily slow in a company such as yours, you think that the best way to stimulate morale is to develop new personnel and demonstrate that a good worker can get somewhere. The two women in your unit are bright and efficient and there is a lot of good-natured kidding. Recently one of your employees, Jane Wilson, turned down an outside offer that paid thirty-five dollars a month more, because she preferred to stay in your group. You are going to get her a raise the first chance you get.

The other supervisors in George Stanley's section do not have your enthusiasm. Some of them are dull and unimaginative. During your first year as supervisor, you used to help them a lot, but you soon found that they leaned on you and before long you were doing their work. There is a lot of pressure to produce. You got your promotion by producing and you don't intend to let other supervisors interfere. Since you no longer help the other supervisors, your production has gone up, but a couple of them seem a bit sore at you. Frank, your junior designer, is a better worker than most, and you would like to see him made a supervisor.

Stanley ought to recognize the fact that the company has some deadwood in it and assign the more routine jobs to those units. Then they wouldn't need your help and you could concentrate your efforts on jobs that suit your unit. At present, George Stanley passes out work pretty much as he gets it. Because you are efficient, you get more than your share of jobs, and you see no reason why the extra work shouldn't be in the form of "plums." This would motivate units to turn out work. When you suggested to Stanley that he turn over some of the more routine jobs to other supervisors, he did it but he was very reluctant about it.

You did one thing recently that bothers you. There was a design change in a set of plans and you should have told Jim Drake (a fellow supervisor) about it, but it slipped your mind. Drake was out when you had it on your mind, and then you got involved in a hot idea of Frank's and forgot all about Drake. As a result, Drake had to make a lot of unnecessary changes and he was quite sore about it. You told him you were sorry and offered to make the changes, but he turned down the offer.

Today you have an interview with George Stanley. It's about this management development plan in the company. It shouldn't take very long, and it's nice to have the boss tell you about the job you are turning out. Maybe there is a raise in it; maybe he'll tell you something about what to expect in the future.

# Instructions for Observers

1. Observe the manner in which Stanley begins the interview.
   a. What did the interviewer do, if anything, to create a permissive atmosphere?
   b. Did the interviewer state the purpose of the interview early in the session?
   c. Was the purpose stated clearly and concisely?
2. Observe how the interview was conducted.
   a. To what extent did the interviewer learn how Burke felt about the job in general?
   b. Did the interviewer use broad, general questions at the outset?
   c. Did Stanley criticize Burke?
   d. Did Stanley praise Burke?
   e. Did he accept Burke's feelings and ideas?
   f. Which one talked the most?
   g. What things did the interviewer learn?
3. Observe and evaluate the outcome of the interview.
   a. To what extent did Stanley arrive at a fairer and more accurate evaluation of Burke as a result of the interview?
   b. What things did Stanley do, if any, to motivate Burke to improve?
   c. Were relations better or worse after the interview? If worse, why?
   d. In what ways might the interviewer have done a better job?

## COMMENTS AND IMPLICATIONS

Stanley will usually begin the interview by praising Burke for certain aspects of his performance such as his originality, productivity, and technical competence. Since this is a form of recognition for good work and involves no area of misunderstanding, the early part of the interview generally proceeds quite smoothly.

However, there are several areas of Burke's performance that Stanley is led to interpret in an unfavorable way. If Stanley proceeds with the interview on the basis of this interpretation, he is likely to make a number of criticisms that seem unjustified to Burke. If Burke feels that he is being treated unfairly, he will become defensive and even hostile. When this occurs, the interview will lead to further misunderstanding and bad feelings.

As in most performance-appraisal situations, there is a built-in source of misunderstanding because the two persons involved are looking at the employee's job from two different points of view. In this case, both are aware of certain facts about Burke's unit, but they interpret the facts differently because of the differences in their perspectives.

To Stanley, the facts add up to an evaluation that Burke's strengths lie in his technical qualifications while his weaknesses lie in his interpersonal relationships. Burke apparently has problems with his peers (the Drake incident), with his superior (resisting assignments), and with his subordinates (highest turnover).

To Burke, however, the same facts add up to the feeling that he successfully develops his employees to their best potential, which accounts for the unit's productivity. He takes pride in the fact that a number of his employees have been offered better jobs. In his opinion, this is partially because of the team spirit that exists within the unit, the fact that he has shared his technical knowledge with his employees, and the enthusiasm that he has generated for the challenges of the job. (It was mainly due to his own enthusiasm and absorption in the challenges that he forgot to see Drake.) Burke feels that he needs even more of the challenging jobs in order to develop and stimulate his employees if he is to be expected to keep them working for the company without wage increases.

Since the known facts are seen as faults by Stanley and as virtues by Burke, the problem is obviously one of interpretation. Each man views his interpretation as the correct one. In order to have a basis for problem solving and the development of solutions, each must learn to respect differing interpretations.

In order to conduct this interview satisfactorily, it is necessary for

Stanley to create a supportive climate so that Burke will feel free to express his ideas and feelings. In this way, Stanley will learn Burke's frame of reference toward various aspects of the work, and he should discover that many of Burke's actions can be seen in a more favorable light. He is then unlikely to make unjustified criticisms and put Burke on the defensive. Thus, the first thing Stanley must learn is how Burke views his own performance.

In general, the best way for the interviewer to proceed is to begin the interview with a general question about how things are going. Frequently, Burke's comments will furnish leads that can be explored later on. The interviewer should then lead into a discussion of the things that Burke feels are going well for him. These aspects of the job are not only easy for Burke to discuss, they also give the interviewer a good opportunity to praise Burke for the things he has done well.

The next area of discussion should center around the things that are causing Burke some difficulties. By listening and accepting complaints, Stanley may learn some of the problems as they appear to Burke. There will be no feeling on Burke's part that he must try to cover up deficiencies (the Drake incident) or defend his actions if he finds that Stanley wants to be helpful. Burke may mention his desire to obtain a greater share of the challenging assignments as a reward for his productivity. Stanley will tend to reject this idea because it poses a problem for him. Nevertheless, the problem of how this can be accomplished without showing favoritism is capable of being solved through discussion.

In the final phase of the interview, mutual understanding and problem solving will be aided if the interviewer asks Burke what he or the company can do to help Burke with his problems. This not only produces constructive problem-solving behavior but also motivates Burke to develop and carry out solutions to his work problems.

In typical solutions, some Burkes are given consulting assignments, some trade a superior draftsman for an unskilled one (in order to obtain a raise in pay for the better draftsman), others influence Stanley to hold group meetings to give out assignments, and many others begin to seek work elsewhere.

It should not matter if all an employee's apparent deficiencies are not brought up in one interview, since the objective is to develop his potential. It is obvious that a person cannot correct all his faults after one interview. The hope is to obtain some improvement after each interview. Of course, if the objective of an appraisal interview is to warn an employee rather than to develop him, this does not apply.

This case is typical of conflict situations that may be resolved innovatively if both sides work toward a mutually satisfactory solution.

Such situations require that differences be respected and explored. A good deal of research[29] indicates that disagreement can lead either to hard feelings or to innovation, depending on the skills utilized by the concerned parties.

---

[29]N. R. F. Maier, *Problem Solving and Creativity in Individuals and Groups.* Belmont, Ca.: Brooks Cole, 1970, 267–270, 325–437.

# 19
# *The Progress Interview*

## FOCUSING THE PROBLEM

Periodic interviews between supervisors and their subordinates can be one of the most effective ways of promoting employee development and good communication. This type of interview may serve both to clear up existing misunderstandings and to prevent others from arising in the future.

However, the potential values of progress interviews are seldom realized in practice. Sometimes this failure is due to a lack of knowledge of and skill in interview methods; more often, diverse attitudes interfere with success. Superiors frequently approach the interview situation with preconceived notions and judgments and do not attempt to discover the frame of reference of the person being interviewed or permit expression of feelings. Previously formed evaluations about a person's progress are likely to be one-sided; they almost always lead to misunderstandings. Many supervisors also lack an understanding of frustration reactions. When an individual shows hostility, defensiveness, undue stubbornness, or other symptoms of frustration, it is inappropriate for the interviewer to attempt to use logic or facts to change the other's mind. If the supervisor uses his authority to pressure the subordinate, he increases misunderstanding. If the interviewer becomes frustrated, he loses control over the situation altogether.

In order to successfully handle an interview situation where feelings and evaluations of another person may be involved, it is necessary for the interviewer to encourage free and full expression of those feelings and opinions. If he does this, he will learn the views of the other person and at the same time will help the individual to think more constructively about his own situation. The interviewer himself will then be able to take a problem-solving and understanding approach to the facts of the situation.

In the present case, the interview is part of an executive development program that is concerned with evaluating the potential of an individual for promotion purposes. The interview is fairly difficult and makes considerable demands on the knowledge, skill, and attitudes of the interviewer.

When possible, the instructions should be assigned to the role players for study and preparation a day or more prior to the interview. If this is done and the interviewer is reasonably well qualified, the case frequently becomes an excellent demonstration of nondirective counseling procedures.

The single-group role-playing procedure is used for this case because it permits an intensive analysis of the effects of small but significant details in the interview process.

## SINGLE-GROUP ROLE-PLAYING PROCEDURE

### Preparation

1. Two members from the group are needed, one to be the interviewer, Walter Pearce, and the other to play James Smith, a chemist in one of the company's departments, who will be interviewed about his progress.
2. The remaining persons in the group serve as observers.
3. All group members read the Background Material. The leader writes on newsprint the list of positions held by Smith during his ten years with the company.
4. The two role players study their roles so they can play them without referring to the written material. They do not read the role for the other person.
5. Observers read the Instructions for Observers.
6. The setting for the role play is prepared by placing a table and two chairs in the front of the room to represent Pearce's office. The furniture is arranged so that the observers will be able to see the faces of the role players during the interview.

### Process

1. Pearce takes his place first and sits at his desk. After a brief pause, Smith enters Pearce's office for the scheduled interview.

2. The time needed for the interview varies considerably; usually twenty-five to thirty-five minutes is required. The role players are permitted to finish whenever possible. If a stalemate develops and no progress is made, the role play is interrupted and the problem thrown open for discussion. The observers offer suggestions and attempt to help Pearce overcome the difficulty. The interview can then be resumed and picked up from any point agreed upon in the discussion. Several interruptions may be made if the interviewer wishes help.
3. The role play is terminated by Pearce.

## Analysis

The results of the interview will vary considerably, depending on the attitude and skill of the interviewer as well as on his personality. In most instances, the results will be either distinctly favorable or unfavorable; there is less chance that an intermediate or neutral result will occur. The following general discussion questions, indicating the areas to explore, may be expanded or omitted depending on their appropriateness.

1. Will Smith quit or, if he stays, will he do a good job? Did Smith behave unrealistically about his progress? Is he unreasonable about what he wants from the company? Is he satisfied with the outcome? (Different views about these questions are explored and discussed.)
2. Did Pearce learn the real reason why Smith feels as he does? Were all feelings explored? What evidence is there that further expression of feelings would be desirable? How could Pearce have brought this about?
3. What did Pearce learn in the interview? Did new problems arise? If so, what were they? What did Pearce do to help problem solving? What things might he have done differently? What more might he have learned?
4. Did Smith's attitude become more or less favorable during the interview? In what ways did Pearce's actions contribute to this?
5. Was Pearce's attitude influenced in any way during the interview? If so, in what way? In what ways did Pearce's attitudes help or hinder problem solving?
6. Did Pearce alter any previous plans he may have had for Smith? To what extent should he do this? How can Smith's attitude be improved? (Pearce reports his side of the question and Smith then gives his views.)
7. Arguments for and against giving Smith the double promotion are developed through discussion.

8. Is the company policy of moving men around in jobs a wise one from a human relations standpoint? What might be some of its more important advantages? What problems might it create? What could the company do to minimize the disadvantages and retain most of the advantages?

9. Is it possible that other college recruits besides Smith have difficulties because of the company's training policies? What clues does the interview with Smith furnish with respect to other trainees? What steps might Pearce take to prevent problems of this nature?

10. What conclusions can we draw from this case? How might we apply the principles derived from this case to our own jobs?

# Background Material[30]

The American Consolidated Chemical Company has chemical plants located in various sections of the country. The main plant is located in Detroit and important branches are in Houston, Texas; St. Louis, Missouri; St. Paul, Minnesota; and Cleveland, Ohio. All the products are manufactured in Detroit, but each of the branches specializes in making chemicals that either utilize raw materials available locally or that have a concentration of outlets there. Thus, the Cleveland plant manufactures products needed in the Cleveland area, and the Houston plant manufactures products that utilize petroleum derivatives.

Since the Detroit plant makes all the products, an experienced employee can be moved from Detroit to any of the other plants. When a vacancy opens up in a particular department in Detroit, it is possible to fill the vacancy by choosing a local employee or by transferring one from a branch that produces a product similar to the one made by that department in Detroit. The company has been expanding, there has been a great deal of movement within the organization, and opportunities for promotion have been good. Morale has generally been quite satisfactory.

Walter Pearce is the assistant to the vice-president for personnel and is located in Detroit. One of his duties is to keep track of the college recruits each year and, from among them, to select those to be designated for promotion and development in higher management. Pearce is about to have an interview with James Smith, a college graduate who was brought into the company ten years ago. The following listing gives the positions Smith has held during his ten years with the company.

| Detroit | Dept. A | 1 year | Regular employee |
|---------|---------|--------|------------------|
| St. Paul | Depts. A, B, C | 2 years | Regular employee |
| Detroit | Dept. A | 1 year | Foreman |
| St. Louis | Depts. B, F | 2 years | Foreman |
| Cleveland | Depts. D, E | 1½ years | Foreman |
| Houston | Dept. G | 1½ years | Foreman |
| Detroit | Dept. H | 1 year | Foreman |

---

[30]Role instructions and background material are taken from a laboratory exercise in N. R. F. Maier, *Psychology in Industrial Organizations* (4th ed.). Boston: Houghton Mifflin, 1973, 502–505. Permission to use this material has been granted by Houghton Mifflin Company, publishers.

Promotion in the company is based on merit, but qualified people with seniority have an opportunity to advance as high as general foreman. The ascending rank of management positions in each plant is as follows: foreman, general foreman, superintendent, department head, works manager. Larger plants also have assistants to works managers. The executive group, located in Detroit, includes several vice-presidents (sales, manufacturing, public relations, research, and personnel), the secretary, the treasurer, and the president.

## Role Sheet: Walter Pearce, Assistant to the Vice President for Personnel

Since Jim Smith joined the company as a college recruit ten years ago, you have kept an eye on him. During his first year with the company, you were impressed by his technical ability and even more by his leadership. After one year in Department A, you sent him to St. Paul where a person with his training was needed. He made a good showing and worked in Departments A, B, and C. After two years, you brought him back to Detroit and made him a foreman in Department A. Since he did very well on this job, you considered making some long-range plans for him. Here was a man you thought you could groom for an executive position. This meant giving him experience in all operations in all plants. To do this most easily, you have made him a foreman in each of the company's eight departments for a short period of time and assigned him to each of the branches.

During the past two years, you have had some disturbing reports. Jim did not impress Bill Jones, the department head at Houston, who reported that Jim had ideas but was always on the defensive. Since his return to Detroit, he has shown a lack of interest in his job, and the employees who work for him don't back him up the way they used to. You feel that you have made quite a mistake with this man and that he has let you down after you have given him good build-ups with various department heads. Maybe the confidence you have shown in him and the praise you have given him during several progress interviews have gone to his head. If so, he hasn't the stature it takes to make the top grade. Therefore, you have abandoned your plans to move him up to superintendent at St. Paul; you think it best to send him to Houston, where there is a job as general foreman in Department C. This won't mean much of a promotion because you moved his pay up as high as you could while he was a foreman. However, you feel that he has earned some promotion even if he hasn't lived up to all your expectations.

Of course, it is possible that Jim is having marital trouble. At a recent company party, you found his wife to be quite dissatisfied and unhappy. Maybe she is giving Jim a rough time. She always did seem to be a bit snobbish.

While you are waiting for Jim to arrive, you have his folder—showing the positions he has held—in front of you.

## Role Sheet: Jim Smith, Chemist

You have been with the American Consolidated Chemical Company for ten years now. You joined the company after graduating from college with a major in chemistry. At the time you were hired, you were interviewed by Walter Pearce and told that a good worker could get ahead in the company. On the strength of the position, you married your college sweetheart and moved to Detroit. You preferred the Houston and St. Paul branches but Pearce thought Detroit was the place to start. So you took your chances along with other college recruits. You were a good student in college and were active in college affairs, so you had reason to believe you possessed leadership ability.

During your first few years, you thought you were getting some place. You were moved to Minnesota and you thought Mr. Pearce was doing you a favor by sending you there. After the first year, you bought a home and started a family. During two years in Minnesota, you gained considerable experience in Departments A, B, and C. Then you were offered a foremanship in Detroit and, since this meant a promotion and you had a second child on the way, you decided to return to Detroit. When you came to Detroit, Pearce again saw you and told you how pleased he was with your progress.

Since then, however, you have been given a royal runaround. You are told that your work is good, but all you get are a lot of lateral transfers. You have been foreman in practically every department and have been moved from one branch to another. Other college graduates who came to the company after you have been made general foremen. They stay in a given department and are working up—while you get moved from place to place. Although the company pays for your moves, both you and your wife want to settle down and have a permanent home for your children. Why can't people be honest with you? You are told what a good job you are doing and then the next thing they do is get rid of you. Take, for example, Bill Jones, the department head at Houston. He acted as if you had done him a favor to go there but you can tell he wasn't sincere. After you got to know him you could see through him. From little remarks he dropped, you know he has been saying some nasty things about you to the home office. It is obvious that Jones is incompetent; you think he got rid of you because he considered you a threat to his job.

Your wife realizes that you are unhappy. She has told you that she is willing to live on less just to help you get out of the company. You know you could handle a superintendent's job, such as George Wilson got, and he joined the company when you did and was just an average student in college. As a matter of fact, if the company were on the ball it would realize that you have the ability to be a department head if George is superintendent material.

Pearce has asked you to see him. You are a bit nervous about this interview because the news may not be good. You have felt that he has been less friendly lately and you have no desire to listen to any smooth manipulations. Last night, you and your wife had a good talk about things and she's willing for you to look around for another job. Certainly you've reached the end of your patience and you're fed up with any more of Pearce's attempts to move you around just because someone is jealous of your ideas.

## Instructions for Observers

Walter Pearce has learned on good authority that Jim Smith is not living up to Pearce's expectations. For the last two years, reports on Smith have shown him to have a rather poor attitude; previously, however, the reports were highly favorable. Since Pearce has given Smith a lot of breaks, including company-wide experience and many pay raises, it is quite a disappointment to him that Smith has failed to live up to expectations.

Smith, on the other hand, feels that he has been given a runaround. He now perceives his many moves as proof that certain people are trying to get rid of him. Although he had received promises of a good future in the company, he now feels forgotten since he has seen others promoted.

With these two different viewpoints or attitudes concerning the many jobs Smith has held, one may either expect the misunderstandings to be discovered or to be increased further. Some of the crucial points to observe in the interview are listed below.

1. Note how Pearce begins the interview. The opening statement might encourage Smith to talk about things that bother him, cause him to become defensive, make him wonder what the interview is about, etc.

2. Make a two-column list of things Pearce does and says (a) that indicate he is open minded and trying to understand, and (b) that indicate he is critical of or in disagreement with Smith.

3. Observe whether or not Pearce seems to change his viewpoint and in what way. Keep track of the events that cause such a change.

4. Make a note of the things you think Pearce learned from the interview as well as the things he missed.

5. What do you think of the solution? How will Smith react? Do you think Pearce is aware of the way Smith feels? (Since you have been given some data on both sides of the question, you are in a better position to evaluate what is going on than is Pearce.)

## COMMENTS AND IMPLICATIONS

This case is difficult to handle because a source of misunderstanding is planted in the roles; unless it is discovered fully, the misunderstanding is likely to grow. Commonly, Pearce shows his disappointment in Smith in various ways ranging from criticism to faint praise, and then he tells Smith he is going to give him a promotion anyway by making him a general foreman at Houston. Smith may well be disappointed with this since he is likely to see this promotion as too little, too late, and the job is located at a place he does not want to go. Pearce, in turn, is likely to further the misunderstanding by taking the view that Smith considers himself too good for the assignment. Pearce and Smith may thus frustrate each other so that the interview degenerates into conflict and recrimination. Frequently, Smith will decide to resign from the company.

Often Pearce will also misinterpret the feelings Smith expresses during the interview. He has concluded that Smith recently has been doing below-standard work, and this conclusion is likely to prejudice him. He may not recognize that Smith's attitude was caused by misunderstandings and may blame Smith for not being more tolerant. He may react to Smith's hostility by showing his own authority or he may feel that Smith is unjustifiably sorry for himself. Occasionally, Pearce will try to question Smith about his marriage or will give him unwanted advice, either of which will deepen the misunderstanding.

In order to conduct a successful interview, Pearce must get Smith to express his feelings about his work with the company. To accomplish this, Pearce must be a good listener and be accepting and respectful of Smith's feelings. Only after Smith has had his say will he be prepared to show constructive behavior.

Once Pearce discovers Smith's view of things and the fact that Smith feels that he has been given a runaround, Pearce has an explanation for Smith's negative behavior during the interview as well as his recent decline in job performance. This insight should convince Pearce that his original evaluation of Smith's ability was sound and cause him to reconsider his previous decision to offer Smith the job of superintendent at the St. Paul plant instead of the job of general foreman at Houston.

This two-step promotion is perhaps essential to correcting Smith's attitude and rekindling in him his former job motivation and confidence in the company. However, it is difficult for Pearce to grant this double promotion because he has rejected the idea once and subsequently decided to offer Smith the job in Houston. Since Smith has developed an unfavorable attitude toward the company, Pearce is likely to be conservative and wait until the attitude has improved. The tendency is for Pearce to withhold the very thing that is needed to improve Smith's attitude. A second difficulty arises: that is, for Pearce to change his own attitude during the interview. In role playing, as in real-life situations, decisions once reached seldom change, even though new, relevant, but conflicting information may be gained. The persons who play the role of Pearce seldom offer Smith the two-step promotion but stay with their decision to offer only the one-step promotion to general foreman. This behavior illustrates a basic principle about human nature, namely that once a person has arrived at a decision, his mind tends to be closed.

Often employees develop poor attitudes because of certain disappointments they have experienced in the company, such as accidentally being overlooked for promotion or receiving rude treatment from an inconsiderate boss. Later, when the employee's capabilities are discovered, promotion is denied because of his poor attitude. Waiting for the attitude to improve spontaneously is unrealistic. Yet, even if the company made a mistake by overlooking a prospective supervisor, it cannot always be expected to correct this oversight by a promotion later. Successful promotions of this type have been made, but it is important that each case be studied separately. While the employee's attitude may have become too bitter to be improved by a belated promotion, this is not always the case. Correcting former injustices is often worth the effort.

# 20

# *The President's Decision*

## FOCUSING THE PROBLEM

One of the important measures of good management is the ability to make wise decisions. This is true in relation to small everyday problems as well as to major policy determinations. Sometimes decisions can be made on the basis of facts known to the individual at that time. To get the facts, weigh them, and then decide is standard practice. At other times, the available facts may be incomplete or the decision cannot wait for all the facts; then inferences, opinions, and other subjective factors influence the decision. When the problem is highly complex or the relevant factors are beyond the knowledge and ability of the responsible person, it is customary and wise to utilize the advice of the company's specially trained personnel: engineers, accountants, lawyers, psychologists, etc. However, even when experts are used, the responsibility for the final decision and the consequences of its success or failure rest with the person who implements it.

When the situation is such that the decision can be based on fact or inference, one set of facts or judgments usually will outweigh the others, and the final solution emerges from an exploration of alternatives. Decision making under these conditions is essentially an intellectual, problem-solving process.

However, in many instances, management decisions are based not only on logic and facts, but also on the feelings of the people who are affected by the decisions. This is true whether it involves a supervisor giving the day off to an employee whose mother is ill or a policy decision regulating coffee privileges.

When emotional factors become paramount—as they often do—the

275

decision may be inconsistent with some of the facts of the situation. This is usually the case when frustration is present, when there are strong attitudes toward the subject under consideration, and when the position or pride of the decision maker is threatened. Many such decisions are made on the basis of prejudices, face-saving needs for individuals concerned, attempts to protect a management prerogative, and fear of change.

Persons who are responsible for making decisions not only must avoid being misled by emotional considerations, but they must know how to use the aid of subordinates effectively. It is easy for the boss to accept the suggestions of his subordinates when their suggestions are in agreement with his views. But when their suggestions are in opposition to his views, he must make a difficult choice. If he fails to give opposing views a sympathetic hearing, it is difficult for him to recognize when he is wrong or biased. If he refuses to be swayed by others, he will be regarded as a stubborn person, but if he is easily swayed by them, he might make poor decisions for which he will be held responsible. If he refuses to share his decision-making function, subordinates soon cease offering the kind of suggestions that get turned down; instead, they spend their time trying to figure out what the boss would like them to suggest.

The success or failure of a decision not only depends on the objective merits of the decision but also on the degree to which persons who must execute the decision are willing to accept it. A second-best decision that is accepted might prove more productive than a better decision that is disliked. Persons responsible for decisions must concern themselves with the problem of how to achieve quality without sacrificing acceptance.

This case, which deals with a president's decision, will introduce many of the complications discussed above. The possible outcomes vary in the kind of decision reached as well as in the degree of acceptance achieved. Since the factors contributing to the different outcomes should be isolated and analyzed, the single-group role-playing procedure is prescribed. In this way, all persons can discuss a common set of events. To test the extent of variation in outcomes, it would be desirable to use the multiple role-playing procedure.

## SINGLE-GROUP ROLE-PLAYING PROCEDURE

### Preparation

1. Four persons are needed to play the roles. (When possible, role assignments for this case should be given before the meeting of the class in order to permit the participants to study the roles carefully.) One participant plays the role of John Ward, president of the company, and the other three are the vice-presidents: William Carson, in charge of manufacturing and product development; James Jackson, in charge of sales; and Russell Haney, in charge of personnel and industrial relations.
2. The remaining persons in the class serve as observers.
3. All group members read the Background Information. The instructor writes on newsprint the name, position, age, and years with the company of all four participants.
4. The participants study their roles so they can role play without referring to the written material. They do not read any role except their own.
5. Observers read the Instructions for Observers.
6. The instructor prepares the setting for the scene by placing a table and four chairs at the front of the room to represent the furniture in Ward's office. The table and one chair are for Ward's use and the other three chairs, arranged in a semicircle in front of Ward's desk, are for the vice-presidents. The furniture is arranged so that the observers are able to see the faces of all four role players.

### Process

1. When all participants are ready, Ward enters his office and sits at his desk. After a few moments, the vice-presidents enter, one at a time, and seat themselves so that Carson will be at Ward's left, with Jackson next to Carson, and Haney at the end, on Ward's right.
2. Ward greets each man as he enters and shows him to his seat.
3. When everyone is seated, Ward begins the discussion.
4. Thirty to forty minutes is usually needed for role playing.
5. The leader is permitted to finish or ask for help whenever he wishes. If conflict develops and persists so that no progress is made after twenty minutes, the role play is interrupted by the instructor and the problem is thrown open for general discussion. Role playing is resumed after the president feels he has gained enough hints to proceed. (If he prefers, another person can be asked to play his part.)

## Evaluation of the Solution

1. Discuss the merits of the solution from the point of view of the future of the company and determine the extent of agreement among the observers. Compare the opinions of observers, vice-presidents, and Ward. In case these opinions differ, each role player introduces any relevant information that was given in his role to see if the new facts will alter the opinions of the observers.
2. Discuss the merits of the solution from the president's point of view. Did he get good advice from the vice-presidents?
3. What are Ward's prospects of being retained by the board of directors if the solution does not result in marked improvement?
4. Discuss the part the vice-presidents played in making the decision. Will they give Ward the support he needs to retain his job?

## Analysis of the Conference

1. Did Ward give the vice-presidents an opportunity to help solve the real problem he faced or did he give them a somewhat different problem? Ward describes why his situation caused him to act as he did.
2. Should Ward have given his side of the problem or should he have confined the discussion to company matters as much as possible? Compare views of participants and observers.
3. Which participants persisted in discussing matters from their points of view? What could have been done to get everyone working together?
4. How did the specialized information that different conferees possessed become integrated into the discussion? Was there an interest in getting facts or did Ward attempt to suppress facts?
5. Stubbornness, aggression, and childish behavior indicate frustration. Enumerate the examples of these behaviors that were evidenced in the discussion and evaluate how they were handled.

## Discussion of Ward's Situation

1. How many observers would have taken the advice given by the vice-presidents (in this situation) had they played the part of Ward? How many would have declined the advice? List the arguments in favor of each position.
2. What would happen if a president's decision was always the joint decision of the vice-presidents? Discuss the favorable and unfavorable aspects of such a philosophy of leadership.

# Background Information

The ABCO Electrical Manufacturing Company produces various parts and subassemblies for radio, television, and other electronics industries. The factory is located in Philadelphia; there are sales offices in several of the eastern cities, in or near their major market area. During the Vietnam War, the company also operated a government-built plant in Kansas City which supplied equipment for military aircraft. However, this operation was abandoned when numerous military orders were cancelled; the plant was bought shortly thereafter by one of the larger electronics manufacturing companies.

Two years ago, the company went through a major management reorganization, brought about by increasing losses in its operations and a steadily diminishing share of the market. The previous top management personnel were extremely conservative in their outlook and methods, and for many years had operated on a small share of the market as suppliers to the radio and broadcasting industries. During the Vietnam War, they made a good showing as a result of increased business and profits from military orders. For several years, there has been considerable growth in the electronics industry. At the same time, new problems have been created for the smaller producers, such as ABCO, by the unusually rapid technological developments and strong competition from the larger companies in the field.

The company's inability to compete for large-volume business has made it necessary to depend more and more on specialty orders. Although the unit profit margin on such orders is somewhat larger, the shifting demands of this type of market call for unusual flexibility in manufacturing processes and procedures and a highly alert, aggressive sales force in order to maintain demand for regular lines and push the sales of new products. Similarly, product development and engineering ingenuity are at a premium in order to meet competition, provide for economical changeover from one product to another, and achieve the quick solution of a variety of complex production problems. It is also necessary for production employees and foremen to adapt to frequent changes in jobs and methods without undue training or confusion.

It was the inability of the previous management to adapt to these changing conditions that led to the reorganization of the company and the installation of a new top management group. Following are the names of the present group of senior officers of the company, together with a summary of their previous background and experience:

John Ward, president of the company. Ward is forty-nine, has been with the company twelve years—first as an accountant, then as controller for six years—before being promoted to his present position two years ago. He has a college degree in accounting and is a CPA.

William Carson, vice-president in charge of manufacturing and product development. Carson has an electrical engineering background and was hired fifteen years ago as a potential management man. He had progressed to general foreman of the night shift at the time he was sent to Kansas City as superintendent. When the Kansas City plant was closed, he returned to Philadelphia as plant superintendent, and was promoted to his present position two years ago when Ward took over as president. Carson is forty-five.

James Jackson, vice-president in charge of sales. Jackson came to the company five years ago from the position of assistant sales manager for one of the divisions of a larger company. He is the only holdover as vice-president from the previous management, having been brought in to set up a sales organization to attempt to recapture lost accounts and widen the market for company products. Jackson started in sales work from business administration school. He is forty-six.

Russell Haney, vice-president, personnel and industrial relations, is thirty-nine. Haney was hired as personnel director for the Kansas City plant during the Vietnam War and then came to Philadelphia in a similar capacity. Previously, personnel functions had been the responsibility of the office manager. Haney remained as personnel director until his promotion to the vice-presidency one and one-half years ago.

## Role Sheet: John Ward, President

You are president of the ABCO Manufacturing Company and have held this position for the past two years. In your previous position as controller, you advised the president on fiscal and policy matters and gained a close knowledge of the inner workings of the company. As president, your duties are much broader and more complex. You now have final responsibility for policy formulation and execution in such diverse fields as procurement, manufacturing, sales, finance, product development, personnel, public relations, and various other aspects of business operation. To a large extent, the progress of the company and your own success or failure as president depend on your making wise decisions. You get a certain amount of credit when things go well but you also take the blame when they go wrong.

One of the most difficult problems you have had to deal with since you became president is whether to expand operations. Within the company and among your close business associates, there are conflicting views on the matter. Those who are opposed to expansion contend that real estate and building values are seriously inflated and that the cost of new equipment is out of line. A further argument is that the television and other electronics sales are highly sensitive to economic conditions. Since company reserves are low, you would have to obtain the necessary funds through stock sales or mortgage loans, and the present financial condition of the company does not place it in an advantageous position for such financing. Furthermore, it would be some time before returns from expansion would begin to pay off to any great extent, and an early business slump could wreck the company.

While there are a number of people in the company who favor immediate expansion, all of them tend to see things in terms of their own particular area of the business and none are in a position to have a broad, overall perspective. Nevertheless, in casual discussions of the matter, they have come up with some impressive facts and arguments in favor of setting up a new plant. One contention, for example, is that the present four-story, thirty-year-old building is not adapted for modern straight-line production methods. Not only is it expensive to heat and light but it lacks the flexibility needed for efficient changeovers to meet production requirements. In addition, it has been necessary to turn down two or three large orders in the past because of insufficient capacity to meet production deadlines. Then there is the contention that a lack of growth is damaging to morale and that good men tend to become discouraged and leave to go with larger or faster growing companies where opportunities are greater.

During the past several months, you tried to keep an open mind to both points of view and, despite the risks, you were becoming convinced that on a long-term basis, expansion was the better course to follow. You have been making headway toward getting the company back on its feet, but, as things are, it is a slow, uphill struggle. Nevertheless, you think that given unfavorable circumstances, the progress you have made is as satisfactory as can be expected.

Despite your best efforts over the past two years, the board of directors informed you late yesterday that they had voted to give you one more year in which to show some results or else resign. You knew that certain members of the board were becoming impatient. However, this action was totally unexpected and came as a real shock. Obviously, expansion is out of the question if results have to be shown within a year. It would take longer than that to make the necessary financial and other arrangements to construct a new plant and get it into operation. The only possible course of action is to play it safe and hope for the best. With a few good breaks and strict belt tightening throughout the organization, it may be possible to demonstrate the desired results within the deadline set by the board. Certainly this is not the time to take chances. Your decision not to expand must be announced immediately. As a first step, you have called a meeting of your three vice-presidents for 3 p.m. Your purpose is to check with them to see whether anything has been overlooked in arriving at your decision. It is now three o'clock and time to begin.

## Role Sheet: William Carson, Vice-President, Manufacturing and Product Development

You are vice-president in charge of manufacturing and product development of the ABCO Company. When you moved into this job from that of plant superintendent two years ago, you had high hopes of streamlining operations and you have been able to accomplish a good deal. For years the previous management had refused to spend money on manufacturing facilities, following a penny-pinching practice of patching and fixing and making you do the best you could with inferior, outmoded equipment and methods. Through your influence with Ward, you have been able to make a number of changes in layout and methods. By carefully shopping around, you have been able to get good buys on several pieces of secondhand but fairly modern equipment. In addition, you have set up a new product-development laboratory. This is a must if the company is to compete with the larger companies and their staffs of research people, both in bringing out new products and in working out designs to simplify production. The company is slowly getting back on its feet and, in large part, this is due to the reduced unit costs you have been able to achieve in manufacturing.

However, you have gone just about as far as you can in this direction, and what is needed now is a new, modern plant. The present four-story building was satisfactory for its purpose thirty years ago, but with newer, integrated assembly-line procedures, all operations should be on one floor. The layout of the present building is awkward for moving things along from one process to the next and creates a lot of needless delay in changeovers when you have new orders to fill. It is also costly to light and to heat, and the construction on the upper floors is not strong enough to support some of the new heavy equipment where you could use it to the best advantage. You have urged Ward repeatedly to expand into a modern building and purchase new equipment; although he has always given you a fair hearing, you cannot get him to commit himself, Ward is a good accountant but he doesn't know the manufacturing end of the business very well and he seems to be a fence straddler. This may be because he was not experienced in administrative work before he became president. As controller, he learned company operations from a fiscal angle, but he merely advised the former president and did not have to make the final decisions himself. Now that he is on the firing line and has to stand or fall on his own judgment, he seems to have difficulty in making up his mind about things. You have given him the best advice you can and you want to help him move things along faster, but he has to make up his mind to expand or else the company will no longer be able to meet competition.

Ward has called a meeting with you and the other two vice-presidents in his office for three o'clock today. He has these meetings at fairly frequent intervals. You don't know what he has on his mind but you hope he has finally agreed to go ahead with the new plant. Almost anything would be an improvement over the one the company is in now.

## Role Sheet: James Jackson, Vice-President, Sales

You are vice-president in charge of sales and came to the ABCO Company five years ago. Before that, you were one of the assistant sales managers of a division of one of the large electrical manufacturing companies. Stepping into the vice-presidency of the ABCO Company meant quite an increase in salary and responsibility and it seemed that there was a real opportunity to do a good job and make a name for yourself. Five years ago, the company had no real sales organization and was losing ground rapidly. One of your first moves was to make an effort to recapture the market and to expand further. This took a lot of work and you had a struggle to win over the old management to your ideas. Now there are sales offices in most of the principal Eastern cities where ABCO products are in demand by manufacturers, and a fairly strong organization has been built up. The reorganization two years ago had its advantages in that Ward gave you more freedom to operate than you had enjoyed previously. He is doing a fair job as president in some ways but seems to be rather unimaginative. He always gives your ideas a fair hearing, but in the end he seems to shy away from new advertising campaigns. During the past two years, he has taken the steam out of some of your best promotional ideas simply by delaying action on them until too late. One of the things you have been pushing, for example, is an expansion of plant facilities. In the past year you have lost several big orders when Carson said he couldn't possibly meet the deadline set by the customers. There may have been something to what Carson calls "unreasonable deadlines" in one or two instances; however, it begins to look more and more as though Carson isn't fast enough on his feet to make the necessary changeovers in manufacturing and Ward refuses to push him. Carson seems to be Ward's fair-haired boy. With a new modern plant, there could be no more excuses and you could take advantage of the breaks when big orders come in. It would help a lot, too, if those in charge of product development would get to work. They have been set up for two years now and despite the ideas for new things that your salesmen have been funneling in to them, they haven't shown any progress. A small company like this must have new and better products to offer if it is to compete for new markets. That way the newspapers and trade journals give you a lot of free publicity, and the salesmen have a chance to get a foot in the door of potential customers. The main thing, however, is to get a new plant so that larger orders can be handled. Turning down the big ones—as you had to do several times in the past—is what hurts, and it demoralizes your sales force.

Ward has been receptive to your arguments for expansion, and there has been increasing evidence lately that he is ready to take action. Today at three o'clock there is to be a meeting in his office with you and the other two vice-presidents. Apparently Ward is about to announce plans for the new plant, because his secretary told you over the phone that Ward wanted you to review in your mind, prior to the meeting, all the pros and cons on the matter of expansion. You are on your way to Ward's office now.

## Role Sheet: Russell Haney, Vice-President, Personnel and Industrial Relations

You are vice-president in charge of personnel and industrial relations, and have held this position since you moved up from the job of personnel director a year and a half ago. All the usual personnel services such as recruitment, hiring, promotions, training, and contract negotiations are handled through your office. On a policy basis, you have set up your office to serve three main functions. One is to prevent as many personnel problems as possible and assist the supervisors with those that arise. Second, you advise the president, John Ward, on personnel matters. Third, you are responsible for maintaining a competent work force in which the employees get along well with each other and do a good job.

One of the things you were able to get underway as personnel director was an individualized program of training and work experience for promising young college recruits. Even though the conservatism of the previous management stymied their progress in many ways, you were able to obtain a few good people each year. Then when the reorganization took place two years ago, a considerable number of these graduates were able to move up a notch. This left a number of vacancies at the trainee level which you were able to fill by going out to the colleges. However you are now faced with the same problem you had previously. The company isn't growing and many of the people you brought in a few years ago who were not ready to move up during the reorganization are becoming impatient. You cannot hold out much promise to new college graduates because there just isn't any place for them to move up in the company, and there won't be any new opportunities unless the company expands its operations. Meanwhile, some of your best employees are disheartened and are leaving; competing companies are picking them off one by one. If this is allowed to continue, the management at the middle and lower levels will be second rate again in a few years. Unless the company can offer good people some inducements to stay, there will be crippling losses in many key positions—the company simply cannot afford that and stay in competition. As far as you can see, expansion is absolutely essential if the company is to keep these employees.

Ward has sent word that there is to be a meeting at three o'clock in his office and that Carson and Jackson are also to be there. Since Carson is in charge of manufacturing and Jackson in charge of sales, it looks as though Ward may be ready to announce plans for the new plant.

## Instructions for Observers

On the basis of what you already know about the ABCO Company and the four top executives, Ward, Carson, Jackson, and Haney, you probably have formed certain impressions about the situation. Most of the things you have learned so far are facts. However, you also know that these facts may be relatively unimportant except as background and that the attitudes, feelings, and personalities of these men, as well as their relationships with each other, may be more important. It is important to observe the feelings that are indicated and not be misled by the actual words spoken if you are to sense the developments as they occur in the role play. The following questions give you clues as to what to watch and listen for.

1. Observe how Ward opens the discussion. Does he seem at ease? Did he state a problem with all relevant facts for open discussion? Is he being open-minded about things?
2. What are Ward's reasons for calling this meeting? How do the other members react to his views? To what extent does he accept their views? What evidence is there, if any, that Ward is defensive?
3. To what extent is this a problem-solving discussion? If not, why not? What do you think is the real problem here? What did Ward do to help or hinder the group?
4. Did any of the participants become stubborn? Why?
5. Note behaviors that indicate a member was holding back relevant information.
6. How acceptable is the decision to each of the members? Note behaviors that support your evaluation.
7. What evidence is there to indicate that fear or threat influenced the relationships of the various persons in the discussion?

## COMMENTS AND IMPLICATIONS

Ward will usually begin the meeting by announcing his decision not to expand company operations. This will produce disagreement and conflict because the vice-presidents all think that expansion is essential and they will argue with Ward. Furthermore, they are likely to think that he is being arbitrary and inconsiderate of their views.

Ward is reluctant to tell the vice-presidents of the board of directors' ultimatum because it would hurt his pride. He also may fear that if he tells the vice-presidents about the board's decision, they will lose confidence in him and either move elsewhere or try to maneuver themselves into competing positions for the presidency. However, if he attempts to protect his pride, the other members are likely to sense that something is not right and to feel that he is deliberately keeping them in the dark. As a result, they will become suspicious of his motives and at the same time become resentful of what appears to be an arbitrary decision on his part. When this occurs, the situation will deteriorate into mutual frustration since neither side will be capable of viewing the differences as misunderstandings.

In order to handle this situation successfully, it is necessary for Ward to inform the group of the action taken by the board of directors and ask for their ideas and help in meeting the situation. He can do this without arousing sympathy for himself if he presents the ultimatum he has received in terms of their having a year to prove themselves. By sharing the problem with his vice-presidents, he can practically be assured of their cooperation and support. He will also focus their attention on the real problem—to show results within one year or convince the directors that this is an unsound request. Viewed in this light, the question of whether to expand is no longer the problem; it becomes merely one of several alternatives to be explored in the search for a solution to a problem created by the board of directors.

In essence, then, the president must decide whether to play a lone hand against pressures both from above and below or whether to share the problem with his subordinates in a joint effort to meet the challenge. To choose the latter, he must have confidence in the judgment of his subordinates and respect their views. When influenced by fears and threats, he is not likely to do this; instead, he will tend to take the very actions that will bring about his own failure and jeopardize the company.

Fear and threat are negative forms of motivation and, as such, are likely to produce cautious reactions rather than positive explorations of new possibilities. These reactions may be expressed in various ways and are based mainly on feelings rather than on fact or logic. They therefore tend to be unadaptive ways of reacting to the realities of the situation. Unfortunately, it is a common practice in life and in industry to use fear and threat in an attempt to get results. The fact that alternative procedures exist for solving most problems does not always occur to those in positions of authority. They may have to learn to set aside their authority and power if they wish to encourage their groups to solve problems by constructive thinking.

In evaluating problem-solving discussions, the contributions of participants can be classified into two categories: (a) the fear-produced behaviors, which at best make for cautiousness and the avoidance of immediate threats; and (b) the exploratory or forward-moving behaviors, which try to locate obstacles and find ways to circumvent them. It should not be assumed from this that all protective behavior is undesirable; there are times when caution and avoidance are appropriate. However, opportunities for positive action should also be explored.

Note - pg. 47

the informal social order in
the organization is an aspect
the women may overlook or
are not aware of or don't think
is important enough to comply
with.